'Tap Dancing on Everest is gorgeous. It is so full of joy, zest, and fun and yet with some profound thoughts. Once started you cannot put it down. I hope it is a huge success—it certainly deserves to be."
—SIR CHRIS BONINGTON, AUTHOR OF *EVEREST THE HARD WAY*, KNIGHTED FOR HIS SERVICES TO MOUNTAINEERING

"With a poetic vision that is staggering in its honesty and beauty, Mimi Zieman brings readers into the heart of a Himalayan ascent, guiding us along some of the unexpected pathways that intense adventures can trace in both body and mind."
—KATIE IVES, AUTHOR OF *IMAGINARY PEAKS: THE RIESENSTEIN HOAX AND OTHER MOUNTAIN DREAMS*

"Mimi Zieman's book is an ideal alchemy of grit and grace. The lessons Zieman learns on the mountain are important lessons for us all. A wild and deeply satisfying journey."
—EMILY RAPP BLACK, AUTHOR OF *THE STILL POINT OF THE TURING WORLD*

"Mimi Zieman is brave, tough, and impressive when on Everest, and lively, engaging, and funny when on the page. After returning from her climb, she says she was 'very grateful for ceilings.' I myself am grateful for her vivid recounting of all her journeys."
—MEG WOLITZER, AUTHOR OF *THE INTERESTINGS*

"The story takes place on a frozen summit but is bound to melt your heart. The courage that drove [Zieman] to this unlikely adventure permeates her candid recounting of her breathtaking tale."
—ETGAR KERET, AUTHOR OF *THE SEVEN GOOD YEARS*

"The small band that formed the Everest '88 team will be remembered as free spirits who went to the unknown and embraced the true spirit of adventure, a far cry from today's narrative on Everest, and

an essential addition to mountain literature. *In* Tap Dancing on Everest, *expedition doctor Mimi Zieman brings to life the toll experienced by non-climbers on an expedition, what it was truly like not knowing if her teammates would return, and ultimately what it took to heal their wounds. While recalling her tap-dancing days, this book is also a metaphor of a different kind of tap dance, that of survival on the roof of the world."*

—NORBU TENZING, VICE PRESIDENT OF THE AMERICAN
HIMALAYAN FOUNDATION AND
SON OF TENZING NORGAY

*"*Tap Dancing on Everest *is that rare book that manages to capture the adrenaline rush of a thrilling adventure and the gut-wrenching pathos of an epic tragedy. Mimi Zieman is telling a story that readers will be unable to put down—not just about life and death on the world's most dangerous mountain, but about how we, as human beings, too often have to put ourselves in extreme danger to feel fully alive. I was utterly captivated by this story. You will be, too."*
—STEVE ALMOND, AUTHOR OF *ALL THE SECRETS OF THE WORLD*

"[This] story touched me deeply."
—DR. TOM HORNBEIN, AUTHOR OF *EVEREST: THE WEST RIDGE*
AND HIGH-ALTITUDE MEDICINE RESEARCHER

"What would lead a young female medical student from New York City who lived a life of shoulds and expectations to join an unaided climb up Everest as the team doctor? That young woman was Mimi Zieman and, in her memoir Tap Dancing on Everest, *she unravels what brought her to that mountain years ago. In beautiful prose, Zieman brings us into her family's Jewish immigrant roots, her city childhood, her dream to become a dancer, and how climbing and adventure helped her reconcile her past with the woman she became."*
—ANN HOOD, AUTHOR OF *COMFORT:
A JOURNEY THROUGH GRIEF*

"The best ascent of Everest in terms and style of pure adventure."
—**REINHOLD MESSNER**, THE FIRST MAN TO SOLO
EVEREST AND THE FIRST TO CLIMB EVEREST WITHOUT
SUPPLEMENTARY OXYGEN ALONG WITH PETER HABELER

*"From page one, Tap Dancing on Everest draws you into the
heart-stopping world of mountaineering. An engaging narrative
rich in details and vulnerability, the story captures the adventure in
reaching beyond one's comfort zone and into the unknown."*
—**JOHANNA GARTON**, AUTHOR OF *EDGE OF THE MAP:
THE MOUNTAIN LIFE OF CHRISTINE BOSKOFF*

*"A captivating story, seldom told, about what it's like to take care of
Everest climbers from the perspective of a feisty expedition doctor.
This page-turner is a must-read for real and armchair adventurers
everywhere."*
—**STEPHEN VENABLES**, AUTHOR OF *ALONE AT THE SUMMIT* AND
FIRST BRITISH MAN TO SUMMIT EVEREST WITHOUT OXYGEN

*"Climbing Everest was not on Mimi Zieman's bucket list. But after a
lifetime of trying—and often failing—to 'follow the rules' of growing
up a good Jewish girl with the right body, the right boyfriend, and the
right personality, the challenge of the vast mountain calls her. . . . By
turns gripping and charming, tragic and joyful, Zieman's rocky, ultimately revelatory journey shows how the true triumph of the summit
is the discovery of her calling."*
—**ALLISON K WILLIAMS**, AUTHOR OF *SEVEN DRAFTS:
SELF-EDIT LIKE A PRO FROM BLANK PAGE TO BOOK*

*"Mimi Zieman's compelling and very personal memoir recounts with
warmth and insight how her father survived the Holocaust, her
challenging childhood, her courage and determination in the face of
continued obstacles, and the passion and persistence that bring her to
the roof of the world.*
—**ARLENE BLUM**, AUTHOR *ANNAPURNA: A WOMAN'S PLACE*

Tap Dancing on Everest

A Young Doctor's Unlikely Adventure

Mimi Zieman, MD

Essex, Connecticut

An imprint of Globe Pequot, the trade division of
The Rowman & Littlefield Publishing Group, Inc.
4501 Forbes Blvd., Ste. 200
Lanham, MD 20706
www.rowman.com
Falcon and FalconGuides are registered trademarks and Make Adventure Your Story is a
trademark of The Rowman & Littlefield Publishing Group, Inc.

Distributed by NATIONAL BOOK NETWORK

British Library Cataloguing in Publication Information available

Library of Congress Cataloging-in-Publication Data available
ISBN 978-1-4930-7843-1 (paper: alk. paper)
ISBN 978-1-4930-7844-8 (electronic)

♾™ The paper used in this publication meets the minimum requirements of American National
Standard for Information Sciences—Permanence of Paper for Printed Library Materials, ANSI/
NISO Z39.48-1992.

The author and The Rowman & Littlefield Publishing Group, Inc., assume no liability for
accidents happening to, or injuries sustained by, readers who engage in the activities described in
this book.

The author's account is based on journals, letters, and imperfect memories. Names and identifying
details of some individuals have been changed to respect their privacy.

For Jeff, my rock

CONTENTS

PART I
SEARCHING

If we go to the places that scare us . . . we just might find the boundless life we've always dreamed of.

—PEMA CHÖDRÖN

At Risk

MAY 1988, KANGSHUNG GLACIER, TIBET
We peered into the white.

White snow, white clouds, white nothingness. The East Face of Everest, where our route snaked through gullies, crevasses, and overhanging ice pinnacles, rose two miles into the Tibetan sky above.

Our small team of six had four climbers, a photographer, and me, a twenty-five-year-old medical student. The climbers were attempting a new route. They were purists, nimble, using no oxygen or Sherpa support.

Joe, our photographer, sat on a blue barrel at Advanced Base Camp and searched through our telescope for the dark outlines of three climbers missing on the mountain. His eyes—finely tuned to details and shapes, shadows and forms—focused on the white slope. We'd last spotted the climbers days earlier, tiny dots ascending toward the summit, creeping over the edge of our route onto the South Col, the link between Tibet and Nepal, East and South, visible and invisible. We distinguished them by the color of their coats and hats, steadily inching up in the bright sunshine. Now there was no sun, just lackluster white, and our world of waiting felt like groping through darkness, except that everything was flat and stark and still.

The tarp of our yellow tent flapped overhead, the wind electric with panic. I stretched out on my belly to Joe's right, propped up on my elbows, and rubbed my dry eyes, willing our friends into view as if desire were a magnet. My teeth chattered and elbows burned from the pebbles dimpling them, so I piled sleeping bags over and under me. Our team's fourth climber, Paul, who'd been forced off the mountain days earlier due to altitude sickness, stood to Joe's left, just outside the tent. The three of us were on our own route, a route of waiting, tethered as if by climbing ropes.

The landscape offered nothing. No tracks in the snow. No blasts of light from their headlamps: two flashes for *safe*, six for *S.O.S.*

With no sign of them by dusk, my hopes for their return dwindled. They were in the Death Zone, an extreme elevation above 26,000 feet, where oxygen is a fraction of that at sea level. Where muscles lag with lethargy. Where the brain hungers for oxygen, and thoughts stall and sink in a slush of gray matter. Where the body rapidly decays and eventually stops functioning. No climber had ever survived more than three days in the Death Zone without supplemental oxygen. We were nearing the end of day six.

Were our friends stranded in the cold, unable to make decisions? Injured? Or had a crushing wave of wind swept them off the mountain?

Be strong. Come back, I whispered into the whirling white.

An unaided climb like ours had never been attempted on the East Face. We'd been warned that no rescues were available in Tibet. Notorious for thundering avalanches, this side of the mountain had been successfully climbed only once before by a large team using oxygen. Although we'd planned this expedition for two years over phone calls, letters, and faxes, creating long lists of climbing gear, food, and medical supplies, we didn't have radios because of the climbers' purist ethos. Now we hung in deafening silence.

"Dude—d'you see anything?" Paul's voice sliced the thin air as he hopped from leg to leg, itching to bolt if there was a call for help. Our team's jokester, Paul's expression was stoic, his eyes vacant and fixed upwards, his black curls matted with sweat.

Paul had been on his way to the summit with the others when he was pummeled with an unrelenting headache he described as his skull being squeezed by the jaws of a tight vise. He doubled over vomiting and coughing up blood. Forced to retreat, he descended the route alone, returning to Joe and me. I examined him, relieved to find him mostly cured by descent, the air at our camp thicker with oxygen. He was a haunting reminder of what can go wrong in the Death Zone.

"I see something moving," Joe said. I bounded up from my elbows, my heartbeat in my ears.

He sighed. "No, no, it's just the wind."

"Can I have a look?"

I pressed the cold metal against my right eye, squinting with my left. The route stared back blankly, as if mocking me. Then I saw something too—spindly white threads dusting down from the rock outcrops. *Is it them?* No, just sheer drapes of snow flapping in the wind. A mirage of the snow desert. I squeezed my parka tight around me and inhaled deeply, my breath an infusion of dry ice. A shiver rippled through me. I passed the scope back to Joe, shifting my gaze to the back of his red fleece hat.

An expert in f-stops and apertures, Joe was a forty-two-year-old ex-Navy submariner, familiar with isolation and risk. I often spotted him standing on a boulder, head buried under a dark cloth, adjusting lenses for the perfect shot. Not much of a talker, his words rolled out quietly in slow motion, making it hard for me to follow. Now he scrutinized the slope with heightened energy as if this disaster had perked him up.

Like Paul and Joe, I was ready for what I'd trained to do. To treat, wrap, mend, and heal. My preparation didn't stop my endless worry that I would fail when most needed, daunted by my responsibility as medical officer, my official title. I'd rehearsed many scenarios—high altitude sickness, traumatic injuries, infections, frostbite—but the climbers were not there to tend to. I pictured the individual medical kits I'd packed with caffeine pills and steroids to boost energy in case of emergency, wondering if they'd used any of it, wondering if I'd done anything helpful.

Staring at the nothingness, I couldn't imagine a world where Stephen, our cerebral and finicky Brit, never returned to his blooming garden in Bath, or where we didn't tease him when he retreated to his tent to listen to his beloved symphonies. I couldn't imagine not seeing Ed, our slowest and most pensive climber, sitting on a boulder as he wrote in his journal or warming his hands around a mug of hot tea. I couldn't imagine a situation strong enough to take down Robert, architect of schemes in advertising (his day job) and in wilderness adventure (his passion). Our team's leader, who'd planned, organized, and executed this expedition, was a confident athlete, his enthusiasm a spell.

When he'd invited me to join the crew, I asked, "Don't you think you can get a real doctor who's good with altitude?"

"Just remember to major in dread diseases and minor in cold feet and you'll do fine." It turned out that climbers brazen enough to attempt the East Face were unfazed by a student caring for them.

I had left New York three months earlier, desperate for air. My decision to join the team—a city girl who would be the only woman, a dancer who would wear mountain boots, a medical student who would serve as team doctor—didn't make sense to most people. But often, when seized by an instinct, I followed it. It's taken me over three decades to understand that the great peace I felt in the mountains was the perfect antidote to the manic pace of my New York City life, to the divisions and dysfunction of my childhood, to the expectations I felt compelled to fulfill.

When we'd set up this camp months earlier, our new glacier home brimmed with promise. Glistening layers of snow formed solid stepping stones over the crevasses below. We shared rehydrated meals and teased each other, intoxicated by the thrill of adventure. On the longest days, we talked about what we missed and what we'd do when we were off the mountain, how our lives would remain intertwined.

"Can't wait to have a beer in Lhasa!" Robert said.

"What about a slice of New York pizza?" My mind always went straight to pizza.

Searching the slopes above, I thought of the climbers' dreams. I thought of their families. I thought of our discussions about the risks of climbing while huddled in tents during endless snowstorms, inhaling the fragility of life together, bonding in a way not possible at home. I reassured myself they were doing what they loved.

Be strong, come back, I whispered again.

If Paul and Joe had similar panicked thoughts and worst-case scenarios running in a loop inside their minds, they didn't say so. There was nothing to do and nothing to say. We listened to the drip, drip, drip of ice thawing in the warmer spring temperatures, the water flowing over unsteady rocks causing us to slide and scramble on visits from tent to tent, our shoulders slumped with worry. The unearthed glacial detritus smelled of decay, the brackish water layered with notes of algae like musky wine.

The flat white of day became a black cavern of night. I moved into Joe's tent, hoping to lessen the crushing weight of emptiness. A tempest outside dropped a wet, heavy snowfall characteristic of a spring monsoon. I lay listening to booming avalanches tumbling down the bowl of mountains above. The ground trembled as the wind rattled the tent and fear pounded in my chest. Peeking outside the vestibule, I saw no line between sky and earth. I curled myself into a tight ball inside my bag, turned away from Joe, and rubbed my bare feet against my hot-water bottle. My fingers grazed the stethoscope and blood pressure cuff next to my thighs; I slept with them to keep them warm and ready to use.

Though I aimed for silence, Joe heard me weeping. He turned toward me, draping me in a deep and lulling melody, harmonizing with the sound of snow drumming rhythmically in the blackness. Snowflakes fell, undeterred, as drafts of wind dusted my face and his words petered out. I expected to be up for a while, with the cold air singeing my cheeks and the constant roars in the distance. At midnight I surrendered, took a sleeping pill, savored the way the heaviness fell first on my chest then spread through my arms to my fingertips.

When I next looked at my watch, a mere three hours had passed. I rolled on my back and stared at the nylon above, listening to the tapping on the roof, trying to contain my swelling heartache. I waited until Joe stirred, then reached for the frozen metal telescope as the slanted pink of morning appeared.

Seven days after we'd last spotted the climbers, Joe stirred a pot of oatmeal. "Maybe we can't see them because they went down a different route." Expeditions from Nepal and Tibet were climbing other faces on the mountain and had larger teams, more support, oxygen, and porters. Could our climbers have joined them?

"It's possible, but there was no one else up there," Paul said. After a long pause, he added, "I think you're right. We should pack up camp and find out if anyone in the valley heard anything."

I had no theories. In this thick muck of waiting, I thought of Robert's father, whom I'd met a few times. I couldn't imagine telling him Robert was gone and watching his eyes fill with loss. Would it be my job to tell the families? Not even a real doctor yet, and three people gone under my care. Was I brave or simply naive to come here?

I sat on an icy rock, the chill a shock running up my spine, and stared upward at the slope, as if from the bottom of a crevasse. As if I'd fallen too and was more vulnerable than ever before. This was the power of loss. We were all fragile and at risk.

Part II

THE VERSAILLES

To be nobody-but-yourself in a world which is doing its best, night and day, to make you everybody else—means to fight the hardest battle which any human being can fight; and never stop fighting.
                    —E. E. CUMMINGS, *A Poet's Advice to Students*

2

Feet First

I READ THE *NEW YORK* MAGAZINE PIECE THE DAY BEFORE LEAVING FOR the expedition. "The ethereal, soft-spoken blonde seems an unlikely candidate for an assault team of any kind." Despite feeling flattered the journalist called me ethereal instead of harried, the last thing I needed was yet another person questioning my suitability. I had done enough of that already. Placing the galley page back on my desk, I looked at the stuff strewn across the floor.

I needed to pack.

I hadn't realized my *unlikeliness* was obvious enough to be revealed in a single hour-long interview. To generate interest in our climb, Robert, our expedition leader, had successfully pitched a "couch-to-climb" story to the magazine. The published article featured a photo of me balancing between walls in my apartment building stairwell wearing green medical scrubs on top, purple exercise tights, white ankle socks, and flat sneakers. Andy Warhol graced the cover.

Scanning the two large gray duffels and last-minute toiletries I'd bought, it seemed clear the journalist had exposed me for who I really was—someone who should not be on an Everest team. Someone who'd heard these messages in childhood: *know your place, follow a safe path, do the things you should do.*

But there I was in full-page color—*unlikely* and doing something I *shouldn't.* Although she'd figured me out quickly, the journalist didn't know how unlikely my journey to this moment had been. Looking back, I imagine my route to Everest as a hiking trail on a map drawn with dashed lines, the blanks between the lines like suspended breaths where I paused to figure out which way to go.

Did my early years—a New York City life of concrete—lead me to choose the expansiveness of a glacier? I had felt confined by various boxes and expectations: cement apartment building, immigrant family, Jewish Orthodox community, and my own list of *shoulds*. All hard surfaces, sharp angles, and deep shadows.

I didn't yet know that on the mountain, we would experience the opposite: long, spreading shadows and melting, morphing surfaces of ice and snow. The rhythm of our days would be at the whim of wind and at the wile of changing seasons.

Everest was not on my list of *shoulds*.

But it was my family, replete with ghosts and outsized personalities, who set me on my trail long before I made choices for myself. I can't write about how I landed on that glacier without writing about them, my map of origin, my genetic and emotional signposts. And although they were stitched into the seams of my backpack, and I treasured that tethering, I needed to loosen those threads to find my own lines.

As I shoved my gear into the duffels, I didn't think about the weight my past added to my load. Tracing my journey now, the dashed lines connecting these extremes—my family's background and Everest—come into focus.

Mom rolled her stockings up each leg and clipped them into the bottom of her girdle, a one-piece undergarment that smoothed her into a large rectangle from sternum to thigh, topped with two pointy cones. In third grade, I watched Mom get ready for work. She opened her closet, clanging the belts draped on a rod, and reached for a dress.

"Why do you wear that thing? It looks so uncomfortable." I crossed my arms in front of my chest. My grandmother wore the same contraption.

"You have to."

"No, you don't. It really doesn't make much difference."

"You have to look your best." Mom brushed her hair then lit a Kent and inhaled. Her chest rose gradually until full, then she released a short *pup* sound, and blew out slowly between pursed lips. When done, she tamped the red-smudged butt, stenciled with lip lines, into an L-shape in the ashtray.

Mom was meticulous about her grooming and dress, but we all had to navigate our large bodies in our own way. When I was nine, I tagged along with my mother to Weight Watchers and Lane Bryant, a specialized store for big sizes. My brother Josh, three and a half years older, wore clothes that came in "husky" sizes, while mine were called "chubby" (terms replaced by "plus" or more neutral words). At Weight Watchers, I learned everything I needed to know about what to eat while dieting, including relying on staples like cottage cheese, cantaloupe, and Tab.

My mother's mother, whom we called Amama (*Uh-muh-muh*), was the first of our family to immigrate in search of freedom. Her sturdy legs and size-ten flat feet with bunions crossed oceans, if not glacial crevasses. In 1956, she walked off a Flying Tiger flight from Munich onto the tarmac in New York City, surely wearing clunky orthopedic shoes, then stood before the six-floor apartment building on the Upper West Side where she was to rent a room. That year, the airline had begun carrying European refugees and Korean war orphans to the United States, two disparate peoples, both displaced.

If Amama had looked that day on the sidewalk the way I knew her later, she stood tall with skinny limbs and a round middle pinched in a sheath dress. She combed her thinning hair over a balding head and wore bright red lipstick, a cigarette dangling between the fingers of her right hand, a chunky gold ring on her fourth finger. Maybe people a block away could even hear her impassioned smoker's cough.

She faced double glass doors adorned with gold letters in rolled cursive: *The Versailles*. The name evoked gilded chandeliers and rich tapestries. Instead, she found a lobby with ornate moldings buried under thick layers of cracked paint.

Like her shoes, nothing about our family's matriarch was delicate. Fired from her job as a choreographer for the Berlin Opera in 1933 because she was Jewish, Amama was in her early twenties when she crossed the Mediterranean to Palestine. Her decision to leave Germany the year Hitler rose to power was bold. It saved her life. In Palestine, she married and bore my mother, but never grew accustomed to the raw life of sand and heat.

After the war, she returned to Germany with my mother, then eighteen. Amama thought she was returning home, but Germany would never be home again. She had divorced—rare for her day—as was moving to another country with a daughter on your own, as was returning to Germany. But Amama was her own guide, following her own path. The first unlikely one.

Examining a picture of Amama from her dancing days, it's clear we have the same legs: slightly thick dimpled knees and long, thin calves tapering into those size-ten flat feet with bunions. Amama's legs and my legs share not only a shape but a rhythm that carried us on our different searches for belonging.

One year after Amama's arrival, my parents sailed into New York Harbor. The ship's manifest lists them as Sabina and Izschak Ziemann. I don't know when Dad became Isaac, when the final "n" in our last name was dropped, or when the pronunciation changed from tsee-mahn to zee-min. Very likely it happened in the port when they were processed through immigration, as these stories commonly go.

Not until I was in middle school did I hear Dad say, "We arrived on the last day permissible under the Refugee Relief Act." Before, I'd thought of them as immigrants, not refugees.

They moved into Amama's apartment with her. As a child, I didn't know I lived among brave immigrants, but I knew the Versailles reeked. Whenever I crossed the inlay of a star barely visible on the scuffed marble floor of the lobby, I reflexively held my breath to avoid inhaling the rancid mix of garbage and cigarette smoke.

The odor concentrated in the elevator, which worked only sporadically, so instead I took the stairs—my first climb—passing the smell of the tamales Mrs. Vegas fried on the second floor, the gingerbread

Christmas cookies Mrs. Scott baked on the third floor, and Mom's simmering chicken soup with matzo balls from our fourth-floor apartment. Sometimes, I found glass seltzer bottles in front of our door, delivered by the seltzer man.

Our neighborhood was full of similar refugees, with stories both commonplace and extraordinary. World War II displaced Jews from faraway countries hard for me to pronounce and others hard to imagine. Czechoslovakia, Uzbekistan, Hungary, Ukraine, Poland. The streets were thick with the cadence of accents: Spanish speakers from Puerto Rico, Cuba, and the Dominican Republic, as well as Creole speakers from Jamaica and Haiti, and speakers of myriad Asian languages.

My family's railroad apartment, built as a series of rooms resembling a train car, housed six other people or families. They lived in different rooms branching off two long hallways, meeting to form an "L." Eventually, Amama moved to Queens, and all but one of the other lodgers left. My parents took over the lease.

The remaining tenant, Mr. Thomas L. Montefront, lived in the tiniest room with an even tinier bathroom off our kitchen—the "maid's room," as these were called in old New York City apartments. Soft-spoken, he shuffled into the kitchen after a day of work, his huge galoshes squishing over the linoleum, and greeted my mother politely, "Hello, Mrs. Zieman. How are you?" Sometimes, he mentioned the weather or placed a single strawberry Dannon yogurt in the refrigerator. He often left us missionary pamphlets on the counter, turned on his radio tuned to the Christian broadcasting station, and we learned secondhand about the power of the Lord. Mom never asked Mr. Montefront to move out. He had no family, and besides, refugees take people in, they don't put them out. She also appreciated his paltry rent, paid in dollar bills left on the stove.

Mom admitted that, like many Israelis, she resembled the sabra fruit: prickly on the outside but soft on the inside. She grew up during wartime, experiencing rations, air raids, and racing for cover in bomb shelters. She had an exuberant opinion and method for everything and expressed her love through order: cooking, cleaning, budgeting.

"Your father's Yiddish is High Yiddish," Mom boasted, distinguishing it from what most people they knew spoke, referring to a dialect with more German than Slavic influence. My parents had met at a party for Jewish students in Frankfurt, my father invited from Munich as the entertainment to sing and recite long Yiddish tales. "He was handsome and charming, and I was a catch too." Mom recounted how they'd flirted and danced, and how boys had swarmed her. She was twenty, and he was thirty-five, too young (Mom) or needy (Dad) to recognize their brokenness or how mismatched they were. But they had the experience of displacement in common. He had been forced to flee Latvia, invaded by Nazis, as a young man.

Mom also boasted about the Versailles, saying, "Mary Pickford once lived in the building, as well as the makers of Hellmann's mayonnaise." This might have been true, but by the time they moved in, the building was in major disrepair, filled with people like them living under rent control. Maybe Mom needed to feel like she had landed somewhere better than she did. The Versailles—pinned on my map as "Start here," before my first dashed line.

Unlike Mom's proud voice or prickly exterior, Dad's voice was gentle, methodical, reflective. Mostly, he loved to be talked about and was less interested in talking, Mom's sphere. My emotional signposts were opposites: overflowing and withholding.

Mom worked in a hospital analyzing blood specimens. Dad was a psychotherapist. She worked on the insides of the body and he on the insides of the mind, but neither type of work helped them completely understand their children's lives in the new country.

I froze behind my bedroom door, listening to the tumult of grievances erupting from my parents' room next door. "Where have you been all night? I'm not an idi*ot*!" Mom spat the "*ot*" sound with an Israeli emphasis. "Bina, you're so controlling!" Dad's favorite refrain.

Doors slammed.

I covered my ears, tiptoed to my bed, and crawled under the covers. Hiding became a mantra, invisibility a shield, and seeking refuge, a mission. The noise, the shouting, and anger drove me into solitude.

One humid evening when I was six, pigeons cooed on the kitchen window ledge and the laundry hung limply on a rack near the dumb-waiter. Mom, Dad, and Josh sipped tea at the kitchen table, while I sat cross-legged on the floor playing jacks. "Does she have to come every weekend?" Dad asked Mom about Amama's upcoming visit. "She picks fights with me, and you go along."

I threw the red ball up in the air and swooshed my hand on the linoleum to pick up the jacks in a single bounce. My stomach knotted, waiting for the familiar fighting to begin.

"Tough! At least she helps me. You don't lift a finger!" Mom's nostrils flared.

I stayed quiet, tossing the ball and sweeping up the jacks, wishing my father and Amama got along. Dad complained before and after her visits, disappearing into his own version of invisibility while she was there.

"What about *your* mother?" I bounced the ball again, trying to change the subject.

"Tell them, Isaac," Mom thrust her chin upward at Dad. I squeezed the ball in my hand. Did I say something wrong?

After a long pause, my father spoke softly. "Mimele, my parents were killed, and my sisters and brother. I have no family. There was a big war, and they killed people for being Jewish."

Dad sat unmoving and Mom looked frozen in battle mode. *Is Daddy okay?* I searched Josh's face. I relied on him most to explain things, but he focused downwards. I wondered if he knew already. My father's voice came from a mile away, but his words didn't make sense. He talked about fleeing Hitler, the death of millions of people, and his own near death.

I looked around the room again. Everyone slouched in their chairs, stared at the table, mouths downturned. No one looked at me. The lump in my throat tightened, my stomach clenched, my knuckles balled into fists. I faced the hallway to leave, but my body froze. The yellow light of the kitchen darkened and closed in around us, squeezing us into a pipe, changing our matter like steam condensing to water.

No point in bouncing a ball. How silly next to death. How silly anything in my life would be compared to what Daddy had gone through.

My troubles would all be insignificant. Daddy's entire family was killed. I would never be worthy of my parents' concern. How could I be?

A new line was etched on my map. A line with a before and after.

Later, when Dad told his story again, I thought it inconceivable that this man in front of me, alive if not accessible, had endured such horrors. He'd recite details flatly, as if distant history, always with events in the same order, yet I could never keep track of the sequence. I felt guilty about this until I learned it is common. Many children of Holocaust survivors can't remember the details of their parents' stories. Yet, our parents' anxiety, their melancholy, their words and emotions not expressed took root in us. We were instructed to "never forget." While I can't forget, I can't seem to remember either.

The early part is simple to grasp; Dad grew up in an Orthodox Jewish home in a small shtetl in Latvia, the eldest of four children. The family lived above their grocery store.

The improbable part follows and my mind wanders. Dad was away at school when Nazi collaborators took his family and the rest of the village to the forest and shot them. He fought with the resistance, enlisted in the Soviet army, and was sent to work in a Siberian coal mine where he almost died.

His talent for languages helped him assume five fake identities, enabling him to survive. He was born Zelick Tziman. At one point, he taught himself Polish from a book and posed as a lost Polish soldier to escape Russia. At the end of the war, on his way from Poland to Czechoslovakia, he pretended to be a lost Greek Jew with the name Yitchak Yehovi. His name in America was Isaac Zelig Zieman. Zelig—like the character in the eponymous movie who transforms his identity to match the needs and desires of the people he meets. Only after the war did Dad learn he was the only survivor of his family.

His survival. Truly the definition of unlikely.

His story explained why I had three first names, Gilda for Dad's mother Golda, Miriam and Tzila for his two sisters. I struggled with my name. It never felt like me. What did I have to do to make up for those lost? In Jewish school we learned, *If I am only for myself, what am I?* We were to honor those killed by improving the world, a defining sense of duty. But being named for three murdered relatives was a heavy load.

The day I learned my father's history, my trust in the world—in people, in the future, and in myself—was shaken. Dad's presence confirmed life could shift unexpectedly. Because of what he'd been through, I thought I couldn't ask him for help, so I'd need to figure things out on my own. As he did. As Mom and Amama did, too. This unspoken expectation landed on me, a weight, as painful as it was inevitable.

When Mom came home from work, she cooked a full meal each night, with meat, a starch, and a vegetable, usually canned. Thursdays were the exception, always crunchy fried flounder, pillowy mashed potatoes, and frozen creamed spinach. I savored every bite. We never had dessert, of course, because we were watching our weight. Yet the pantry was stocked with Devil Dogs and Ring Dings, which we ate whenever we wanted. Like other parents of the time, Mom said, "Clear your plates; there are children starving in Africa." The nightly news in 1969 showed Biafran babies with skinny arms, swollen bellies, and eyes too sunken and dry to shed tears, victims of a civil war in Nigeria. The images troubled me as a six-year-old, but the babies seemed as far away from me as my dead relatives.

I wondered about my family's obsession with eating. *Is it because Dad nearly starved to death working as a slave laborer in the coal mine?*

In Novosibirsk, Siberia, a military officer had sent him to the miners' infirmary. "I had no idea such a thing existed," Dad said. "I was emaciated. A kind woman took pity on me. She brought me a bowl of thin broth each day." He described her intervention as random—and the reason he survived. Also, the reason he savored food, taking time with each slurped spoonful of the soft-boiled eggs he ate from special, oval egg cups.

I've since learned that Holocaust survivors, or their children, often develop pathologies related to food, whether over- or undereating. Despite our joy at being allowed to eat all the treats we wanted, we were ashamed of our girth and felt guilt about our privilege. This abundance was an accident of where and when we were born: not in Biafra and not during the Holocaust. Another random circumstance of good fortune, like Dad's soup lady.

It makes sense that those palpable events, the ones that make our throats tighten and stomachs clench, that change our matter and our sense of self, that have a before and after, can transfer not only psychologically but also physiologically. They may be woven within the expression of our genes, an encoding, a remembering, a shifting within, a process called epigenetics.

While Dad's trauma might have been passed in cellular form, my body had its own memories buried deeply.

On the snowy New Year's Eve my mother went into labor with me, six weeks early, Amama babysat Josh. Mom was *farpitzed* for a New Year's celebration, her Yiddish word for dressed up, her dark hair set in a high pouf with spray, her brown eyes smoky with blue shadow, her lips and long nails swiped siren red. I imagine she would have leaned into the mirror to powder her olive skin, which glinted as if she, herself, had been plucked from a tree in the Mediterranean. She loved to be the life of the party.

Dad also would have been dressed smartly, his dark hair slicked back, smelling impeccably clean, sealed with aftershave. His eyes, the color of not-here-not-there hazel, befitted his displaced-person lot. I picture Mom leaning closer to the mirror to apply mascara, as she always did, when the first contraction came.

Amama dipped doughnuts into an enormous gleaming pot of oil, her traditional German treat for New Year's Eve, as my parents dashed to the hospital.

"Can you put more sprinkles on, Amama?" Josh asked.

"Ya, Pushkin. As much as you vant."

She heaped powdered sugar and colorful sprinkles on the doughnuts while ashes from her cigarette dropped onto the stove and the plastic ladle melted near the flame. When she moved to the table, Josh climbed onto her ample, crumb-filled lap.

Dr. Lapid, Mom's obstetrician, rushed into Mount Sinai Hospital. Mom was bleeding heavily, and I was positioned feet first. He quickly scrubbed in the delivery room, pulled on my ankles, and declared, "At least you will get a tax deduction."

"If she wanted to come early, in this blizzard," my father said, "she will be fierce like a Cossack!" He knew about such things from his time in Siberia.

It was a dramatic delivery for a future OB/GYN.

After birth, they placed me in my first box. A literal one. The incubator was typical for four-pound preemies, who were ogled through faintly distorted glass portals.

Another box came quickly. At six months old, my legs were bound in plaster casts, forcing me to lug my body by my arms for a year.

"You were pitiful," Mom told me later. She described my legs as "turned wrong," while twisting her arms inside-out to demonstrate. She said I wriggled up from my belly onto my elbows, grunted onto my wrists, and inched across the floor like a worm. When Mom pointed outside the window at my friend with fiery orange hair crossing Broadway to visit us, I hoisted myself up to the windowsill to see him. The outside world was already more colorful and beckoning. And I was already searching.

A sense of freedom accompanies my earliest memory. *A bad odor rises to fill the halls and lime green walls of the hospital when they saw the casts off my legs. My damp thighs touch air again and can breathe.* As a child, this was a clear memory. Now, it's a memory of a memory.

I can trace everything important to my legs, born first, bound in plaster, inspired by Amama, gaining strength in dance long before climbing over mountain ranges.

Amama signed me up for a dance class at the "Y" when I was two, telling my mother, "Never mind she had the casts. She vill learn to dance." Snuggling in Amama's lap, the metal snaps of her housecoat cooled my skin, and the chain attached to her eyeglasses left track marks on my temple. She smelled sweet, of syrup and cinnamon, but also sour, of pickles and liverwurst and the diabetes that slumped and rounded her tall figure.

When I was six, she schlepped me to classes at Martha Graham's studio on the East Side. I cowered next to the naked grown-up bodies in the dressing room. We lined up and did triplets across the studio, a saunter in rhythm, from bent knees to tippy toes. I always hated "across the room" in dance. Too many eyes on me, my body awkward, already judged too large, and full of shame.

In grade school, I couldn't ignore the skinny models who graced magazine covers and the messages to diet in every advertisement. Especially in our plus-size family. We stood out. When the school custodian delivered boxes of cold milk at 10:00 a.m. snack time, mine was skim. Maybe my devotion to eating was a way to devour my feelings, folded neatly into the cream centers of Oreos. Later, denying myself food would feel like power. Later still, society would finally embrace the message to feel good about our bodies in every size.

The reasons for shame piled up in my mind. Parents with accents. Almost no extended family since Dad's relatives were all murdered. In private school on financial aid. Wearing glasses. As a chubby kid, I received compliments on select parts of myself: blonde hair, blue eyes, and dimpled smile. "You have a pretty face," leaving unsaid, "as opposed to your body."

One entire summer at camp when I was eleven, I loathed my stomach rolls, the way my thighs chafed, how different I looked. I couldn't swap jeans with the other girls, instead wearing my ugly chubby-girl clothes. The best way to escape judgment, it seemed to me, was to hide, and I thought wearing a large blue sweatshirt did the trick. One day while crossing a bridge, my hands tucked in the kangaroo pocket, I overheard a conversation between two boys. "You mean the fat girl in the sweatshirt?" one asked the other.

I stopped in my tracks.

Our bodies: defining us, composing us, clenching memories within our casings of skin, sometimes trussed in girdles.

Our bodies: our first consciousness.

My body, so much a part of my story.

My body, my map.

3

Immersion

I LISTENED ON AMAMA'S LAP WHILE SHE SPOKE TO MOM IN GERMAN. I listened to Mom gossiping with her friends in Hebrew. I listened quietly for many years. Listening to languages was a window.

Amama's German words crackled: *vunderbar*, *schrecklich*, and one of her nicknames for me, *Quatsch Backe*. That one sizzled with love. German, with its hard, guttural sounds like sandpaper, disliked by many Jews after the horrors of Hitler, felt like home to me.

On weekends, Amama and I were roommates. She was a queen in my bed, while I slept on a folding cot next to her, not needing to shout and beg for a tuck-in. As we lay side by side, she taught me German. "Say *ich*," she instructed, and I repeated "*ish*," never getting the sounds right. She circled words in her German word-find book, the sound of the pen scratching the page, a gurgling cough, a soft kiss good night. Contained in this room with Amama, I had no need to hide or leave.

She told me about her different jobs, introducing me to the wider world. Her favorite was chef on a cruise ship. One night when I was around five, she surprised me in bed.

"Sveetie, I brought you a doll from Haiti."

I wrapped my arms tight around her, squeezing her waist, inhaling her vinegary scent.

"What was it like, Amama?"

"*Nein* . . . I didn't get off the boat, but I make *gross salate* and sculptures from pineapples *und* vatermelons. I vill show you a picture." She told me about an enormous party where the guests had danced to island music. Although she was thrilled with the festivities, I felt sad she didn't leave the ship.

Mom's Hebrew, the language of Jewish prayer, square sounds with emphatic consonants and sharp corners, seeped through my skin and crouched in wait.

Dad's talent for languages dazzled in the way unique sounds and syntax rolled effortlessly off his tongue even when decades had passed since regular use. He spoke Yiddish, Latvian, Russian, German, Hebrew, Polish, and English, acquired in that order. Some he picked up on the run, listening to words carried on the wind while crouching in a field to steal potatoes, absorbing what he needed to know—where to go, what to avoid—to stay alive. From him I learned that deciphering foreign words was a key to passage.

Dad's Yiddish sounded melodic and old country. He nodded with his eyebrows raised when repeating one-liners, like *tsvey kluge kenen nit shtimen*, or two smart people can't agree. He laughed with his shoulders heaving up and down when he told classic jokes: Five Jewish women are eating lunch in a busy café. Nervously, their waiter approaches the table. "Ladies," he says. "Is *anything* okay?"

Their landscape of phrases fertilized my first impressions. It meant something when they changed channels to a different accent. Usually, it meant they didn't want Josh and me to understand. They wanted us to be American, which meant speaking English, but our ears were primed.

We learn languages by immersion, gradually increasing clarity. From this priming, I sought different immersions, again and again, shifts from confusion to new worlds of knowing, shifts to the feeling of belonging.

When the curtain had fallen after the first act of *A Chorus Line* during a school outing freshman year of high school, I turned to my best friend and said, "I want to do that!" Awed by the power and grace of the dancers' movements, the confidence they had in their bodies, I wanted this immersion. The popularity of jazz dance was at an all-time high in 1976, and I didn't need a map to find my way to the Phil Black Dance Studio on Broadway.

Almost every evening until I graduated from high school, I traveled by subway to 50th Street, passed the doughnut shop and the sweet scent of sugar and glaze on the first floor, climbed the stairs past "Girls XXX" on the second floor, and reached Phil Black on the third. The sleaze factor didn't bother me—I'd already learned how to expertly navigate seedy neighborhoods: keep my face down, make no eye contact, and hold my bag close. I turned my body sideways to avoid the men headed to the second floor.

Dance was pure abandon. Freedom from second-guessing everything. Feeling the bop-bop-bop rhythms. Pulsing to the beats and the pauses, training to isolate and control every muscle, owning the air between landings. My goal became to reach the level of the Broadway dancers in the advanced classes.

Tap dancing was like joining a cabal of jokesters. The Shirley Temple beginner routines were so silly I couldn't help but feel joy. Later, complicated syncopations challenged me. This, too, was a new language. Shuffle ball change. Time steps. Pullbacks. Wings. Cramp rolls. I got to be the drummer and the drum. Inside the beat. My body *was* the music.

One afternoon in my senior year of high school, I finally felt ready to take Phil Black's advanced jazz class. Phil was an intimidating, mustachioed teacher who beat his bongo drums to the rhythms he wanted us to jeté, twirl, or tap to. I'd taken his tap classes, but his demanding approach intensified in advanced jazz. He screamed at dancers or banished them if they didn't measure up. "What are you looking at?" he sneered at those watching themselves in the mirror. "There's nothing to see. Trust me."

Lining up in the back of the class, well behind the professional dancers claiming the front row, I made myself small, hoping Phil wouldn't notice me, while also hoping that if he did, I'd be good enough. We kicked our legs high in the air to Natalie Cole's "This Will Be," sauntered with jazz walks—torsos opposite hips—and leapt across the floor. We rotated lining up in the front row for our pirouettes: singles, doubles, triples, quads, bent knees, tippy toes, to the right, to the left. I concentrated on balance, digging my toes into the floor, avoiding looking at myself in the mirror or meeting Phil's eyes. My body rotated—muscle memory—one, two, three times. Spine straight, shoulders back, center grounded. As I turned my head to spot within the twirl of motion, my eyes met Phil watching me. His look was unmistakable. Downturned lips, pinched eyebrows. But no words, no shouting. My heart pounded, my breath shallow, I rotated out of the row. *Am I not worthy of a scream? Did my attempts to stay under the radar work? Or did I earn my spot?*

I didn't have an answer, but when I came home, I finally told Mom, "I want to be a dancer."

"You'll starve!" she shouted without missing a beat. "You have a perfectly good brain—use it!" I'd heard that message enough times. Do well in school so you can get a good job. Mom didn't like me spending so much time dancing and had made it clear she didn't think I could earn a living that way.

"You've never even seen me dance!"

Since Phil's was a professional studio, there were no recitals, and she'd never come to watch me. One evening, Mom came to Phil's and stood outside the studio's glass wall. I don't remember her reaction to the seedy neighborhood where I'd spent those years or any comments about my dancing. I only remember her silence, which for Mom, said a lot. Couldn't she think of one positive thing to say? One of her stock phrases—*Who do you think you are*—coursed through my mind. I stewed as we rode the subway uptown, longing for her to say something encouraging. Choosing to dance as a career was a big decision. I wanted to believe Phil keeping me in his class meant I had potential, but I didn't ask him or my other dance teachers for advice. I cowered from authority.

Who did I think I was? Not someone good enough to be a dancer. After years of work, I gave up my dream to be a dancer fairly quickly, although I vowed to never stop dancing. The risk of struggling to earn a living, as my parents did, was too great. I wasn't ready to give up hiding, to expose myself to auditions and be beaten down by rejections. There would be no one to prop me up when I was down, no one who believed in me. Including me. Especially me. I chose safe. I chose *should*. I chose college.

Studying at McGill University in Montreal was a language immersion with convolutions: an English-speaking school in a French-speaking city. A French-speaking city in an English-speaking country.

I wish I could say I chose McGill because of a romanticism about crossing borders and exploring the world. Shortly after I arrived in 1980, Ronald Reagan was elected, leaving the United States divided and me embarrassed while watching his inauguration in a basement dorm among jeering Canadians who thought the new president clownish. But the real reason I was there was because McGill was significantly less expensive than comparable US schools. Dad had forgotten to fill out the financial aid forms for my top choice school. I raged at him and then headed north.

Montreal also teemed with immigrants. Their colorful shops smelled of cumin, clove, and curry, turning a sidewalk stroll into a sensory immersion. Spicy restaurants awakened my tongue. French roused my ears. Every street promised reinvention, and I walked them in my oversized thrift-shop men's blazer with wide shoulder pads and purple plaid balloon pants—it *was* 1980—sporting a bad haircut I'd given myself. Far from the New York City I was used to, here was a different gray, a different spray of shadows.

When I came home from college for freshman winter break, a girl my age who'd come to New York from the Midwest to be a dancer, was renting my bedroom, next door to Mom's room.

"How's the dancing going?" I asked my doppelgänger when we met in the kitchen outside of Mr. Montefront's room, his Christian radio audible, late at night. She told me which classes she was taking, and about the studios and teachers she liked or didn't. Far from a "starving artist," she was heavyset. Not only was she brave for following her dreams, but she did so despite not fitting the mold of what was expected of a dancer.

One day when she left for ballet, I snuck into my old room and looked in the closet.

"Ma! Where are my jazz shoes?" I hollered.

"I threw those out. You have a new pair."

"What?" I yelled, stomping down the hallway and slamming the door to the apartment. I'd been planning to frame my first pair of white

Capezios. Mended with silver duct tape, they represented years of work, steps, and dreams. All now lost.

The instant I disembarked from the twelve-hour train ride back to Montreal into my first Canadian winter, my entire face got brain freeze, and my eyelashes icicled. I trudged through the long season in my Timberland boots—to science classes, to the theater for dance troupe practice, to sit-ins urging the university to divest from South Africa, and to the Women's Center where I worked on a literary magazine. I walked and walked, no matter the chill or snow, up Mount Royal and down, over sidewalks and through neighborhoods. Huddled with my parka hood tied in front of my face, the wind toppling me, I budgeted an extra twenty minutes to thaw my fingers for exams.

A perfect curriculum in severe cold.

The summer after freshman year, I craved a language immersion. I'd studied Hebrew in *Yeshiva*, Spanish in high school, and French in Montreal. I took a job waitressing in a hotel in Switzerland to improve my German.

But I failed.

At a long wooden table with other guest workers, most of them from Yugoslavia, the Swiss hotel served us a meat stew every night that I couldn't eat. At twelve, I'd announced, "Ma, I'm a vegetarian. I'm not eating meat . . . or fish. I don't want to eat animals."

"That's ridiculous!" Mom flipped the schnitzel she was frying at the stove. "What will you eat? I'm not making you any special food!"

"Did I ask you to?"

With little to eat in Switzerland, I lost ten pounds. My new slim felt good. Slim prompted hunger to root in me. Slim prompted a hollow and a svelte that would become addictive.

When I spilled soup on an ancient woman in the fancy hotel restaurant, she scowled. My boss, who was watching, scolded me dramatically in German. I gave up, quit, and returned home.

If this had happened to Amama, she would have said, "Never mind I spilled some soup," and brushed it off. Once when I was a young girl,

Mr. Montefront walked past Amama, sitting at the kitchen table, to enter his room. "Mackafuck is home," she blared, as he closed his door. I held two fingers up to my lips to shush her, while we both burst with laughter. She got away with saying anything in her heavy German accent.

Amama spoke her mind so fiercely that whenever someone stood up for themselves, we called it "pulling an Amama." Once I sat beside her in a taxi when she got angry with the driver about the route he drove. I crouched into the black leather, trying to fold into the crack. *It's not a big deal*, I thought. *Let it pass.* She yelled at the driver to stop immediately, then stormed out. She took my hand, proud, as if nothing had happened, and guided me down the sidewalk.

I didn't yet know that everyone should learn to "pull an Amama."

She smooshed my face between her plump knuckles and cooed, "Miss America." This nickname was not about me becoming a beauty queen but her affirmation of my place in this new country, and the expectation that I listen for, and seize, opportunities.

But expectations could also feel like duty.

After returning from Switzerland a failure, my duty was to find another job quickly. I became a room service waitress for the breakfast shift at a new hotel in the World Trade Center. The only other passengers on the subway at 5:00 a.m. were pimps and prostitutes. I told Dad that I sat on the edge of my seat every morning, so he bought me a can of mace to protect myself. After a few weeks, I quit.

I hurried into my third job, selling ice cream as a street vendor, but days after starting, the police towed my cart into a truck and handed me a summons for selling in a forbidden street zone. Appearing before the judge, I trembled. "Your Honor, I had no idea I wasn't allowed to park there."

"Ignorance of the law is no excuse!" The judge pounded his gavel and charged me a fine.

I longed for Mom or Dad to be beside me in court, but they were both at work, supporting and building their separate lives.

Not long after I'd learned about my father's Holocaust past, when I was seven, Mom had summoned the family to Josh's room. She sat on the bed while Josh and I played with wooden blocks on the floor. Her lips stretched tight and thin as she said, matter-of-factly, "Your father is moving out."

Dad stood by the door. "We are getting a separation."

I didn't understand and looked at my brother for help. Josh rolled a block in his hand, and stared down at it, his bottom lip jutting out. "It's like a divorce." Despite my parents' constant battles, I was stunned.

Josh crossed his arms in front of his chest. "That's so stupid," he yelled.

My body rocked back and forth. My body wailed. Mom's red lips remained tight and straight. Dad looked as though he couldn't disappear fast enough. I wondered why they were treating it like it was no big deal. I didn't know anyone whose parents were divorced.

Later, I overheard Mom explain to friends. "Well, it isn't good for the children if I stay in a marriage where I'm unhappy, either." This made sense, even if I didn't like it, even if I wished they'd get back together. Since Mom and Amama were both divorced, they always emphasized that a woman should never rely on a man, either financially or for her happiness.

After Dad moved out, he became a barely there shadow, and a new normal emerged from Mom's need for control. Although Mom liked her work, she despised her hospital situation, fighting constantly with her supervisor. She never shied from battle.

Friday nights, after Mom had endured a long work week, Josh and I braced ourselves in anticipation of the turn of her key in the lock. Friday nights were not about welcoming Shabbat in peace. As Mom walked the hallways, she noted the mess, or the table not set, or the bathtub not properly scrubbed. When the steam within her rose, she bubbled over like a teakettle until the explosion of its whistle, and the release of certain phrases on loop. When she was really angry, she used our Hebrew names: "Yehoshua! Miriam! Two good-for-nothings, what's the matter with you? You can't do anything right; do not talk back, you live in my house—I say what goes! Who do you think you are?" And most stinging: "If you don't like it here, go live with your father." After he'd left, I'd never stayed over at his place.

Not living up to her expectations led to frequent warnings of a spanking so severe "it would sizzle." I was more shocked than afraid on the rare occasion she grabbed a belt. I have no memory of pain, just of my own bubbling anger. With each smack, I felt betrayed, toughened, closed off. The aftermath of my thoughts played a different loop: *Not good enough. If only I'd done better, been better, she wouldn't be so mad. She had a hard life. I need to help her more. Do more. Be more.* My guilt grew into a habit, then a well-honed muscle and finally, a reflex.

After Mom shouted or struck us, she quickly became jovial, as if nothing had happened. I didn't bounce back as quickly, my head full of her words, leaving no room for my own. I hid in my room, slumped with doubt, nursing a mistrust for authority and what was expected of me. Resentment swelled like a welt.

I turned to Josh. One of our favorite games was when he pulled me by the arms down our long hallways, releasing me in a big swoosh.

My body found relief. My body dragged in glee.

At other times, Mom's soft sabra center burst with generosity. She was attentive, especially when I was sick, which was often as a child, mostly ear infections, allergies, and head colds. "Do you want chocolate pudding?" she asked tenderly. "I hate to leave you home alone to go to work."

I wanted to grow up and make my own choices. Now at eighteen, I was failing at all my job choices. I needed to find another one quickly. I was anxious about money. Dad had paid child support, but any additional expense required negotiation. When I'd wanted saddle shoes to be a cheerleader in high school, Mom said, "Go ask your father." I asked him. They haggled on the phone. The result was, as always, "We'll split it." In the end, they were generous. But, by that point, I felt split between them, split by the expense, split by the burden I was.

I quickly settled into my fourth job of the summer, a safer choice, ensconced in an office as a bookkeeper. Through my successive failures, I had to face my lack of persistence. What was a justifiable reason to quit something? Feeling isolated and hungry in Switzerland? Feeling terror on the subways? Feeling lost as a vendor and finding myself in court? I failed again and again but made a critical discovery. I was willing to try almost anything, even when unprepared, even if risky.

I also gave myself a fifth job in my spare time, spreading books out in front of me on Mom's dining room table. Her volatile voice rang through the walls while she chatted on the phone to friends. While she overran her space, my new shrunken self strained to read the book I'd assigned myself: James Joyce's *Ulysses*.

On a cold winter night during the previous school year, my crush, my date—a scientist in a chunky sweater—had read to me from *Ulysses* by candlelight, between sips of strong tea. His voice reading the poetic prose melted me. We dated for a few months that I thought would last forever, as happens with first love. But on a sunny spring Sunday, while having brunch on the rooftop of his building, he revealed that he had a girlfriend who'd been away and was about to return. We were over. He pried me open then left me bleeding with that familiar feeling: not good enough.

I naively reasoned that if I read *Ulysses*, I'd understand him more, and why he hurt me. We would see each other back at school and he would love me again because reading this book would somehow make me enough.

Ulysses didn't help me understand him or my hurt, but it did return me to the feeling of immersion in a foreign language with the possibility of new belonging. Its complex sentences and stream of consciousness provided a glimpse of how other people think and what courses through their minds. I bought a companion book to decipher the winding words and laid them both out in front of me on the table. Side by side, like a map.

4

Freedom Tinged with Terror

In mid-June of the following summer, after my sophomore year of college, I descended the steps of a Greyhound bus in a parking lot in Gunnison, Colorado. The wind whipped my face, the sun scorched my skin, and the dry air cracked my lips. I maneuvered my suitcase to the fishing store to meet my arranged ride, a flannel shirt tied around my waist. The passersby were deeply tanned with fine lines scrawled across their skin, strolling slowly in their muddy boots, kicking up clouds of dust from their heels. What felt like the Wild West was simply a strip mall filled with pickup trucks. Like earlier gold rush explorers, miners, and speculators, I wondered what treasures this corner of the earth held.

A few months earlier, I'd stopped in the hallway of the biology department at McGill when I spotted a poster with a photograph of a jagged snow-topped mountain and green meadows. *Rocky Mountain Biological Laboratory, Gothic Colorado*, and *Summer Courses in Field Biology* caught my eye. Maybe I could make a career of fieldwork like Jane Goodall? The poster advertised "scholarships available," so I applied, was accepted, and was now west of Pennsylvania for the first time.

The lab, fondly called "Rumble" in a nod to its RMBL acronym, looked just like the poster: an assortment of log cabins dotting green meadows surrounded by jagged gray Rocky Mountains, at an elevation of 8,500 feet. I dropped my bags in my cabin and settled in for our evening student orientation in the dining hall. One thing was urgent. "Where's the bathroom?" I asked.

The administrator met my eye. "The outhouse is behind the building. There's only one flush toilet—for visitors."

Clearly far from the Versailles, I returned to my seat, my head throbbing, and eyes burning. The lab director warned us: High altitude may cause headaches, nausea, and shortness of breath. "You may wake up feeling like you are choking. On hikes, beware of hypothermia and loss of mental acuity."

I hadn't thought about the dangers of high altitude, but I was used to navigating fear and risk. As a child, when I wasn't hiding under the covers while my parents fought, I went outside to the streets, my pockets full of unease. *The City*, as we called New York, simmered with menace. In the 1960s and 1970s, our neighborhood was tense with wildness and tales of muggings on every corner. Needles littered the sidewalk cracks, and catcalls besieged the girls from block to block.

Mom drilled Josh and me like soldiers once we reached grade school, arming us with keys clenched between knuckles, warning us to avoid the avenues with gangs. While we loved the freedom of life outside, our freedom was tinged with terror. While I was trained to be vigilant, my stomach was trained to knot. It turned out the risks of our neighborhood provided unusual training for the unknowns of Everest.

When I was in second grade, Josh, a ten-year-old with choppy bangs and a Batman backpack, took my hand when he met me outside our school's front door, two blocks from home. We scurried to the rhythm and cacophony of traffic on Broadway, ripe with the stench of towering garbage mixed with the aroma of gardenias stacked outside the florist. We passed the neighborhood butcher, who gave us a slice of oily salami, and Rudlee's Diner where we had dinner with Dad on Tuesdays.

On our corner, we were met by two or three prostitutes who rotated shifts. They had large bosoms erupting from tight bras, hot pants wedged up their rears, cigarettes dangling from their lips, and perfume smelling of overripe strawberries. They propositioned guys walking or driving by while flicking ashes onto the sidewalk. Josh stared downward when they called, "How about some after-school delight?"

At times, we held slices of Sal's pizza steaming our tongues, while we cranked the double locks to enter the Versailles, then examined the triangular mirror in a ceiling corner of the elevator to see if someone was inside waiting to jump us. After two break-ins, Mom armored the window facing the fire escape. The steel bars laden with locks and steeped with black soot were sentries guarding us from the chaos outside. But the bars didn't mute the sounds drifting up in a nocturnal wave through my alley-facing window. Terror rode in with the surf, rising with the sounds of glasses clinking, radios blaring, and voices ricocheting across the walls. My heart pounded and my mind raced: *Is that a cat or a baby crying? A pigeon or a rat? Can the neighbors reach across from their window to mine? Would they lay down a ladder, window to window, to cross the fourth-floor chasm?*

In middle school, we rode the subway, where cars, swiped with block letters of graffiti, blasted us with hot air as they whirred past the stations. The tracks below swirled with clouds of dirt and rumbled with crowds of rats. I climbed the stairs onto the bus after school for my piano lesson or Israeli dance class, flashing my city bus pass, and hung onto the strap reading the ads above. "It could be you," a public interest campaign warned about the risk of rape, "whether you are young or old."

Before the divorce, our family escaped from the City for two months every summer to a bungalow colony in the Catskill Mountains, what we called *the Country*. Nestled behind the Homowack Hotel in the Borscht Belt, the colony had a motley group of around fifteen families, almost all of whom, I found out later, were Holocaust survivors. Bold, laughing, opinionated, they exposed us to incomprehensible things. Like the woman who fled Poland as a young girl and always hired Polish cleaning women. "They deserve to scrub our toilets for what they did to us," she said, haunted by murdered family members. We children, though part of the story, couldn't reconcile these worlds of mass extermination and rootlessness with our lives of cereal and cartoons.

The Country introduced me to the freedom and delights of the natural world. My feet trod on dirt paths instead of dense concrete. I felt feathery breezes magically transform into shuddering gusts as the sky blackened with the tremble of thunder. Crawling through the grass, I watched shadows sway beneath leafy woods, touched leathery lizards, and smelled wet earth after the rain.

Here, our parents seemed more themselves, socializing with friends from the old country, weaving past and present. Many families owned their cabins, but we rented the same one every summer, the last on a hill in a forest of evergreens, fragrant with spicy spruce.

Here, wilderness replaced wildness. Adventure replaced adversity.

The hippie vibes felt groovy on the upstate wind near Woodstock, where the kids hung out together all day, roaming endless lawns, freshly cut and smelling herbal. Afternoons we dipped in the murky pond catching tadpoles or in the pool for underwater tea parties. The moms, lounging nearby, let us snack on candy necklaces, the spiral pastel sweets sucked and savored. In these moments, I was not clenched keys and a knotted stomach or cowering under covers; I was beaded necklaces, knotted macramé, and climbing a fort in a treetop so high my hair rustled the leaves. We named it the Secret Place.

I tagged along, one of the youngest in our gang, excited yet scared when the older kids played spin the bottle on a dim cabin floor, balmy with oak and dare. They cast me as Toto in *The Wizard of Oz* and assigned me the tambourine in our band, the Crazy Cats, while Josh played proper instruments like guitar and drums. I loved it when we performed "Proud Mary," and sang about rolling down the river. The music was in me.

But even the idyll of the Country was not without risk.

One day, while we swam in the pond, a car drove up and stopped by the road. Sharon, an older girl, said "Who wants to see what's going on?"

"I'll go." I was six and curious. I draped my Archie comic strip towel around my waist, pond water beading on my calves. Sharon and I skipped up the hill to the car. The driver rolled down his window and asked:

"Which way is Monticello?"

We both pointed to our left up the road then looked back at the driver. His eyes bulged behind huge glasses, like magnified spider eyes. He grinned at us. I looked straight at his face, then down. My breath suspended for a long moment, time expanding and shrinking between beats of fear. I saw the dashboard, the passenger seat, the clutch, and his hand vigorously rubbing his exposed self, a large pink peeled shrimp. We screamed for the kids in the pond. I clung to the teenagers on my towel—Archie, Betty, Veronica, and Jughead—as we raced barefoot up the grassy hill, sobbing breathlessly, toward the safety of our parents.

I can still see the large black and white dice hanging by a red lanyard from his rearview mirror.

That day I learned that danger lurked everywhere. Not just in the gray city but in the green country. Tiny by age, by innocence, by wonder with the world, I learned a man could drain the air between us, could dominate my breath, my space, my body with his wants. This would be another reason to hide, to melt into the background, to stay small.

At night we resumed listening to the honking toads and our favorite records by the Beatles and the Rolling Stones, while the moms' mahjongg tiles clacked along with the crickets, and the dads dealt poker cards in a wave of cigar smoke. Someone strummed a guitar, and others hummed "Leaving on a Jet Plane," a song that felt like unity when everyone harmonized, that met my sense of wonder, that sparked a dream to flee.

Now, at nineteen, I'd fled to the Rocky Mountain Biological Laboratory. The day after I arrived, I was eager to join other new students on a hike to a waterfall. Someone spread out a topographical map, and I got my first look at dashed-line trails with peaks, saddles, and blue rivers squiggly as varicose veins.

We hiked past the cursive meander of ancient streams and varying iterations of earth, water, and mountains. My confused body moved from green lowlands to steep snowy slopes above the timberline. A summer storm with hail-like snow pummeled us, then passed as quickly as it came. The chilled wind shocked me. I donned more layers. By the last stretch, at an altitude near 12,000 feet, I hyperventilated gulps of pure, intoxicating air. We pushed through a steep basin where the sun, reflected off the white snow, blinded and parched us. Almost nothing grew at that elevation, but a black hawk soared provocatively over its range. Without warning, mushroom-thick, heavy clouds released a torrent. Jolted by

the perilous transformation of sun into lightning, I learned a new mantra: *Always be prepared in the mountains.*

We raced downhill through willow thickets and beside rushing
water; my ears popped, and my knees and ankles basked in the pull of
gravity. I was drenched, my stomach vacuous but my spirit full. Hiking
inspired change. The undulating ground challenged me, whether ascending—muscles strained to their limits—or descending—steadying myself,
spent and alert. I adapted to maintain the ground's support, developed
resilience as my feet balanced on uneven ground. I also gained new
skills—how to recognize landmarks so I could find my way back, how
to pack for the unexpected. But I discovered a conflict. The mountains
pulled me toward solitude, even when I wanted to be in community.

My work-study assignment was in the kitchen, so after meals I was
headfirst scrubbing a large metal pot or unloading the dishwasher, a
rush of hot steam in my face. Billy Barr ran the kitchen. He resembled
a true western mountain man, sporting a long brown beard, shaggy jean
shorts, and a baseball cap, but was actually Jewish and from New Jersey.
We bonded quickly over our shared backgrounds and gossiped while
scouring pans.

One afternoon, Billy and I hiked steep Gothic Mountain, which
towered over the lab. We encountered an array of nature's obstacles and
wounds: dried trees, thorns, snow bruises, mosquitos, talus. On our way
down, we ran into a group of researchers going for a naked dip in water
they called Friends Pond. Billy dove in. *Do I want to expose myself like
that?* Shyly disrobing, I lasted five seconds in the glacial water before
standing on a rock, arms covering my shivering body to air dry. My now
hundred-pound body felt the same shame as the fat body hidden under
the blue sweatshirt. I wore thinness as armor protecting me from judgment, but I was still hiding. My restricted eating, started with the unexpected weight loss in Switzerland, was a confinement like Mom's girdle.

I watched the researchers splashing and lazing, unselfconscious. A
biologist of slight build with long, tousled brown hair met my gaze. His
blue eyes lingered, and embarrassed, I turned away. Our class had spent
a week studying in the fields with him, joking that he flitted like the
butterflies he studied.

During one of our evening dance parties, the biologist boogied over, and we jumped to the rock-and-roll beats. He brushed my arm and touched my hip. A flash of chemistry sparked.

A few days later, he invited me to his lab and leaned beside me to point out the stigma of a scarlet gilia under a dissecting microscope. Peering at the magnified image with his body close, I admired the curved flower blooming with potential.

He asked me to talk "seriously," and we ambled up the road behind the lab. "I'd like to explore a relationship with you." He took my hand and looked me in the eyes. "I have an open marriage," he added.

A teenager who'd never been in a normal relationship, I told him I wasn't ready for anything that complicated. He was in his thirties.

"Okay. But maybe you'll change your mind." He continued holding my hand as we strolled back down the slope, passing the now familiar landscape of aspen, veratrum, sunflowers.

What did he see in me? I wondered if his attraction was based on anything real. Before my weight loss in Switzerland prompted slimness, I'd already moved from the chubby racks to a regular size. At twelve, a growth spurt had thinned me, and the following summer I was unexpectedly popular at camp. The boys voted my best friend "prettiest," and me "sexiest," even though I had a flat chest and was the same girl who'd recently hidden in a sweatshirt.

"Huh?" I asked.

"You look like you just woke up," they answered. "Your messy hair." *Maybe I am waking up.* Even though it felt better to be popular than not, much better to not be labeled as the fat girl, I was the same person. If people's treatment of me was based on superficial things like looks, this was another reason for mistrust.

My high school math teacher, always dressed in a white button-down, a protractor in his shirt pocket, lived a block away. Our family had met him when he taught Josh a few years earlier. He and his wife had hired me as their cat-sitter a few times when I was in middle school. One day when

I was in tenth grade, we rode the crosstown bus together, then walked up West End Avenue toward our homes.

"You know, you've turned into a pretty girl," he said. These words, so unexpected, so odd, caused the familiar knot to clench in my stomach. I bit my lips and tasted fear, tinny as a battery. I didn't look at him. I didn't answer him. Acid filled my throat.

After a minute of silence, I turned back toward him as he leaned into me. Instinctively, I turned away, but his squishy, wet, open lips landed on my cheek, his prickly red beard stung like a hornet.

I held my breath, trembling. Avoiding his gaze, I continued walking. So did he.

He spoke from someplace distant. "Are you liking school?"

"It's okay," I whispered, staring straight ahead.

My feet carried me forward as I pretended nothing had happened. He, too, behaved as if nothing happened.

Decades later, the teacher was exposed for being inappropriate with girls at the school where he'd worked for over forty years. When I heard, I knew that the baffling kiss had been real. I immediately phoned my best friend, who'd also been his student, to tell her what he'd done to me. "Why didn't you tell me?" she asked.

Until then, I had never told anyone. Like so many other girls.

Although my father was a psychotherapist, I didn't confide in him about my lecherous teacher, part of my decision to not rely on him, or burden him, or maybe because I didn't feel close enough. Even so, I missed what it had been like when he'd lived with us. He wore strappy white undershirts when he greeted each morning with Soviet-style stretching exercises. Mom complained that he spent too much time with his *girlfriend*, as she called the *New York Times*, heaped in uneven piles around their bedroom. "Your father's showers are a whole production!" She rolled her eyes, complaining how he took well over thirty minutes scrubbing each toe fastidiously with a washcloth. Perhaps his obsessive self-care was an attempt to mend deeply entrenched wounds.

His voice crescendoed in a wave of Yiddish melodies echoing from the tiny shower stall. It resembled the way he belted out prayers in the synagogue, forcing his voice above the crowd, causing sideways glances from those around us.

He didn't explain his loud singing until I was much older. When he was near death in the Siberian coal mine, he heard Jews praying together on Yom Kippur. He hadn't realized it was the holiday, and the swelling sounds of *Avinu Malkeinu*, "Our Father Our King," roused him with hope. Everything in the new country sang of hope. He was determined to make his voice heard.

On lucky days when I was small, I stood beside Dad on a stool in the bathroom, where he handed me shaving cream and an empty metal razor, the handle bumpy and heavy. I spread the white cloud on my cheeks, inhaled the menthol scent, and mimicked him, scraping vertical columns down my face. Sometimes he'd dab toilet paper on a speckle of blood on his cheek, and I'd stick a wad up my nose. He laughed, his shoulders heaving up and down, and called me *Mimele*.

Visiting Dad one day when I was thirteen, I marched briskly, fighting the wind, glancing sideways and backward when crossing the avenues, sweaty fingers clutching the keys inside my pockets. I rode the elevator to the sixth floor of his building and pressed the doorbell: one long beep followed by a short one, our secret ring alerting him it was me, not a client for his therapy practice. He never gave me a set of keys.

Dad buzzed me in from his seat in the study. I passed through the waiting room, really a short and cramped hallway with a low orange sofa and narrow coffee table strewn with *National Geographic* and *Time* magazines. Dad had become a psychotherapist to help others process their traumatic pasts. He led workshops every summer in Europe to facilitate the coming together of conflicted groups, including Jews and Germans and Jews and Arabs.

Entering his dim kitchen with faded yellow walls, I put the kettle on, and sat at the table with boxes of herbal tea stacked high, bottles of vitamins, and an open package of black German bread secured with a red rubber band.

"Hello, *Mimele*." Dad hugged me. I caught the scent of his aftershave and soapy skin. Shiny from his long showers, cleansed and risen from the grime of coal and forced labor, he wore a paisley button-down shirt with his collar open, a navy knitted vest, and gray slacks.

"How many of these do you take?" I pointed to the stockpile of supplements from the health food store.

"I don't know. I take two of these at breakfast and dinner." He picked up bottle after bottle and recited doses. I counted him ingesting around eighty pills a day, ranging from vitamins to "adrenal boosters" and "digestive enzymes." His over-the-counter "thyroid enzymes," taken for energy, once landed him in the hospital with a rapid heartbeat.

He draped a large white paper napkin over his chest, attaching it to his collar with a special clip he'd purchased for this ritual. A sip of tea scalded my tongue, and I stopped to blow on the mug. He asked, "Would you like me to call you a girl, a young lady, or a young woman?"

My eyes widened. *How the hell should I know?*

I figured he was trying to be thoughtful in his therapist way, but I wanted a father who would protect me from the terrors outside, not a clinician looking expectantly at me from behind invisible glass.

I knew our meal was over when he cupped one hand in front of his mouth while using the other to squeeze two Binaca breath mint drops onto his tongue.

In college, I noted my best friend Amy's father light up when she walked into the room. He said, "Hi babe!" with adoring eyes and a crinkling mustache. She described herself as a "Daddy's girl." That must have felt special.

As Dad got older, he wore a yarmulke for meals and said, "I'm grateful for this food, for freedom, for this country and democracy." I didn't understand, then, why he prayed and blessed, even though he said he didn't believe in God. I didn't get how those lines blur. How ritual can provide comfort, and how the concept of God, mixed up with gratitude, isn't black and white.

As an adult, I came upon this excerpt in Dad's writings. "Even though a son and daughter were born in 1959 and 1962, I regret and confess that I had little interest in dealing with the children, though I sometimes reluctantly went through the motions of taking care of them."

In the Rocky Mountains of Colorado, I discovered that when I hiked quickly over a canvas of pebbles, I was unharmed. But when I strove to secure myself, the relentless rocks countered, and I slipped. The lesson was to go with the flow, not overthink, believe in my swift feet. To let my body lead. With time, my stride took on more air, gaining weightlessness, the suspended moments holding greater possibilities.

I woke up early in the mornings with the beauty of dawn flashing through my closed eyelids, soft like velvet. As the stillness waned and the sun climbed, shimmering aspen leaves latticed the sky outside my window. I was smitten by this splendor, by the scent and gray-green tapestry of sagebrush.

By August, the vegetation was greener, taller, thicker. My toes adjusted to the uproot and felt more planted. Everywhere, wildflowers popped—larkspur, sunflower, lupine, columbine. The flowers claimed their places, their seeds cast. I admired the beauty of pattern, of the seasons, of researchers leaving and returning each summer. A craving took root. To return again and again to the mountains. To this peak of wonder and peace inside.

I didn't have an affair with the biologist but was swept into a relationship of letters. He offered to mentor me, attention I coveted. Fairly regularly, back in Montreal, I'd open an eight-page note, handwritten in slanted blue ink that matched his eyes, describing his life and research. I replied with equally long, intimate reflections.

Before returning to school that fall, I rode the subway in New York with my father and his fiancée, Ingeborg, going to City Hall, where I would be the sole witness before the justice of the peace marrying them. Josh was out of town. They had met a few summers earlier during one of Dad's workshops in Switzerland. Inge, in her late forties, was a slim, sweet German woman who'd never married. A pediatric nurse, with a self-effacing demeanor very different from my mother. But there was a problem, at least as far as Mom was concerned. Her family had been in the Nazi party, although they claimed, as others did, that everyone in their Bavarian town was pressured to join.

After the simple office ceremony, we returned uptown on the subway. I closed my eyes as the car rocked through the tunnels, while diverse people got on and off the train. I looked at this odd couple dressed in everyday clothes for their wedding, my father holding his girlfriend—the *New York Times*—in his lap. He, the sole Holocaust survivor of his family, had found true love with a German gentile woman.

Dad used to brag that he "was the fastest walker in Latvia." As a little girl, I took this literally and imagined him winning races. Now I think of the power of his momentum to move forward like a race walker—chin up, shoulders back, focus straight ahead. "We must always do our part. We can't be silent," he said while pasting leaflets for meetings and rallies about civil rights and peace in Israel—in his Russian-styled cap and cross-body man purse, which he called a satchel—to traffic poles on the Upper West Side.

As a child of immigrants, I was taught to believe another life was possible through hard work, intelligence, and wits. But Dad and Inge showed me it was never too late to follow your heart in an unlikely direction.

5

Tibet Calls

TWO YEARS AFTER FIRST VISITING RMBL, I SKIPPED COLLEGE GRADUA-
tion to return for a second summer employed as a research assistant,
still hoping to become like Jane Goodall. My first Sunday back, the lab
grounds were dusted with white from an unexpected June snowfall. Few
people had arrived this early in the season, but I met John, a guy starting
graduate work. Since he was new to RMBL, I offered to take him hiking
and showed him several options on the trail map.

"Let's do this long hike," he pointed to a trail that would take us all
day round-trip.

"Okay. Have you had any altitude problems since you arrived?"

"Nah. I hike all the time." He stood with his legs wide apart and
tipped his chin up. The more we talked, the more I thought I didn't want
to spend a whole day with him, but I'd already agreed.

After several hours, we reached a ridge at 12,000 feet. We ate sandwiches in a vast and quiet snow basin. Parched from the blue sky and hot
sun, I wiped my brow, took off my jacket, and tied it around my waist.

After lunch, we gleefully ran down the slope, our feet sinking into
snow up to our knees. John, several yards ahead of me, tripped and tumbled forward as if in slow motion, crashing into a large log. Bright red
blood pulsed onto the snow. I ran toward him. He lay dazed, eyes vacant.
His gash, about five inches long, had ripped through several layers of
flesh on his shin. I took my bandanna off my head and wrapped it tightly
around his leg, halting the blood flow.

"John, let's get you up."

He weakly attempted to sit, then laid back, and closed his eyes.

"Come on John, I'll help you."

No response.

I sat back down to think about what to do. We were high on a ridge, and it didn't look like he could hike down with his injury. Should I run down to get help? But if I left him sitting alone in the snow, his condition could worsen. While I mulled options, he muttered something about first aid, then faded out. I coaxed him to sit up, gave him water, took off his backpack, and layered it over mine. He buried his head in his hands. I massaged him and told him to breathe deeply.

"Lean on me." I wrapped my hands around his chest and pulled him up. With his weight on his good leg, we hobbled as if tied together, three-legged style. We crept down the slope, thick with tree limbs and rocks, our descent dawdling and difficult. Not long after we began, he stopped, lay down, and said, "I can't go on." I crouched beside him and rubbed his back.

"You can. I'll help you." I gave him a swig of water. "Together, we'll get down." I talked and talked until we both believed it.

His state of shock and hesitancy to move persisted the whole way down. It took every last bit of muscle I had to haul his extra weight, and every last bit of nerve to not emotionally crumble. When we approached the lab, my feet were two blocks of ice, frozen by snow and deadened from the extra weight. I sat him on the ground and ran to call for help. Two researchers bolted up the trail to get him, while I collapsed in the grass.

After John was loaded into a van, he yelled to me through the window. "You're coming to the hospital, right?"

I sat up to answer. "I'll check on you later!" Then, plopped back down.

That evening, he knocked on my door. "It was so intense up there."

"It's as if my heart is still racing."

"Had to get twenty-two stitches. They said it was really deep." His voice was perky.

I was surprised I'd had the strength to get him down, to figure out what to do. It energized me to have helped him and to see him back strong and happy. Field biology met so many of my interests—immersion in nature, learning about plants and animals, scientific inquiry. But I'd also been considering a career in medicine.

Mom took me to my first gynecology appointment at sixteen with a doctor from her hospital, because I'd been having trouble inserting tampons. I felt lucky to have a female gynecologist since most were still men. On the way, Mom said, "You should also get on birth control." I didn't have a boyfriend and wasn't ready to have sex, but her openness impressed me.

An elegant Iranian physician in a pencil skirt and sensible pumps entered the exam room. She washed her hands, then dried them with a brown paper towel, and faced me. "It's nice to meet you," she said with a lilting accent. She leaned in for a breast exam, her updo unmoving, her cold slender fingers prodding.

"Can you wear tampons while swimming?" I asked.

"Yes, no problem."

"How do you know if you have PMS?" She frowned and didn't answer.

"Is this normal?" I pointed to a single hair near my nipple. She finished my exam, walked toward the sink, glanced back, and raised her left eyebrow and chin. She stared as if straight through me. The bright lights felt instantly hot.

"Of course. You're Jewish, Middle Eastern, a hairy people. Why wouldn't it be?"

Sweat beaded on my forehead despite the freezing room and flimsy paper gown. I mulled the word *hairy*, feeling ugly and insulted. *You're Middle Eastern too!* She recommended I use a diaphragm—everyone did at the time, including Mom—and she demonstrated filling it with spermicide and squishing it to insert.

I returned to the waiting room with my new flying saucer, the color of Silly Putty, in a brown paper bag.

"How was it?" Mom asked.

"Fine. She's kind of mean," I whispered, my cheeks flushed.

My mother raised her eyebrows. "People think highly of her."

We walked to the bus, me clutching my bag, past the statue of Columbus, a male conqueror standing forty-one feet tall and proud in the middle of the traffic circle named for him. We passed people moving quickly with purpose, and joggers entering Central Park.

My heart quickened as I replayed the appointment, thinking about the impatience the doctor displayed after my first question. The sigh she emitted after my third question. Her general dismissiveness. If I were her, examining a teen for the first time, I would be kinder, more patient, and more understanding of a frightening experience. *Maybe I could do this.* I imagined myself wearing the same starched white coat, washing my hands at the sink, confident and knowledgeable, but rather than frown at a girl's questions, I'd encourage her by putting into practice the feminist influence of my mother and grandmother.

"What else do you want to know? No question is too silly," I'd say. I would encourage women to feel good about their bodies, not hairy and ugly or fat. I wouldn't wear pumps and clack around. *Maybe this is what I'm meant to do.* So many physicians trace their interest in medicine to interacting with a kind doctor or an experience with illness or a sense of altruism. My spark was ignited by indignation. Five years later, my experience with John made me consider medicine again.

That second summer at RMBL, I had my first real relationship, not with John but with my research partner Tom, a Jersey boy, who lived for playing Ultimate Frisbee and his guitar. We stomped down slopes in our ponchos in the rain and shared his Walkman headset to listen to Springsteen's new hit, "Born in the U.S.A." We transformed endless hours crouching in bushes—counting the holes chewed by beetles in mustard leaves—from drudgery to bottomless belly laughs that moved us out of the friend zone and into my first romance in the wild.

One July evening, I sat on a wooden folding chair in the dining room at RMBL, among rows of other researchers, my nose drippy from mountain dust, waiting for the evening's entertainment. A bearded scientist walked to the center of the room and introduced his slide presentation.

"Tibet is the highest plateau in the world." He pointed to a photograph of a sweeping flat plain with a distant view of snowcapped peaks. "I went to sample the acid rain levels there."

I squinted and leaned forward in my seat for a closer look. I'd assisted this researcher sampling nearby lakes for acidity, a marker of pollution, but didn't know he traveled the world doing the same kind of work.

"First my team arrived in Lhasa, the capital." He spoke over the click of the slide projector and the whirr of its fan. A close-up of a man wearing a tall brown furry hat stared straight at the camera. He had chiseled cheekbones, wind-weathered skin, and fine lines trailing from his eyes. The researcher clicked again, and an image filled the screen of a woman crouching next to a basket of potatoes on a cobblestone street in a marketplace. Her hair was braided around her head, and she wore a bulky necklace of turquoise beads with a large coral stone in the middle.

As one striking photo of towering mountains after another flashed on the screen, I stared slack jawed. *What is it like to stand beside the tallest mountains in the world?* In that moment I committed to finding out. *I'm going there.*

At RMBL, I'd started down the path to becoming a field biologist, but during that second summer I found myself restless with the research and itchy in the bushes counting insects. I'd wanted to keep medicine as an option, so I'd already taken the med school prerequisites, admission test, and participated in premed activities. Choosing medicine seemed like a good way to answer the question I'd learned in Jewish school: *If I am only for myself, what am I?* I couldn't imagine anything more interesting than studying our bodies to gain a deeper understanding of human nature. I'd even bought an endocrinology book to read just for fun. Surely understanding hormones, or how the body's "messengers" carried information, would lead to some revelations.

Aspiring to become an OB/GYN, I could combine taking care of others with being an advocate for women. But I wouldn't let go of the mountains. First, I would travel to the Himalayas.

Back from my summer in Colorado and living with Mom in the Versailles, I applied to medical schools by day and waitressed by night. Planning my Himalayan trip, I discovered Tibet was closed to foreigners because of civil unrest, so I decided to go to Nepal. I wandered the dusty rows of my local library and made phone calls, but information was difficult to get before the internet. I finally found a friend of a friend in Chicago who'd traveled there. "Buy *The Lonely Planet Trekking Guide* and follow what it says," she advised over the phone.

Curled up in my childhood bed to read the trekking guide, I switched on my reading lamp and propped my head up on pillows. I'd spent a lot of time in this very spot reading. When I was a little girl, Mom used to say, Josh was the fun one, "full of personality." Unlike him, I hovered near her and her friends. "Why are you here?" they'd ask, before providing their own answers: "She is mature for her age," "too serious," or "too sensitive." Then, my mother ordered me to "Go play."

I retreated to reading. Mom said I started when I was three. Reading became subversive, a way to break rules and avoid bedtimes, a way to remain in solitude. Patton, a twenty-pound orange Maine coon with a compulsion to eat his own fur, purred and curled around my ankles like a hot-water bottle. Patton waited behind the door for me to get home from school, then splayed across the kitchen table as I did homework. He was by my side when I stayed up late, flashlight under the covers, devouring *Charlotte's Web* and *Little House in the Big Woods*, when I imagined myself as the heroic and brave Florence Nightingale, caring for injured soldiers, and when I was an amateur sleuth solving mysteries with Nancy Drew.

Books inspired bravery and filled lonely latchkey hours. In fourth grade I wanted to be just like Harriet the Spy. Layering sliced bread, mayonnaise, and tomatoes, I made her trademark sandwiches as an after-school snack while Mom was still at work. From Harriet, I learned to record observations about people in a lined composition notebook while riding the bus. I recruited my best friend Gaby, a spunky girl with a stylish bob, to create Spy Pocketbooks filled with important surveillance equipment like notepads and magnifying glasses. She nicknamed me Eager Beaver because

I got excited easily and ran down the hallways in our apartment instead of walking. I called her Gullible Gaby, which may not sound nice, but was a tribute to her trusting nature. Together we strapped on crossbody pocketbooks, big sunglasses and floppy hats, studied the "Most Wanted" signs in the post office, and slipped into Central Park to hunt felons.

One day, after spying on a man with a metal detector combing the ground for treasures, we decided to take a break and ride the carousel, but we couldn't find it. We asked another man for directions.

"Follow me." He headed toward a thicket of bushes, his shadow stretching across the lawn. I stood still as I watched Gaby follow him, my arm hairs prickling.

"Gaby, Mommy wants us home. Come back!" I kept calling her until she slowly turned around. She ran back to me, and we didn't stop running until we reached her apartment, both breathless.

"Promise not to tell!" I said.

"Pinky promise." Gaby held out her little finger.

"They wouldn't let us out alone anymore if they knew."

We didn't find treasure or capture a criminal that day, but we made an important discovery. Curiosity and our freedom might lead to danger. But that wouldn't stop us.

The Nepal trekking guidebook led me to other books. Maurice Herzog's *Annapurna* told the story of a French expedition in 1950, the first successful climb of a mountain higher than 8,000 meters (26,246 feet). My heart pumped alongside Herzog and his partner in Nepal when they reached the summit of Annapurna, the tenth-highest mountain in the world. I was astounded that their expedition doctor had to do emergency amputations after the effort resulted in severe frostbite and gangrene. Herzog described the virtue of their journey: "In attempting to do the hardest tasks, all our resources are called upon, and the power and greatness of mankind are defined." The climbers survived by reaching deeply into themselves. This made a big impression.

That book led me to *Annapurna: A Woman's Place*, by Arlene Blum, about an all-female ascent of the same mountain in 1978. They wanted to be respected as much as the men doing the same climb were, and to discover the best of themselves. Like Herzog's team, they reached the summit of Annapurna but endured trauma: two climbers died during a second summit attempt.

Blum's team inspired me the way my mother's and grandmother's messages did—to not depend on men, and to forge my own way.

My tenth-grade history teacher gave us a daily quiz on the front-page news in the *New York Times*. I stood on the crosstown bus each morning, the newspaper folded into a slim rectangle, the black ink staining my fingers, skimming stories as the bus sputtered along. Often featured were articles about the battle to pass the Equal Rights Amendment, which stated that "equality of rights under the law shall not be denied or abridged by the U.S. or by any state on account of sex." A no-brainer as far as I was concerned.

Our congresswoman Bella Abzug had campaigned saying, "The test of whether or not you can hold a job should not be in the arrangement of your chromosomes." When our eighth-grade class visited Washington, DC, Abzug, known for her humor and trademark hats, stood tall and confident in front of the Capitol, while my class sat on the surrounding steps for a picture. "This woman's place is in the house. The House of Representatives," she said. So, in a gift shop nearby, I bought my mother a plaque that said "A woman's place is in the home. And she should go there directly after work." Mom worked out of necessity, but women being treated as equals was an ideal we shared. Together, we watched *Maude*, a popular TV show about an outspoken character who was passionate about women's rights. Decades later, I still wrap myself in long cardigans like the ones Maude wore, feeling fierce like her.

Even though I was captivated by the extreme feats and heroics of these Annapurna expeditions, my plan was simply to hike. To veer off the trail of expectations and back to the mountains. The two main trekking destinations in Nepal were the Annapurna Circuit and the Everest region—both offering spectacular views. I read and reread the trekking guide, trying to choose one, imagining myself in each place.

"The Circuit" surrounding the Annapurna Mountain range was usually followed from east to west in a counterclockwise circle, the crux being a 17,769-foot-high mountain pass called the Thorung La. (La means pass in Nepali.) I chose this route because I liked the idea of the challenge required to climb the pass and complete a circle. A clean and perfect path.

I booked my flight to Nepal the day I received my first medical school acceptance.

Tap and jazz classes were my training for trekking, and my limited savings meant I would travel with a borrowed backpack and camera.

One evening in March, the rain rustling the trees on Broadway, Mom invited Gaby and Amy, my best friend from college, over for dinner.

"Tell her!" Mom's brows furrowed at Amy, across the table set with Mom's trademark Israeli salad drenched with fresh lemon juice.

"Mim, we really don't think it's a good idea for you to backpack alone in Asia. Is there any chance you will consider postponing? Wait for Tom to finish classes?" Amy nodded askance at my mother while twisting her hair. Tom, my RMBL boyfriend, was pursuing a master's in Illinois.

"We just want you to be safe." Gaby, my Harriet-the-Spy partner, added.

Mom's chest rose, then she fumed, "Other kids don't put their mothers through this!" She stood up, walked to the sink, and filled the kettle with water. Her voice came down an octave. "School starts in a few months. How will I reach you to tell you if you got in anywhere else?"

"Ma, I told you, you can send me letters to the post office in Kathmandu."

Maybe Mom had a point. Maybe I'd put her through greater stress than her friends' daughters. It would have made more sense if I stayed home, prepared for medical school, and focused on my long-distance relationship with Tom. But an inviolable voice from deep inside drove me to leave. I knew without knowing that this journey was important.

Even though I typically became anxious before new endeavors, I wasn't worried at all.

I'd always been convinced to follow the expected route. Not this time.

PART III
VASTNESS

The question then is how to get lost. Never to get lost is not to live, not to know how to get lost brings you to destruction, and somewhere in the terra incognita in between lies a life of discovery.
—Rebecca Solnit, *A Field Guide to Getting Lost*

Taking Risks

6

The Land of Truth

I STUMBLED ONTO THE TARMAC IN KATHMANDU, INHALED THE DIESEL fumes, and gagged. Searching the sky for the great Himalaya, I saw only clouds and mist. Despite this shrouded welcome to the mountain kingdom I'd imagined as Shangri-La, I hoped that something mysterious awaited me. Something other than diesel fumes. At that moment, I didn't fear falling off a cliff but finding my way into town.

Walking to a traveler enclave called "Freak Street," named for its hippie visitors, men on street corners bombarded me: "Madam—change money? Buy smack? Hash? Heroin? Marijuana?"

Why are they calling me Madam? Groggy from jet lag, I ignored the shock of drugs offered openly, failing to grasp the seedy undertow. The streets were crowded, and the men's heckling added to the chaos and stench of wandering cows and dogs, and the background noise of honking cars and ringing rickshaws. I'd read about the poverty but was saddened to encounter the many disabled beggars in the street, and children stretching their palms toward me. Squawking black birds swooped through the suffocating air, almost grazing my head.

For 60 cents a night, I found a room in a lodge on Freak Street with plain white walls, a narrow bed with white sheets, and a night table. I put my pack down and washed my hands in cold water in the rusty sink down the hall. I picked up *Seven Years in Tibet* from the lobby bookcase, and noticed other guests, many with yellowed, bloodshot eyes, lounging, reading, writing, and washing clothes. Resting in a chair, I read Heinrich Harrer's words: ". . . I succumbed to the magic of the Himalayas. The beauty of these gigantic mountains, the immensity of the lands on which they look down . . . —all these worked on my mind like a spell."

That night, I visited a Buddhist monastery and joined locals as they circumambulated clockwise around a prayer structure. They rang bells, the only sound piercing the quiet, and lit candles while mouthing prayers under a bright starry sky. Dawn filled with the sounds of roosters crowing and men spitting and blowing long honks of snot out of their nostrils. From the roof of my guesthouse, I watched the street awaken with the sun, a yawn of outstretched orange. Shopkeepers rolled open their doorways, bicycles beeped, and cooks fired up street grills to sell breakfast.

Freak Street didn't have the Shangri-La atmosphere I'd imagined. I headed to Thamel, the trekking neighborhood, dodging cows roaming the streets, and passing a group of young boys with shaved heads wearing bright orange robes. After applying for my trekking permit in the government office, I entered a hiking shop, filled with brightly colored ski bibs, hiking poles, and boots in every size. I picked out a pink ski parka to rent, then my heart raced when I saw a stack of T-shirts across the room with the slogan "A Woman's Place is on the top: Annapurna." I remembered from Blum's book that the all-women team sold these shirts to raise money. I walked straight to the display then shuffled through the shirts, holding up different sizes against my chest. *I'm here, where these climbers were*, heading to Annapurna. I proudly whipped out the rupees from my purse to buy a T-shirt in their honor. It would become my cozy nightshirt for decades.

The Annapurna Circuit, which covered 145 miles of slopes crossing multiple terrains, had opened to foreigners only eight years earlier and took around three weeks to complete. At 26,545 feet, Annapurna is the highest mountain in view, with another thirteen peaks over 23,000 feet and sixteen more over 20,000 feet.

Before leaving to trek, I called my mother, collect. "You got into Einstein," she said about my top-choice medical school, located in the Bronx and known for its humanistic approach.

"Send the deposit for me, Ma! Please! I don't want to lose my spot there." I didn't want a repeat of my college scenario, when my father had forgotten to fill out the financial aid form for my dream college. Of course, Mom was too organized to let that happen.

On a clear morning in early April, a week after landing in Nepal, I boarded a flatbed bus in Kathmandu and headed west toward Annapurna, my pack throwing me off balance, the sleeping bag attached awkwardly by bungee cords. Riding outdoors on the cargo bed, I baked under a hot sun, pungent sacks of scallions heaped beside me singeing my nostrils. The foothills were lush and layered with terraced rice paddies, highlighted by varying hues of muddy brown and punchy green.

Next, I hitchhiked and landed a ride on the back of a pickup truck, smushed between sacks of rice. I faced a Nordic-looking couple with a son around three. *That's ballsy*, I thought, traveling with a toddler in a place where many visitors got sick. I jumped off at the trailhead, awed by huge valleys where tangled banyan trees braced the sky, more magnificent than anything I'd ever seen.

I scrutinized the map, crossed a suspension bridge, and found my first teahouse. Instead of camping in tents, trekkers stayed in teahouses, which filled each evening with travelers from around the world. These lodges consisted of a single large dark room with a raised platform where trekkers spread out their sleeping bags. The proprietress, called a *didi*, sister, or *ama*, mother, cooked a meal for everyone over an open flame, often fueled by yak dung, filling the room with acrid smoke. Pressed together intimately against strangers, I heard my neighbors' breathing and smelled their consumptive coughing spurred by the smoke. Without running water, toilets, or outhouses, we relieved ourselves in the woods. I needn't have worried about being lonely; when mornings arrived, I eagerly returned to the trail and my solitude.

Annapurna is a female Sanskrit name meaning "(She who is) replete with food," so it was ironic that food on the trekking route consisted almost exclusively of *dal bhat*—rice with a soup of lentils poured on top. Two meals a day, brunch and dinner, no matter which teahouse I stopped in. Rice and beans, rice and beans, rinse and repeat, a heavy meal that weighed down my insides like cement. Uninspiring, but a relief of sorts not to think about food choices.

April on the Annapurna trail meant hot days and freezing nights. I dressed modestly, as advised, in blue long underwear, top and bottom, covered with a long flowy Indian skirt I'd bought in Kathmandu, to not reveal my body and draw attention to myself as a twenty-two-year-old woman traveling alone. At first, I worried about getting lost, until I got on the trail. There was usually only one way to go. Following the circuit meant ascending and descending a series of slopes, an average of ten miles a day, day after day—a lot of climbing with a heavy backpack.

It turned out my borrowed backpack wasn't really a backpack but a convertible suitcase with straps, which, I learned, is not comfortable for hiking long distances. The hip straps, which are supposed to carry most of the load on a pack, performed like an afterthought, a mere decoration on the bloated maroon bag that became my beast to bear. I'd filled it to the brim with summery shorts and T-shirts, hiking boots, books, camera, lenses and filters, flashlight, batteries, stationery, towel, snacks, and my sleeping bag. For the higher elevations I brought winter clothes: parka, extra sweaters and layers, hats, mittens, and a scarf. I had packed enough to outfit a small family. I wanted to be prepared for anything.

Huffing up the first slope, my pack bore into my shoulders, and my upper back muscles spasmed. Most of the other trekkers traveled with a companion and a porter who carried their packs. One moment the unbearable weight was in my neck, then my hips or knees. *Maybe I don't need to carry four books.* And the air. It was so light, so ephemeral, my lungs didn't feel nourished. *How much oxygen am I getting? Is anything passing through my nostrils? Maybe dance class wasn't the best training for trekking. Maybe Mom and Gaby and Amy were right when they said, "Go for a hike in the Catskills!"*

Doubting myself was a fully ingrained habit. At ten, I'd told Dad I wanted to be a veterinarian—my first medical interest.

"Why would you want to take care of animals instead of people?"

"Because I want to!" I screamed, "I love animals!"

"That doesn't make sense."

I didn't have the language to debate him. My father may have validated his patients during their therapy sessions, but both he and my mother had trouble seeing things through my eyes. Maybe these are common ways parents respond, maybe more common with immigrant parents who have dreams for their children's lives in the new country, which includes specific measures of success. Their objections shaped my decision-making. When Mom thought I'd starve dancing, I gave it up.

Then, I looked up and saw them: the Himalayas, previously shrouded by fog. Towering cliffs rising from a steep gorge, filling the sky. *This is why I'm here. To witness this majesty. I can do this.*

My third day trekking started like all the others. I awoke with the chickens, hiked to a spot to relieve myself, washed in a river, and sipped hot milk tea in the sun outside the teahouse. I climbed up and down slopes that passed villages with views of mountains towering like beastly phantoms. The single footpath was filled with porters carrying various wares—light plastic sandals, long logs of timber, heavy round potatoes. The path had served as a trading route between India and Tibet for several millennia, passing through subtropical bamboo and rhododendron forests and into bare mountain environments above the tree line, contiguous with the Tibetan plateau—home to the Thorung La high pass.

Tibetan prayer flags were strung on rocks and homes. Blue, white, red, green, and yellow, the flags were meant to promote compassion, peace, strength, and wisdom. Both the flags and the white-capped peaks waved invitingly. I passed cows grazing and roosters crowing. Mothers patiently picked lice off the heads of their children, who yelled "Namaste—me pen," asking for the popular writing gifts trekkers gave locals.

The heat was unbearable, my maroon beast more beastly, and I envied the trekkers with porters. Resting under a grove of tall trees with fluttering lime-green leaves, I relished the verdant breeze. I filled my water bottle, added iodine drops to kill germs, shook the bottle, and waited thirty minutes for the purification effect. I powered ahead into the mountains and open space, imbued with the feeling of possibility, reminding me of the intoxicating air of RMBL.

Up. Down. Repeat.

Part of the beauty, rhythm, and peace of the trek was encountering religious elements on every ridge and in every village: temples, *mani* stones inscribed with Tibetan prayers, and *chortens*—Buddhist structures that hold prayers and offerings. The harsh physical environment had inspired religious devotion.

Dropping my backpack in front of the teahouse in Bhulbule, I spotted a couple moving on, not stopping where the guidebook advised. I was looking forward to putting my feet up and cracking open a book, but they inspired me to keep going. I hoisted up my pack, threw it on my sweaty back, and followed them. A short while later, they stopped and spread out their sleeping bags. I did the same, about twenty yards away, beside a two-hundred-foot waterfall under a crown of bright light from a full moon.

A massive tropical tree stood rooted beside the falls, and the moon reminded me that today was the first night of Passover, the holiday commemorating the Jews' escape from enslavement in Egypt and subsequent wandering in the desert. Lying in my sleeping bag, feeling the cold wind on my cheeks, and hearing the branches creak, I realized I was wandering like my ancestors, not knowing what each day would bring. I was walking toward freedom as they had. Freedom from my *shoulds*. And at the same time I was firmly rooted in my origins like the massive tree beside me.

I'd already bounced between various kinds of Jewish practice. Our home was not observant; we didn't light Shabbat candles, keep kosher, or refer to God. But after dissatisfaction with our local public school, Mom enrolled Josh and me in an Orthodox elementary school. There, we spent half the day studying Jewish texts including Torah, the book of Prophets, and commentaries. The teachers, along with many of our classmates, expected us to spend Saturdays dressed up, attending synagogue, and observing rules such as not spending money or turning on electricity.

Once a year, we crammed over a thousand Jewish blessings from booklets jammed with little block Hebrew letters and their English translations. Different blessings for every type of food, blessings of wonder for seeing a rainbow or a shooting star, and those to mark holidays and milestones. We then participated in a school-wide "brochos bee," quizzing us on the blessings. In sixth grade, I felt proud to be the winner. But I also felt weighted with the irony that my family recited no blessings, observed no rituals, adhered to no admonitions. Yet my parents immigrated to New York City because of the persecution of Jews in

Europe. Didn't that mean we should uphold tradition as a tribute to our survival? As a way to ensure the continuity of our religion and people? We were survivors and the descendants of survivors.

I was eleven when I decided to do something about the guilt and fear I felt from not practicing what I learned in school. I began following Orthodox rules, stressing out my mother by adding my requirements of Orthodoxy onto her single-mother, double work-shifted, overtime-laden life. "We need to take that new pot to the mikvah!" I demanded, expecting her to adhere to the ancient, obscure law requiring dunking a new vessel into a ritual bath. Not only did she lack the faith that would inspire her to obey these laws, but she lacked the time. Still, I was relentless. A zealot, and a nag, I even yelled at her in Central Park: "Ma! It's not kosher to drink from a water fountain on Passover!"

After a few years of this strict practice, I pondered the central stories of Judaism and whether I believed them, deciding by age fourteen against Orthodoxy. Now, out in the open sky in Nepal, I questioned the boundaries of organized religion, the ramifications of breaking from boxes, the *shoulds* and *shouldn'ts*. I loved my Jewish roots, many of the rituals, my family. I loved the mountains, the pure energy there. Now, I was introduced to Buddhism, a different way to experience the world. But wasn't it all the same spirituality?

I missed the peace and comfort that had come from my practice of Orthodoxy, from thinking God was always with me, and always cared about me. I wasn't alone.

Yet here, alone at the waterfall, steeped in these thoughts, I didn't feel lonely. I lay on my back searching the sky flooded by brightness, pondering this Passover night full of hope, wonder, and curiosity.

This freedom, too, had a tinge of terror. *Hoina!* I cried out. No! in Nepali. Fear had startled me awake in the middle of the night, when I sensed someone was standing over me. But it was only the very bright light of the full moon that had roused me.

This night was indeed different from all other nights—the phrase that anchors the Passover seder. This night engendered a sense of home and peace, attached to no deity, leaving me rested, tired and fulfilled, in the shadow of the mountains that had been there for millions of years and would continue to stand for millions more.

The following day, the maroon beast got the better of me, and I considered hiring a porter. I thought about the weights I'd been burdened with that couldn't be stuffed in a bag and hauled up a hill: the weight of duty that had made me religious and made me choose a secure profession. The weight of guilt that made me feel inadequate. The weight of my body as a source of shame. But if I hired a porter, I'd need to manage another person. Did I want to give up my independence and yield to another person's needs?

I decided to plow ahead on my own.

I would choose how far to trek, how slow or fast to go, where to sleep, who to befriend or avoid.

The only decision not up to me was what to eat: there was only dal bhat.

The immensity of the landscape forced reflection, and the constant motion, one foot in front of another, felt like gears fueling obsessive thinking, which ran the gamut from the inane to the sublime. *My feet! Maybe I should just wear sneakers? Then I'd have to carry my hiking boots and they weigh a million pounds. How long until the next village? I could use some hot tea. I'll never get over the pass—I can barely climb this ridge. God, I hope I don't run into that annoying couple from France. They're always like "our porter is setting up our bed," and taking pictures of each other. What will medical school be like? Will I like anyone? What am I going to do with my life?!? Maybe I could move here for a while. I could become a yak-cheese maker. I love cheese. I could eat cheese all day. What's the point? We're all just blips in this vastness. The point is to just be present now. It's so magnificent here.*

The trails were perfect for thinking, but the nights in the crowded, stinking teahouses felt oppressive. Trekking exposed the tension I'd noticed in the mountains of Colorado between wanting company and craving solitude.

The conversation among travelers huddled in the teahouses at night revolved around how difficult crossing the high, cold, steep Thorung La was. "You think I can make it?" one asked, "I'm pretty beat, I may turn around instead of doing the Circuit," another chimed in. "I don't think I brought enough winter gear," complained another. I was glad I'd rented a parka, but I lay in my sleeping bag filling with dread.

7

In Tandem

On the fifth day of my trek, I soaked in the hot springs of Chame with the only other travelers I'd met hiking alone and without porters. The three of us discussed how we were each hoping to cross the pass.

"I'm Mark," one of the guys introduced himself coolly, as if no breath passed from his lips. He said he was from California. "I'm a fruitarian," he added.

"What's that?" I asked.

"I only eat fruit."

Duh.

"So, what are you eating here?" asked the other trekker whom I'd noticed on the trail. He was an adept hiker who stared deeply at the vistas. I'd imagined his thoughts churning like mine.

"If it's not available, I eat what is." Mark lifted his chin and gave his head a little shake. His long brown ringlets, parted in the middle, bounced attractively around his shoulders.

"I'm Bruno," the second trekker said, "from Canada." He stood up, towering over us, and removed his cap revealing cropped brown hair and a serious brow.

"Mark, you know you need winter gear to cross the pass," Bruno said. Mark carried only a daypack and wore white athletic shorts with a red stripe and Birkenstocks with socks.

"Figured I'd just wing it and see what happens."

Bruno and I exchanged grins.

I faced Mark. "Carrying this suitcase is killing me. I have a ton of extra gear. How about on the day we go over the pass, I lend you winter stuff, and we exchange packs?" My voice got higher as I choked out this question.

"Cool," said Mark.

The three of us, one minute strangers and the next friends, had a plan.

The following morning on the trail, Bruno pointed to the hills.

"Wanna go to that village?"

"Lemme look it up." I flipped the pages of the guide. "It says it's not part of the usual route and there are no teahouses there."

"If it means we can avoid the riffraff, let's go." Mark grinned, referring to the other trekkers.

"Can't be worse than our usual dal bhat." I laughed nervously. We had days to go before the high pass, and I wondered if we'd stay together, our differences so obvious. We resembled the fabled three bears: Mark, ill-prepared; me, overprepared; and Bruno, just right. But the bears were a family. We were just loners tentatively testing each other's company. Instead of launching solo, the three of us stepped forward in tandem, if not quite aligned.

We hiked through fragrant pine-, spruce-, and juniper-covered hills. As we gained elevation, the wind whipped my skirt and scarf in gusts, sending a fierce chill under my collar to my skin.

The village was full of fortress-like Tibetan homes framed by prayer flags. We passed men practicing archery and women wearing colorful jewelry, then rested on a hill overlooking potato fields. Communicating through gestures, a family agreed to host us for the night in exchange for a small fee.

"It's so nice and warm here." I rubbed my hands together near the kitchen hearth, grateful to be protected from the vicious winds pounding the one-room stone house.

"I'm knackered," Bruno said. We all rested our heads on the floor and drifted off to sleep, listening to the patter of rain.

The following day, we continued off the beaten path and climbed steep hills to a ridge at 12,375 feet, our highest elevation so far. I had trouble keeping up and feared my two new friends would desert me. Our breath became visible in the cold air, and I rummaged deep in my pack for my rented parka.

Stomach problems were common on the trekking route. Germs flourished without bathrooms or running water for washing. Travelers in the teahouses composed songs about giardia, a rampant parasite that caused foul, egg-smelling gas and diarrhea. I'd been having the runs for a few days and felt weak.

When we arrived at another hill village, a couple with a one-year-old daughter invited us to stay. I tried to befriend the mother, practicing Nepali with her, but didn't get far.

Their house, structured like others in the village, had one large room with a hearth where the family cooked, ate, and slept together. A wooden ladder connected to the lower level, where an enclosed courtyard housed animals and where they assigned us to sleep for the night. Again, no outhouse. We learned that people did their business on the outskirts of the village.

The didi served us dal bhat—no surprise there—and tiny boiled potatoes for dinner. I didn't know whether I should avoid eating to rest my stomach or eat for strength. Our hosts were religious, and before the didi served us, she raised her arm dramatically and struck the pot about ten times. As we ate, the family was fascinated by my eyeglasses and Bruno's flashlight, passing them around the room. When Bruno snapped a photo, the flash caused them to jump. Afterward, they prayed for hours, swaying, chanting, and rotating prayer beads while we watched awkwardly. Nobody was there to interpret their rituals. I returned to my churning thoughts. *What am I doing here? Where am I going?*

I awoke in the middle of the night, my stomach stabbing with pain and aching to explode. I desperately needed a bathroom but had no time to climb the ladder to exit the house, possibly rousing the family asleep near the hearth, let alone stumble around in the dark to reach the edge of town. I panicked and finally was so seized by spasms that I ran to relieve myself next to the animals. Trembling and breaking out in a sweat, I hoped not to wake anybody up.

The moment I finished, the didi shouted, screaming and whooping. I crawled into my sleeping bag, terrified that my defecation was disastrous and desecrating, trying not to wake my friends. Her bellowing upstairs continued. I hoped she'd simply woken up to begin some sort of routine, emphatic praying, and that her screaming had nothing to do with what I'd done.

In the morning, I confessed to my friends, and the three of us scurried out of there as quickly as possible. No longer the three bears, now we were like the three blind mice, running from a situation we didn't understand.

Days later, Bruno, Mark and I reached a windy place called Phedi, the last stop before the pass, where there was only one tiny hovel crowded with anxious trekkers preparing for the climb.

"We're here!" Bruno announced between sips of hot tea.

"I'm glad we're together," I replied, meaning I was glad Mark would carry the maroon beast over the pass in exchange for my clothing.

We warmed by the fire that night, and I felt better than I had in days, finally on antibiotics for my diarrhea. I'd brought them along as advised but didn't know when to use them. My appetite improved, and I hoped keeping food down would strengthen me for the climb.

We barely slept, kept awake by the seesaw hum of a French man snoring, but at 3:00 a.m. we joined a different hum of trekkers gathering gear for the climb. We'd each slept with two hot-water bottles by our feet for warmth filled with drinking water for the next day. Our flashlights pierced the crisp black air as we piled on layers of clothing.

"Bruno, you okay?" I asked. He was slumped over, immobile.

"I've been up all-night retching and having the runs."

"Drink this." I passed him hot tea. *There's no way he can make it over the pass.*

"I'm going with you guys today. I can't spend another night in this dump!"

"Okay. We'll help you. I'll take *your* pack," I offered.

I glanced at Mark, a mirror image of myself. He was dressed from head to toe in my stuff: hat, layers of sweaters, windbreaker, pants, sneakers, the bloated awkward maroon bag, pulled together with a flowery scarf. Our eyes met and we laughed simultaneously. We shuffled our packs like a game of three-card-monte: Mark carried my beastly pack, I carried Bruno's just-right pack, and Bruno carried Mark's daypack.

We panted heavily climbing the first steep hill. Bruno stopped periodically to stoop over and belch. We followed the footsteps in front of us lit by flashlights in the dark, marching in a straight line on a narrow path across an icy slope. The wind swept me from side to side like a leaf blower. As we gained elevation, the air became frigid and harder to breathe. We couldn't hear each other over the thundering wind, pausing often to turn away from the gusts and catch our breath. Other trekkers, scattered along the route, struggled in the same way.

Still in the dark of night, we crept along a narrow ridge with steep slopes on both sides. Falling meant a precipitous and frightening drop. I lost my footing on the ice, my body jerking with fear. As I neared the ground, trembling, a hand grabbed my backpack straps to steady me. Bruno held me tight from behind. I steadied myself on my knees, panting, while he held on. When I caught my breath, I climbed up his legs to stand, and we huddled together to regroup. The warmth of his body, and Mark's, calmed me. Startled by the danger, we locked arms to move as a unit. When it was too hard to walk, we stood still, the three of us huddled together, bracing against the wind.

Several chilling hours later, morning approached. The path widened, and we hiked on our own. Bruno gained strength and pulled ahead. He reached the top of the pass first, set down the daypack, and returned to relieve me of my pack. "No." I shook my head. I needed its weight for balance.

At the top of the pass, we were greeted by sunrise and a broad sweeping view of the valley on the other side. Enormous peaks towered in every direction, the "outstanding" view I'd read about in the guidebook that had motivated me. I hugged Mark and Bruno and yelled "Woohoo!" We'd made it, locking arms and moving as one when needed.

Being so intensely present and alert invigorated me like nothing ever before.

We had to decide whether to stay at a teahouse near the bottom of the western side of the pass or hike to one farther away, described as nicer in the guidebook. Choosing nicer, we walked another five wearying hours.

"My feet are throbbing," I complained when we arrived. "And my skin is radiating fire." The western side of the pass held little snow. We'd traded freezing cold for scorching heat.

"Emitting heat is a sign of healing power," Mark said. "It's good you're going to be a doctor."

Bruno released a guttural grunt, "I think it's just sunburn, Mark." We all howled with laughter.

With the danger of the pass behind us, our steps became lighter, our senses keener. We climbed a mossy stone staircase, worn smooth by countless porters, inhaling fresh spruce, our steps crackling on the forest's softly needled floor. It was a welcome contrast from the arid Tibetan plateau.

On the third day of the western side, we arrived at a lodge and quenched our thirst with hot lemon water. We asked for a bucket of steaming water to soak our feet.

"Why didn't we do this before?" My cramped toes, freed from sweaty socks and hard boots, wiggled like guppies in water.

"We were too busy with the runs and panicking about the pass." Bruno stretched his arms overhead.

Crickets chirped as we inhaled the aroma of a pungent curry. This side of the pass offered a wider variety of food. As the sun waned, pony bells rang, dogs howled, and the planets appeared.

I woke up in the black of night and descended a carved ladder to the barnyard, where cows lay still, and angora goats stirred. Going outside to pee, a strange warmth of thick darkness enveloped me. Peaks of white ice glistened in the moonlight like the glaze on the pumpkin skin we'd eaten at lunch. My heart felt full, peaceful, and open in that night air, but I longed for my friends and family, mostly Mom and Josh, wishing they could experience this with me.

When we approached the roadhead a few days later, we went our separate ways. Bruno headed to Western Nepal, Mark returned to California, and I considered trekking more.

Bonding intimately then separating felt natural. Part of the magic of trekking was a respect for individuality—even while we relied on, or saved each other. Since we didn't become attached, there was no risk of disappointment, unlike relationships in the real world, where I might want a connection that I wouldn't get. As with my first love who inspired me to read *Ulysses* then left me. As with my family that broke up. I'd appreciated the company of Mark and Bruno, but I still had things to figure out by myself.

Alone again at the end of the Annapurna Circuit, I watched the sunrise from a perch called Poon Hill. Birds and gibbons hooted a lively soundtrack in the rhododendron forest, peaks appeared and disappeared behind morning clouds reminding me of what I'd seen when I landed in Kathmandu. It was time to return.

Riding atop an open bus, I admired the tropical green landscape again, but now felt like I knew those hills intimately, that they were a part of me. At the post office, I sifted through rows of envelopes addressed to people with last names beginning with "X, Y, Z," to find letters from my mother, Josh, and Gaby. Hearing about their lives, knowing I wasn't completely cut off, made me look forward to telling Mom everything over steaming mugs of Nescafé in her kitchen.

Since I'd spent less than a dollar a day so far, I could afford to visit the Everest region too. The guidebook said, "Solu Khumbu is justifiably famous, not only for its proximity to the world's highest mountain but also for its Sherpa villages and monasteries."

I craved more time to reflect. The propulsion of this trek entranced me like a hallucinogen. The vastness made my insides more accessible, paring everything down to an essence. The expansiveness made me want to take up space, not hide. Trekking challenged me to make decisions, to carry my own weight, to give that weight to others when necessary, and to carry others' burdens when I could.

I lightened my maroon bag, placing stuff in storage in Kathmandu, before repacking it to leave again. I flew to Lukla, the airstrip closest to Everest, redeemed from the choke and noise of the city.

When I deplaned in the Everest region, the crisp scent of juniper quenched a longing, and something in my heart clicked into place.

I ached for Amama. Remembering her loud voice and willingness to take up space, I admired her decision to rebuild in new places—from Berlin to Palestine and finally, New York. She was bold, and here in Nepal, I'd been bold also.

If she hadn't taken me to dance classes after my leg casts came off, I might never have been able to build the physical confidence to walk on the knife-edge of a mountain in the sky. In movement, I trusted myself to make good choices, and dance taught me the power of movement.

When I was in eighth grade, Amama babysat us while Mom visited Israel during Thanksgiving break. The morning of the holiday, I found her slumped at the kitchen table with her head resting on her hand.

"Are you okay, Amama?"

"Nicht so gut." She placed a nitroglycerine tablet under her tongue. She was being treated for angina in addition to her diabetes and often had chest pains. She phoned her cardiologist who advised her to stay home and rest. Josh and I were reluctant to leave her, but she insisted, and we went for the holiday meal to Mom's best friend, Sara.

Sara had escaped the Nazis at age seven in 1943, with a few hundred other Polish children who'd boarded a ship to Palestine. She was raised there in a youth village. Slim, shy of five feet, crowned with tight, rust curls and eyebrows painted in high arches like permanent parentheses of wonder, Sara often said, "What you are at seven, you are at seventy." She had seen a great deal by seven, and it cloaked her in melancholia well past seventy. As if to keep the frenzy of the world at bay, she talked and moved very slowly.

During the holiday meal, we worried about Amama, but when we returned, she said she was fine. Since Mom was out of town, I slept in her bed, while Amama took my bed next door, as usual.

Before I went to sleep that night, I prayed with all my heart. I covered my eyes, focused my intention, and recited the *Shema*, a Jewish prayer, adding *Please God, make Amama okay. Please, please.*

The next morning, the phone woke me up. Sara said, "I'll wait on the line while you check on Amama." I opened the door to my bedroom, and saw Amama on the floor, face down, back rounded like a turtle, legs folded beneath her.

"Amama!" I called.

She didn't respond. I stepped slowly toward her, my hand covering my mouth, and tapped her shoulder. She was still. I ran back to the phone breathless, my voice trembling. "Amama's on the floor. Not moving!"

"Get Josh!"

I ran down the hallway and woke him. He rushed into my bedroom and took over while I retreated to his room, and rocked back and forth, wailing, pleading to God. *I will do anything! Please make it okay. Please make Amama okay!*

The medics arrived, followed by a lot of commotion, and talk about "the body." I realized praying wasn't going to help anymore.

Maybe ever. For anyone, ever again.

An open German word search puzzle lay by her feet. Later, Mom said one of the circled words was *tot*. Dead.

When Mom returned from Israel, we had Amama's funeral, followed by seven days of shiva, ritual Jewish mourning, during which Mom sat on a low cardboard box receiving visitors. Occasionally she raised a handkerchief to wipe tears. I'd never seen Mom cry before. The world now felt even more perilous, precarious, and unpredictable. And I felt more alone.

I often wondered about what Sara said, whether we can change throughout life or if we remain our seven-year-old selves. I wondered because I was always searching *for* change and hoping *to* change. Of course, both are true. We are our same seven-year-old selves, yet we are so different, but how different depends on how much we want to change.

Now, in a teahouse in the mountains, these questions spun as I fell asleep before embarking on my next journey, my pack on the floor beside me, Amama stitched in the seams. I thanked her for introducing me to dance and what it is to have a voice and to take up space. I thanked her for giving me an early lesson in feeling alive.

8

Dreaming under the Plume

BUDDHISM WAS ALL AROUND ME. WITH THE RELIGION'S EMPHASIS ON experiencing the present and not worrying about the future, I left going to Everest Base Camp—the main attraction of the region—for last. I would embrace the journey over the destination.

I aimed for Gokyo, a spot containing only a few huts but rumored to have stunning glacial lakes. The downside of this detour meant I'd have to attempt another high pass—the Cho La—to cross into the Everest Valley to reach Base Camp. On my last night in the main village, Namche Bazaar, almost a metropolis compared to the other villages, I was the only guest in my lodge. From my window, I watched the moon illuminate a peak spiking through the clouds in the hush of dusk.

While I was trekking the next morning, a dry, hacking cough stole my breath and punched my ribs. I fingered the bones on the right side of my chest and wondered if I'd cracked a rib from coughing so hard.

Mid-morning, a Sherpa stopped to talk to me. "Irene?" he asked.

"Me?" I asked. He nodded his head. "No," I answered.

He pointed to my glasses and hair as if to say those things made him think I was Irene.

Next, I met an Israeli couple on the trail, Arik and Eti. Both pasty and wearing glasses, they moved leisurely, enjoying the views. After exchanging pleasantries, Arik said, "You're the one who said *L'hitraot*," Hebrew for goodbye. Another Israeli trekker had told him about meeting a girl hiking alone who speaks Hebrew. Arik spoke more freely with me, while Eti smiled shyly, tossing her shoulder-length curls.

"Guilty," I chuckled.

"You should meet Irene! She's a Canadian girl, also trekking alone," Arik said. Our paths would cross a few times in the next month, and Arik turned out to be something of a yenta and matchmaker. His first match for me: Irene.

After a few hours, I snaked around a ridge to reach Dhole, a flattened green meadow with a handful of houses.

"Welcome!" someone shouted when I entered the single teahouse there.

"Come sit here." Another trekker patted the bed next to her. "You won't believe the amazing leftover expedition food they have."

I soon learned no one else was hiking alone. Lying in my sleeping bag that evening, I questioned why, surrounded by friendly people, I felt engulfed by loneliness and longing for a companion, whereas the previous night, all alone in the lodge, I felt at peace.

The next day, I scrambled around menacing boulders, feeling alternately hot from the sun and exertion, and cold from the wind and clouds. Around noon, I came upon stunning teal lakes, which meant I'd reached Gokyo.

I spotted a blonde girl with bangs and glasses like mine sitting alone on the slope. She wore a down jacket and knee-high, patterned yarn booties, and munched a *chapati* in the sun.

"Are you the famous Irene?"

She nodded her head and laughed, her eyes sparkling. We gossiped in the wind, admiring the lustrous lakes, breathlessly swapping trekking stories about characters we'd met on the trails. She'd been on several hiking, bicycling, and skiing adventures. We eavesdropped on a group of trekkers lazing on the hill above us, translating each other's words while smoking hash, and discussing what food on the trail made them sick.

Snow forced us inside the teahouse in the late afternoon. So cold I needed to wear my down jacket inside my sleeping bag and unable to read in the dim light, all I could do was lie there and think. I was tired, my throat ached from coughing, and I dreaded climbing another high pass. I considered returning to Namche Bazaar. I watched with awe and sympathy as the didi collected water and wood, washed dishes, and cooked over an open flame. *Who am I to feel bad? Look how much work she has.*

The following day, I felt better, so Irene and I climbed Gokyo Ri together, a peak rising above the lake to 17,552 feet. Snowflakes swirled, but we didn't utter a word. There was no question we'd continue to the top, even as our breath labored, and my legs grew heavy from lack of oxygen. Hoping to cross the Cho La with Irene, I didn't want her to know how challenged I was. I gulped air silently.

The snow petered out as we approached the summit and sat on the ground. The hovering clouds parted, revealing glaciers with craters of various shades of cobalt ice, sugared with white snowdrift. The wind whistled through my hair and over my face, the taste effervescent on my lips. Irene's face beamed as we listened to the trill of birdsong. Everest was straight ahead, the view a reward for our effort. We marveled at the path of her glacier, the mementos of her power.

The next morning, we traversed a glacier on the way to the Cho La Pass, the earth beneath our boots gurgling and creaking. A rolling terrain of rocks and ice, the ground felt alive, unpredictable, as if it were daring us.

After a few hours, we were in a dense fog, and I noticed I'd lost my mittens along the way.

"Will you come with me to find them?" I asked Irene. Shivering and frightened I'd get lost, I didn't want to search the glacier alone.

"Where do you think they are?"

"I don't know."

Irene sighed and rolled her eyes but followed me. Miles later, we found my mittens perched on a rock. "Well, that was a waste," she said.

When we reached the teahouse before the pass, we found a guy lying flat on the floor, gripping his head, saying, "I'm dying. My head is killing me!" We gave him aspirin. It wasn't uncommon at this altitude for people to deteriorate and need to descend. Seeing the man's condition made us more nervous about climbing the pass, so we planned a 5:00 a.m. start.

The next morning, the climb was steep and rocky at first, and my limbs shook with jolts of electricity. It wasn't anything like hiking the

Thorung La, the pass on the Annapurna Circuit. Here, we had to climb vertically. I planted my right foot and clung to a rock above, but my right leg trembled, threatening to give way. I froze. I needed to lift my left foot, but it had a life of its own, refusing to listen. My backpack pulled backward and downward as I struggled to raise my leg. Rocks tumbled down from above, making a cracking sound as they bounced off ledges below. *I guess this is why climbers wear helmets.*

My whole body shuddered and sweat, then froze with a chill. I clenched my muscles and held my breath, as rocks sailed past with a whistling sound. Exhaling, I quickly moved my left leg to a ledge above.

Continuing upward, one foothold at a time on slippery rock and ice, we barely spoke, grunting instead. Irene climbed above me, while I inched below.

"Try not to kick rocks down here," I yelled.

"Why are you moving so slowly? Haven't you climbed before?"

"No."

"Well, if I knew you were so inexperienced, I wouldn't have gone with you. I've done stuff like this in Canada."

I bit my lip as a red bolt of shame electrified my cheeks. Ironically warmed by my humiliation, I focused on continuing slowly upward. Once on the route, I'd realized the climb was too advanced for me. But what could I do now?

The top third of the slope was covered in snow, with ice hanging all around us, as if we were inside a chandelier. We couldn't see the way out. We weren't wearing crampons, and I was particularly clumsy with my suitcase backpack and discount boots.

Reaching the top of the pass, Irene crept over the edge. "Shit, we went totally out of the way, too far up." She towered above me, hands on her hips. I needed to get through these final moves, when slipping would not end well. I planted my hands on the ridge, pressed my body into the mountain and pulled myself up, panting frantically as I flung my legs over the ledge. I lay there, snow falling into my gaping mouth like a goldfish on the water's edge. My heart pounded, exploding from my chest.

Finally, I stood up and understood what Irene meant. Blinded by the ice, we had made the climb harder than necessary, veering to the left of the route. I leaned over, hands on my knees, and took some deep breaths while my heartbeat slowed. After recovering, we descended a path through heavily falling snow and sheltered in a hut we found. Inside, the snow rained through the yak dung ceiling. A few hours later, two French men and their porter came in, built a fire, and shared their noodle soup. We were very grateful.

Later, I researched the Cho La Pass online and read this:

Do not go from west to east. That's what we did.

It's too steep and slippery, looks impossible, requires ropes. That's how it felt.

Be aware that Cho La is prone to rock fall and avalanches. We could have died.

Our muscles ached, but we left for the next village, Lobuche, at first light. After a few hours, we stopped to rest at the crest of a hill. I was snapping pictures when a noise startled me. I turned around and watched in horror as my maroon beast somersaulted down the mountain, hitting rocks as it tumbled. A quick glance at Irene's grimace told me I'd screwed up badly. When it finally stopped on a ridge below, it was hard to face the fact that I'd need to descend, get the pack, and climb back up again. I trudged down, cursing myself, but was relieved to find the pockets hadn't opened, and I'd only lost my extra water bottle clipped to the outside.

We climbed a hill slippery with loose dirt, where I had a hard time gaining traction. My muscles quivered from the day before.

"It wouldn't have taken so long today if your pack hadn't fallen," Irene scowled. She was suffering from conjunctivitis and was extra grouchy.

"You have something to say about everything!" I snapped back, wondering how long we'd stay together.

A short time later, we ran into Arik and Eti, my Israeli friends. When I waved *L'hitraot*, goodbye, to them, the "r" sound gurgled from the back of my throat.

At sixteen, my mother had practically pushed me on the plane to Israel for my first trip alone. I'd planned to do medical research in NYC, but she had other ideas. "That's a ridiculous way for a teenager to spend the summer," she said. She believed what was best for me was to be more like her. She had loved growing up in Tel Aviv, skipping high school to party on the beach. I bristled at going because it was *her* idea, *her* country, and I felt under *her* control.

Mom sent me to her friend Rachel in Israel, who arranged for me to spend the summer volunteering on a kibbutz. Rachel, with jet-black hair, fair skin, and red lipstick like an Israeli Snow White, pointed out landmarks as we drove to Ramot Menashe, a socialist settlement where everyone was an equal member of the community and shared in the work. I silently studied the sandy landscape rushing by.

When we arrived, the director of volunteers approached and extended his hand toward me. A tall man with a paunch and mop of gray hair, David smiled. "Welcome, I'll take you around."

I watched Rachel drive away and felt that stomach pang of the unknown. David and I strolled on a path between green fields lined with colorful flower beds and a smattering of tiny houses and dormitories.

"This is the dining hall, where everything happens," he said.

Before entering, a crash of voices resounded like clashing cymbals. Inside were rows of tables filled with diners gesticulating wildly.

"Many have come from all over the world." David waved his hands at the room.

There's a saying: Two Jews, three opinions. Here were hundreds of Jews and what felt like thousands of emphatic voices, laughing and assertive, rising above the steam of coffee mugs and clanging trays. Many wore blue work shirts, short shorts, and dome-shaped sun hats. How would I ever find my place amongst these people?

I reported to the dining hall for work in the cotton fields at 3:30 a.m., the blackest hour of night, as David had instructed. With the other gathering workers, I warmed up, sipping *café botz*—strong, sweet Turkish coffee—in the cool dry air, waiting for stragglers to fill a pickup truck.

We traversed bumpy farm roads for an hour and arrived at the valley fields before sunrise. We hunched over cotton plants, a row of human Cs, up one long aisle and down another, silently pulling weeds from the grainy soil. We plodded along, the air slowly filling with birdsong and rising heat, the sky at first thickish and gray, then a warm orange. Our reward arrived at 7:00 a.m., when a truck pulled up with a spread of hard-boiled eggs, briny olives, plump red tomatoes, crunchy cucumbers, and soft pita bread.

We returned to the kibbutz before the heaviest heat of day. Afternoons invited a hitch to the beach or a laze by the pool. Even though I only slept a handful of hours at night, I relished pushing my body to extremes and feeling that effort in my sore muscles at night, the way I had with dance. After a few weeks plowing the land, my dreams furrowed in Hebrew.

My next assignment was in the kitchen. One afternoon, while I was diligently stooped over a large stainless-steel sink, carefully scrubbing each lettuce leaf, my boss scolded me.

"What are you doing? If you spend so much time on each leaf, no one will eat tonight."

Rather than feeling criticized, learning that my work mattered energized me. Dinner depended on me. I sped up, happy to feel a part of this community where I hung out with the teens my age who lived there. At night, we sang songs to a strummed guitar, cracked open watermelons, and slurped sticky juice. I joined in spitting the seeds. We danced disco wildly on Friday nights in the bomb shelter, which doubled as a makeshift nightclub.

One minute I was in New York with people racing over cement sidewalks, the next I was on a farm, working the land, discovering a new sense of belonging. On the kibbutz, no one knew my parents were divorced, that they had accents, that I was a scholarship kid. Wealth and material goods didn't matter. For the first time, I felt the exhilaration of reinvention, seeing myself anew through other eyes, eyes that weren't judging me—only my work—and weren't fitting me inside a box of their expectations. I was simply me, a good worker who makes dinner for her community, yet I was prouder than ever before. Why didn't I have this feeling at home? Who was judging me? I thought it was my mother, my father, my Orthodox community, people like the gynecologist.

But I was putting myself in boxes too.

The first time I met a "kibbutznik" and she asked who I was, I replied *ani mitnadevet*, a volunteer. She and her friend laughed at how

I'd emphasized the wrong syllable. A little embarrassed, I laughed with them, then memorized their lesson so I'd say it right the next time.

When I'd struggled to understand my parents speaking foreign languages, it felt like glimpsing through a window. Now, living this language felt like I'd cracked a window open. I faltered when trying to express ideas, but the different syntax helped crack a window of thought as well. Speaking another language changes the shape of your mouth, the roll of your tongue, the feel of breath in the back of the throat, even the tilt of your chin. Speaking with new grammar inspired a new way to interact; it was almost like becoming a new person.

Speaking additional languages had literally saved my father's life, and it was merely expanding mine. Or maybe it was saving my life, too. My mind, soaking in all this difference, was getting a makeover, as was my body. Weeding cotton and scrubbing lettuce made me feel capable and full of agency. I didn't have to live in a girdle like my mother and grandmother did. I could bust out, and strip away expectations.

"I'm not coming home," I told my mother on the phone. "I'm happy here."

"You'll do as I say, young lady!"

We spent weeks negotiating over the phone, until I agreed to return the day before senior year of high school. She'd pushed me on the plane to go, then begged me to come back. She'd been right about what was best for me.

I'd practiced my Judaism by genuflection in the weeds. My prayers had resided in the peduncles of pears I picked straight from the tree. I left the expansive sky of the kibbutz with the promise to return promptly, to return to the feeling of being capable and free. I still hadn't made it back.

Instead, I was exploring being capable and free in Nepal. And now I happily conversed in Hebrew with my Israeli trekking friends—a welcome break from squabbling with Irene.

After leaving Arik and Eti, Irene and I slogged together, and a few days later, we reached the famous Khumbu glacier, the final part of the trek to Everest Base Camp. We hadn't realized we'd need to walk through this confusing terrain that had no trail signs.

The structural elements that make glacier walking confusing and dangerous—crevasses and ice pinnacles—are formed by the slow movement of glacial ice "downstream," much like a waterfall into a river. Just as river rapids form eddies around rocks, the ice flows and cracks downward, forming holes or crevasses. In other places, it mounds upward, forming towers or seracs. Snow often crusts over the top of a crevasse, making it look like solid ground when, in fact, it veils a deep cleft.

We picked our way through the glacier, admiring the novel terrain of ice castles, but were relieved when we spotted the colorful tents of Base Camp surrounded by prayer flags. We approached awkwardly to have a look around.

The only Everest climbs in 1985 were expeditions consisting of serious mountaineers, often part of a national team, with only a handful of teams permitted each season. This was the final year that the Nepalese limited climbs to one team per route. We came upon the American West Ridge Direct Expedition, consisting of twenty-one climbers using oxygen and Sherpa support. The team members we met at Base Camp were disappointed to have just learned that their team's final attempt at the summit had failed, although the climbers reached a new high point above 28,000 feet, within a thousand feet of the summit. One of the climbers, Dan, chatted with us as we warmed in the sun, munching our chapatis smeared with honey.

"I've been meaning to climb Kala Pattar, near your teahouse. I'll visit you tomorrow if the weather's clear," he said, referring to a small peak with close-up views of Everest.

Irene and I left around 4:00 p.m. to return to the teahouse in Gorak Shep, where we'd slept the night before. We quickly got lost in the towers of ice. Nursing a pounding headache, Irene sat down on a boulder, covered her eyes, and rubbed her temples, leaving me to find the way. I panicked. Searching the huge seracs towering around us, I saw no path, no cairns. The light was shifting, and I feared getting stuck in the dark.

What kind of doctor will I be if I panic?

I retraced our steps and still couldn't find the path. Systematically, I walked in each direction, noting landmarks so I could find my way back to Irene. I panted, becoming increasingly chilled, walking between tall ice blocks stippled with slanting sunlight. When I finally found the path, my shoulders released, and I raced back to Irene. Once we knew where we were going, we relaxed and appreciated the incandescent ice castles with the sun descending on, through, and between them. I felt redeemed. Not destined to always be the weaker link.

We often managed to do something that made our trek more demanding. This time, we accidentally took a high rocky ridge, expending extra time and energy. Back at the teahouse at dusk, we plopped on our beds, and someone else's porter brought us Sherpa stew loaded with potatoes.

The following morning, my eyelids were heavy and my body sore.

"Look how cloudy it is," Irene said.

"I guess we can't climb Kala Pattar." *Thank God, a rest day.*

Dan arrived with a friend. "Hey, you two should come to the big expedition party we're planning for Pangboche on the sixteenth," he said, referring to a village on the way back down the valley.

"Hold on—let's check our schedules." I mimed leafing through a book to see where we'd be in five days.

"It might work out." Irene's rosy cheeks glowed.

"Don't miss it. We're having American food, American music—a real party!" They were likely eager to have two women join them. We looked forward to some fun too.

The weather cleared in the late afternoon, and we felt better rested, so Irene and I ascended Kala Pattar to 18,192 feet, my new high-altitude record. We enjoyed the view of Everest, seen sporadically between milky clouds. Her famous and prominent plume—a cloud floating on the mountain's powerful jet stream—like a flag anchored to the pinnacle, flapped fast in the winds. We rested on top until forced down in a hailstorm, ice crystals pelting our faces with the sensation of downhill skiing.

Our teahouse had filled with people. We passed the night wedged in head to toe, listening to every cough, sneeze, and burp. I jumped over bodies to go outside to pee around midnight and was startled by how close the Milky Way appeared. It swept the sky a hazy white like an eraser on a chalkboard. We were truly on another level of earth, where I might reach out, sink my hand into the sky, and pull a star free.

Our destination behind us, we began our descent through the Khumbu villages to return to the airstrip at Lukla and fly back to Kathmandu. Irene and I enjoyed sunny weather, relaxing conversation, and wonderful days feeling liberated and adventurous. I met a woman on a remote ridge, and we realized we lived on the same street in Manhattan, a block apart, and danced at the same studios. Inconceivable, that the world could be so vast and small at the same time. Decades later, I would scan old journals and recognize the address she gave me is my adult son's apartment building. I would visit and discover she is still there.

We reached the village of Chukhung, the most beautiful place I'd ever been, surrounded by mountains and the glaciers draining them. We settled on the ground to shelter from the winds and admire the scenery. I sat with my back against a hill and my knees bent. Dirty after two weeks of trekking, we disrobed to air out our bodies in the sun. I focused on the geometry of the boulders as thistle heads whistled in the wind just beyond my knees, swaying gray and transparent. The endless sky of blue above and blue beyond evoked a sense of timelessness, where memories and options coexisted.

I delighted in observing the gray diaspora of clouds and felt like one of them—wispish, condensing and expanding—leaving a trace but rarely an impact.

Irene and I were having fun, and I wanted to trek with her, but I also wanted to be alone among these peaks. To study them and listen to all they had to tell me. In that moment, the glacier spoke to me.

Open your heart that turns away from people.

"But I am hurt," I responded in my mind. "How can I embrace openly?"

Remember your fear on the Gokyo glacier. That glacier supported you. You bowed down, thanking its strength, your heart open.

"But it's hard to open myself up, to connect, or even to accept attention."

You have come this far, ready for my grace, but you have yet to embrace yourself. You shed pieces of yourself as if they are worthless, instead of collecting your visions within your seams.

A breeze brushed my face, and I shifted on the rock, glimpsing Irene a few feet away.

Your dance teacher tells you to come forward, but you don't move until you feel ready. It isn't about being ready. You must surrender. Likewise, here you must not simply follow. You must choose your own dance and paint it in your colors.

A low cloud descended over our naked bodies, wafting a cool airstream around us.

With a shudder, I dressed.

I later learned that several Hasidic rabbis recommended praying in solitude, in nature. Rebbe Nachman—the most famous of these—wrote, "When a person meditates in the fields, all the grasses join in his prayer and increase its effectiveness and power."

The glacier not only joined my prayer but begged me to listen and to release my guard. The more solo wandering I did, the more connected I became. To my roots, to myself, to others.

9

A Himalayan Rave

I LEFT IRENE TO VISIT THE HIGH-ALTITUDE MEDICAL CLINIC IN PHER-
iche, with a plan to meet later. What was medicine in the mountains
like? I entered a room with stone walls and a small exam area. A man sat
behind a desk, wearing a puffy vest, and drinking tea, and another man
wearing an oxygen mask lay on the table beside him.

The man at the desk tapped his fingers, barely lifting his eyes. "Can
I help you?"

"Hi. I'm starting med school in the fall and wanted to pop in for a
visit, see what's going on. I'm Mimi." I extended my hand.

He perked up, shaking my hand. "I'm Stefan, I'll show you around."
He pointed to the patient lying on his exam table.

"This trekker got here this morning. Classic signs of AMS. He'll be
fine with some oze."

I stared at him confused. He added, "Sorry, he has acute mountain
sickness. I'm treating him with oxygen." He chuckled, and pointed to the
other side of the room, "These are two Sherpas. One has bronchitis, the
other a nasty foot infection."

Stefan was the physician staffing the clinic for a year. I was surprised
he took care of locals in addition to treating altitude sickness, given the
name of the clinic.

"We've evolved into being a local clinic," he explained. "But we also
see a lot of high-altitude problems, usually people who aren't following
acclimatization advice." As he made me a cup of tea, I wondered if I
could ever do what he did. The conditions were rough, but I'd be in the

mountains, and I'd be helping the local people. My heart quickened with the thought of practicing mountain medicine, the idea of being of service to this population in this place.

"Stefan, how did you train for this?"

"I'm an ER doc." I took out my journal and jotted down his contact information. I was still planning to become an OB/GYN but could see myself working there, living there, feeling useful there.

The clinic was established in 1975 by the Tokyo Medical College and the Himalayan Rescue Association for the treatment, education, and research of high-altitude medical problems, including AMS. The founders were concerned that both climbers and trekkers were dying from severe altitude sickness.

I left the clinic and met Irene in Pangboche to go to the Everest party. We climbed the steps to the lodge, the thumping bass of the Rolling Stones blasting from inside. The room was packed, half the village drinking out of red plastic cups. Irene and I found a couch.

"You made it!" Dan greeted us.

"Happy to have a break from Sherpa stew," I said, grabbing a handful of potato chips.

"You weren't kidding, Dan." Irene's face flushed, sipping a beer.

We served ourselves the potent local brew, scooped out of large Tupperware containers. While I chatted with Dan, Irene stumbled back from the dance floor.

After the Stones, Sherpa music played, and the locals flooded the floor for a circle dance. Enchanted by their wide grins, I jumped into the circle, my arms on the shoulders of people on both sides. I lost myself in the stomping rhythm that reminded me of years of Israeli folk dancing: stamp right foot twice then brush left, rest on left. A surge of instrumental music led to clapping and more stomping. Dancing in my stiff, heavy hiking boots was incongruous and deliciously fun. Dust crumbled off my soles.

When I returned to the couch, Irene was prostrate, resting her head from the spin of high altitude mixed with alcohol.

Robert, one of Dan's teammates, stood in front of the couch. He talked loudly over Dan and me, to a person behind us.

"Yeah, I run an advertising agency in New Zealand," he said.

I couldn't hear Dan or the person next to me.

"I was on the Summit Team, got within eight hundred feet," Robert called over me.

He's being so rude.

Robert directed his gaze downward and spoke directly to me. "Where are you from?"

"New York."

"What are you doing here?"

"I've been trekking for a few months. Irene and I met Dan at Base Camp. He invited us." I pointed over to Irene, but she wasn't on the couch.

"Are you with a group?"

"No. By myself." I turned and scanned the room but couldn't locate Irene. I hoped she was okay, knowing she wasn't feeling well. "Nice to meet you," I said, standing up to return to our lodge.

"I'll walk you back," offered Robert.

"No thanks, I'm fine."

"It's pretty dark out, and a long way back to the teahouse. Let me go with you."

"Okay."

We stepped into the inky black night. I sensed Robert was tipsy and wondered how he'd find the way. He led me on a road near stone-encased fields for a long time, me walking a few steps behind. When nothing looked familiar, I got nervous. *Who is this guy? Where's he taking me? Why are we near the river?* My suspicions and fear grew but after about twenty minutes, the main homes of the village emerged as faint outlines in the blackness. Outside the door to my lodge, we said good night. He moved to kiss me.

"You've been on the mountain for three months—another planet," I said. "That's why you want to kiss me."

"No, I like you." He paused, then grinned. "You've been away a long time too."

I laughed because he had a point. He appeared sad about getting so close to the top of Everest and needing to turn around, making me feel a little sorry for him. We shared a quick good-night kiss, then I softened and wrapped my arms around him saying, "Welcome back to Earth."

He laughed. "I want to see you in daylight."

"I'm sure I'll see you on the trail." I turned to enter the lodge. I found my sleeping bag and was happy to see Irene in hers.

The next day, Irene and most of the Everest climbers headed toward the comforts of Namche Bazaar. Instead, I detoured to the village of Thyangboche, famous for its monastery; I had run into Arik and Eti, who invited me to a Friday-night Shabbat dinner there. Irene and I had parted on good terms, but I was happy to be by myself again. Approaching the lodge, I waved to Arik.

"Mimi, you won't believe it, we taught the didi how to bake challah! Wait till you see the feast we planned." He grabbed my arm to show me inside.

A long table was set with dishes, a big upgrade from teahouse meals eaten in bed.

Most of the guests were trekkers, but both Robert and another climber from the American team, Ed Webster, showed up. Ed was from Boulder, Colorado, famous for his rock-climbing skills and his book about climbs in New Hampshire. He had a dark brown beard and enchanting light blue eyes, and he delighted the diners with climbing stories and an understated sense of humor. Robert sat beside him, with an even darker beard and another set of piercing blue eyes. He was more subdued this evening.

I met Arik in the kitchen, where he cornered me with another matchmaking siege.

"Robert asked me all about you. He likes you. Did you know his girlfriend in New Zealand is a former Miss Universe? There must be something to him." Gossip on the trails was as endemic as yaks.

Did Arik think more of him because he was involved with a world-class beauty? I wondered why he was interested in me. *He must be desperate after his time on the mountain.*

"Is that supposed to make me like him more?" I furrowed my brows, skeptical, but also flattered. "How do you know he likes me?"

"He came here looking for you. He said he heard you were staying here. I think you should go for it."

We returned to the table, where the conversation flowed between the international guests. When I stood up to say good night, Robert approached. "When are you leaving for Namche?"

"Not sure." Skepticism had won out.

The following morning, I reached the trailhead around 6:00 a.m. hoping to beat everyone else and return to solitude. Stepping out of the trees and onto the trail, Robert announced, "You didn't think you'd get rid of me that easily!" He wore a big grin and spoke with a cheerful lilt.

His voice startled me, as did the fact he was up so early. We set out walking together in the gray light of a chilly morning. The trail meandered through rhododendron forests and crossed rushing streams.

When the sun blazed through, we stopped. I took off my pack, leaned it against a tree and tied my jacket around my waist.

"Want a Milky Way?" Robert asked.

"You've been holding out on me! I'll eat anything that's not Sherpa stew."

"We lived on these on the mountain. High altitude. Poor appetite. They go down easily."

"Wouldn't you love a pizza right now?"

"We could get one in K-du," he said, referring to Kathmandu. "But I'd rather meet you at a sidewalk café in Paris and share a bottle of good red wine."

I smiled. "Sounds good."

The conversation flowed easily as we discussed our favorite books and authors. One of his was Lawrence Durrell's *The Alexandria Quartet*, which I later read thinking of him, appreciating the evocation of place and romance. Robert grew up in Denver, was a competitive skier and biker, and was now working in New Zealand. He wasn't only the arrogant climber I'd first met, but also a thinking, considerate person. Oozing with charm.

He repeated, "I was so close, just eight hundred feet from the summit," then added, "You know it was kind of a big deal that I was chosen for the summit team."

"Oh yeah?"

"And now I know I can make the top." His jaw was set, his eyes fixed on me. "I'm going to come back. Plan my own Everest expedition." His face lit up as he leapt over a boulder, his long lean body a rubber band needing to stretch and pop. "It takes years to get a permit."

That made sense. He'd proven himself, why not come back? Just the mention of it returned a bounce to his step.

What made no sense was what happened next.

"Well, if you need a doctor for your next expedition, call me."

Robert pursed his lips and leaned his head to the side, examining me.

What did I just say? As the plucky words rolled out of my mouth, I surprised even myself. I hadn't started medical school. I knew nothing about being a doctor, much less about being one on an Everest expedition. I knew nothing about wilderness medicine. But I figured if it took years to secure a permit, I would at least be an actual doctor by then. If I were invited. Then, I could return here. To this magnificence.

During our enchanting walk, we talked about how surprising it was to get to know and like each other. But when we reached Namche, I was content to say goodbye to Robert and any potential connection or relationship with him. I liked him but didn't want to lose myself. Since he lived in New Zealand and I in New York, pursuing anything romantic was pointless. I still had my long-distance boyfriend from RMBL. Robert had Miss Universe.

The expedition members were staying together in one lodge in Namche. They invited me to their team dinner, but I didn't want to stay with them. Instead, I chose an empty lodge. The large dormitory-style room was filled with separate cots, and I spread out my stuff, thrilled for my first shower in weeks.

I scratched my scalp in the hot water, washing away layers of grime and dust, then dressed in clean clothes and lay down to enjoy a book. The tip of Robert's head bopped up the steps. "There's no place like home!" He threw his pack on the cot next to mine.

We were now the only two lodgers there.

From between the leaves of my book, I spied him returning from his shower, having washed away his caveman vibe. Shiny hair, shaven, sporting crisp blue jeans and a light blue denim shirt. *Wow, he looks good. And he's wearing Birkenstock clogs!* That clearly negated any arrogance.

After the expedition's group dinner Robert and I crashed in our separate cots.

I was awakened in the middle of the night by menstrual blood soaking through my underwear. Miserable and bloated, I climbed up and down the stairs to the shower to wash my clothes and sleeping bag. I had read the body is prone to misfire at high elevations, so I hadn't expected to ovulate. At least it happened at the end of the trek, in a place where I could shower. Drained and embarrassed, I climbed back into bed, hoping Robert wouldn't wake up.

"What's wrong?"

"I'm fine." I turned on my side away from him, weeping and hormonal. He persisted asking me questions until I explained what happened.

"Let me help you." *Help me? Could anything be more awkward?*

He turned in my direction and wrapped his long, spidery arms around me. Instead of our fantasy date in Paris, we were in this dormitory, sharing a thoroughly embarrassing intimate moment. But his kindness warmed my heart.

The next day was like being in the City after the Country. Sitting on the large wooden deck of a café , we ate cinnamon buns (not dal bhat!) in the sunshine and conversed with characters I'd met over weeks of trekking. Robert and the other expedition climbers were descending the following day to Lukla to fly to Kathmandu, but I refused to join them, explaining that I was trekking more. As soon as they left, I regretted my decision.

I awoke to drenching rains. Trekking was pointless now that the monsoon season was beginning. Wearing a big poncho, I trudged down the trail in the mud, rain pounding my pack which hung heavy on my shoulders. I entered the lodge in Lukla to find the expedition stuck there, unable to fly in the rain. Robert jumped up, his eyes wide and happy, and enveloped me in a bear hug. I relaxed my head into his shoulder.

Back in Kathmandu, I again stubbornly refused to stay in the team's lodge, intent to maintain my separate space. I picked up a letter from Amy in the post office and visited Robert on the roof of the Tibet Guest

House, lined with plump pink flowers in boxes. As the sun set, his large hand lifted my chin to meet his eyes. Soon we connected under white bedsheets after a month of ground, nakedness after layers. Cascading monsoon showers romantically thrummed the roof.

During the next week, Robert and I hung out with other expeditioners, ate in various pie shops (a thing in K-du), and he coaxed me on another adventure—riding a motorcycle for the first time to visit Swayambhunath, the famous monkey temple.

"It makes no sense to get involved," I said, canceling a dinner date with him.

"You never know what can happen. We're having a good time—why not stay open?" *That's exactly what a player would say.* A player with a beauty queen girlfriend. We didn't discuss her or my boyfriend because we weren't going to stay together. I obviously hadn't gotten the memo to chill out because *what happens in the Himalayas stays in the Himalayas.*

Many of the climbers and trekkers I'd befriended were headed to the beaches of Thailand to recover from the mountains, as was Robert, who was meeting his father there. I was going there too, but after a trip to Burma, now Myanmar, so Robert and I planned to meet for the one night we would overlap in Bangkok.

On my last night in Kathmandu, I dined with Arik and Eti. Feeling faint from a return of diarrhea, I left shortly after dinner. The sky cracked with thunder and a monsoon deluge, my flip-flops no match for the torrent, my feet submerged in rushing sewage-filled water. I hailed a rickshaw, and the driver maneuvered it like a raft through a raging river.

My whirlwind of seven days in Burma included sleeping on sticky floors of trains and boats, exploding with diarrhea, and visiting magnificent temples. I lived for the entire week on the money I got for selling a carton of 7-7-7 cigarettes and a bottle of Johnny Walker Red, purchased in Duty Free as advised by other travelers.

On the plane to Bangkok, I looked forward to seeing Robert, but assumed he wouldn't be there. He probably *was* a player and by now had moved on from any thought of me to consorting with a bikini-clad woman he'd met on the beach. I would need to navigate a new city on my own. I forgot about him when I experienced the joy of a clean airport flush toilet. But not long after clearing immigration, I spotted Robert's head above the crowd.

"I booked you a room in the airport hotel where my dad and I are staying tonight," he said. We walked there together, and after checking me in, he told me we were having a fancy dinner, then left.

My first thought upon entering my room was how spacious and comfortable the carpet looked, since I'd been sleeping on floors. Staring at my outfit in the mirror—bamboo hat, long skirt, sneakers—I plopped my backpack on the bed wondering what I could wear to dinner. I browsed through a limited selection in the hotel lobby store and bought a batik outfit with a matching skirt and top, feeling quite savvy.

When Robert picked me up, he pointed to my flip-flops. "What are you wearing?"

"Stop. I don't have anything else."

"Well, I'm sure you'll be the first and last person to dine at the Oriental Hotel in those. Come on!"

"Does this count as our Paris meal?" He laughed and took my hand.

The dining room glistened like a different kind of Shangri-La. Instead of glacial ice sculptures, resplendent chandeliers hung overhead, and floor-to-ceiling windows overlooked twinkling Bangkok lights. I hid behind Robert so no one could see my flip-flops. Robert's father, a banker, tall and formal in a suit, extended his hand. "Nice meeting you." Robert pointed out my shoes, and his father said, "They don't mind. Our money counts the same."

I'd never dined in such an elegant, impeccable place. This was way beyond the hotel where I'd failed as a waitress in Switzerland. If only Amama, the chef, could have experienced the drama of this five-star French service and food. She, who deserved a little pampering. It was a shock after spending my previous night on a crowded train floor in Burma eating a dinner of peanuts coated with a red chili spice.

Robert and I stayed up late in my room, mostly talking through the bathroom door since I was glued to the toilet. Neither of us understood our closeness. Now I would feel a loss, which is what I'd been trying to avoid.

"I'll write to let you know when I'll be in New York. Might be sooner than you think."

He and his father left for their flight at around 3:00 a.m., and I reveled in my spacious, modern hotel room, planning to check out as late as possible.

The bustle of Bangkok contrasted sharply with the boundless energy of the mountains. The city felt heavy with limitations, worries, traffic. I planned to get a good rest and recover from my diarrhea by "drying out"—my very nonmedical notion—at the beach.

I rode an overnight bus to the island of Koh Samui. After a few days my diarrhea situation became dire. I realized I hadn't peed in two days. My body's water poured out of my rear instead. *What kind of doctor will I be if I can't take care of myself?* A bout of stomach cramps brought me back to my straw hut and to my knees, to guzzle more antidiarrheal medication.

Watching the moon from the porch, I wrote letters until the mosquitos drove me under my bed's net for refuge. I'd just met two travelers with malaria and wanted to protect myself. Abdominal spasms woke me in the middle of the night, threatening an imminent explosion. Trapped by the net tucked under the bedsheets, I pulled and sweated and swore, fearing I'd shit the bed. I barely made it to a tiled hut nearby, with a place to squat and a hose.

The next day, I noted how relaxed people on the beach appeared—sunning, swimming, talking. Determined to feel more like them and take better care of myself, I wrapped a sarong around myself and hobbled over to the restaurant to find something I could keep down. Seeking relief from the beating sun, I sat at the counter on a high stool under a canopy. I splurged on cold bottled water, which went down more smoothly than the iodinated version. I ate a plate of brown rice, and my insides cramped. I pressed deep into my belly to massage the growing pain, trying to quell it. I felt hot and began to sweat. A sharp stab grabbed me from inside, and my fingers trembled. I ran to the bathroom. When I returned, I ate a cookie, hoping it would stay down, but again had to run to the bathroom. A second cookie stayed down.

I chatted with an older American couple who stood out from the backpacker crowd. Barry had sandy full-facial hair and wore a button-down shirt, while Sharon wore a sundress, her curls blowing in the breeze. We discussed my stomach woes and Barry, a chiropractor, convinced me to let him adjust me. He proposed "closing a valve in my intestines which backed up toxins in my stomach." Back at their hut, he kneaded, prodded, or twisted my stomach, diaphragm, neck, back, ribs, ankles, knees, and hips. It felt good to be in someone's care, but the aftermath of soreness added another layer of misery on top of my intestinal issues. I had passed only blood that day.

At night, I dropped to my knees in the sand and cried, "Mom! Mommy, help me! I'm so weak!"

My guidebook explained that rectal bleeding combined with my other symptoms were suggestive of dysentery but could also be cholera, a disease that led to death 25 to 50 percent of the time. When morning came, I went to a local clinic, but the line stretched for hours. I didn't have the strength to stand and wait. Returning to the bungalows, I asked Sharon and Barry if they'd bring my backpack to Bangkok because I was too weak to carry it. We arranged a time and place to meet the following Sunday. I boarded an overnight bus, relieved to sit in air-conditioning but unhappy about using the bus bathroom for twelve hours. After studying a map of Bangkok with marked hospitals, I chose one labeled "teaching hospital," hoping they'd speak English.

Waiting in the registration line, I got dizzy and collapsed. The receptionist ran for a stretcher and wheeled me to the ER. In the bed, I closed my eyes, relieved to rest. A series of people examined me, pressing on my stomach, talking over me in Thai, coming in and out of the room, and huddling. With no one speaking English, I was scared. They directed me to the third floor where I provided a stool sample and was brought in to see the doctor.

"Have a seat," he said.

"You speak English!"

"I studied in New Jersey." He explained my test result was consistent with shigella dysentery. "You should feel better quickly with this antibiotic." He handed me a prescription and explained where the pharmacy was. Later, in medical practice, I would remember that fear of not under-standing, and took extra time comforting patients with a language barrier.

I called my mother collect. She said she'd woken up in the middle of the night hearing "Mommy! Mommy!"

When younger, I'd struggled to reconcile Mom's prickliness with the idea that she was always doing her best, but I knew it in my gut. Every-thing she did was out of love, but didn't always feel like love. Now, despite the tension between us, Mom had the superpower to connect with me across twelve time zones in a dream when I needed her most.

"You must check into a real hotel with air-conditioning. I will pay for it," she said. "Enough with these hostels."

By then, I'd understood Mom had been tough with us because she was raised in the same demanding way. That it might have even been a *Yekke* thing, like other Jews of German origin who lived by attention to order. Amama wasn't fastidious like Mom, but she lived by strong Ger-man *shoulds* and *shouldn'ts*.

I checked into a six-floor hotel, entered my room, and slid between silky white sheets. The antibiotic took effect quickly. Full of gratitude for Mom, I basked in the cool air-conditioning, comforts, and cleanliness of a real hotel, staying for two whole days and nights, before slinging on my backpack, brought to Bangkok courtesy of Sharon and Barry.

PART IV

RETURNING

You cannot always stay on the summits. You have to come down again. . . . So what's the point? Only this: what is above knows what is below, what is below does not know what is above. While climbing, take note of all the difficulties along your path. During the descent, you will no longer see them, but you will know that they are there if you have observed carefully.

—René Daumal

10

Breathe In Slowly: One, Two, Three, Four

DURING ONE OF MY FIRST CLINICAL ROTATIONS AS A MEDICAL STUDENT in 1985, I ran to keep up with my intern in the Bronx County emergency room, green scrubs chafing my inner thighs. We had learned to draw blood by practicing on fellow students in a classroom across the street, and I'd already applied this skill in the ER for a few weeks. But on that morning, we were notified that, due to the emerging AIDS epidemic, we would now be required to wear gloves when drawing blood. Everyone was talking about it, wondering if gloves were necessary.

So much was still unknown about HIV. The wards were full of patients with hollowed cheeks, purplish-brown spots, and gaunt arms clutching IV poles while walking the hospital hallways, their gowns barely cinched behind them. The strange manifestations of AIDS required us to gain new vocabulary: Kaposi's sarcoma, *Pneumocystis carinii*, cryptosporidiosis. It was heartbreaking to care for so many people who had fallen gravely ill with this new syndrome which invariably resulted in death.

The first time I donned gloves, I set up to draw blood as usual. Our patient presented with a gastrointestinal bleed, and I recognized the characteristic foul odor emanating from his black tarry stool with its own medical name: melena. I placed the tourniquet on the patient's left arm and palpated his vein, holding my breath. I'd have to learn to deal with fetid odors. The cubicle was small and sweat beaded on my neck. The bulge was much harder to feel through the latex glove than with my bare fingers. I pulled my gloves on tighter, then pulled down on the skin below his elbow crease for counter traction and slid the needle into the vein.

Crimson blood oozed into the syringe, and I filled three vials. Holding gauze on the puncture site, I moved to release the needle, and the syringe caught the edge of my glove, flipping over on itself, flinging the needle into my forearm. *Shit!* I stuck myself because of the glove.

I looked over at my intern. "What should I do?"

She shook her head, eyes wide.

The patient wasn't known to have AIDS, so I turned back to him and kept working. This was an immersion with risks. Eventually, the hospital would create detailed policies for handling needle sticks and the risk of infection.

Since beginning school, I'd buckled from the weight of the unrelenting workload. I'd traded in wide mountain vistas for constricting corners of a library cubicle, colorful skies for monochromatic fluorescent lights, moving forward in the sunshine for standing still at the photocopy machine, breathing in light air for inhaling mountains of information. I named the feeling I had when I left anatomy lab reeking of formaldehyde: cadaver-dead.

To dissect a human body was to feel curiosity, awkwardness, gratitude, wonder. Someone had donated their actual body, their self, for our benefit. When we sawed open the skull of our cadaver, a tiny chip of bone flew into my throat. Or did I imagine that? A scratchy, sharp feeling lodged near my tonsils for months, leading me to wonder if I'd get Creutzfeldt-Jakob disease—a very rare, fatal neurodegenerative disease that can be caused by exposure to infected brain tissue. This was my version of "medical student syndrome," when students think they've contracted whatever disease or condition they are learning about. Of course, our cadaver didn't have this disease, but I wondered what else I might've caught with that piece of bone.

Questions about the person on our dissecting table gripped us as we discovered what killed them by analyzing their tissues. We invented stories about what kind of life they might have led. It was inescapable to face where and how each of us ends up, and I pondered how I wanted to spend my breathing hours. I didn't want to feel choked by bone or school.

I longed to be back in nature, to be in—and of—the world and sky. Not to be scrambling through hallways worrying about syringes and a disease nobody understood. People had warned me not to go into medicine, that it would change and harden me. While sawing the skull of our cadaver, I worried they might be right.

When I'd first returned to New York City after trekking, I leapt back into dance class, wanting my body to stay strong. "Did you desert me, baby? I missed you," my teacher cried, arms wide. Luigi, the master teacher in the studio next door, took my hands in his. "I wish you would dance with me all the time," he said, inspiring me to do a triple pirouette without overthinking, spotting his warm grin and crooked eye. I hadn't expected either of them to notice I was gone.

My body felt at times like a conjoined twin—part of me, but not me. My body propelled me along my dashed lines. My body woke up each morning recognizing the familiar twinges, crawled in casts, stepped on sidewalks with bunions, leapt in dance studios, ran down hospital hallways, and hiked to the top of the world. She was fat and thin, sick and healthy, weak and powerful. I was challenged to feel her and me as one and the same. That happened when I danced and hiked, activities that grounded me in my body, as I now learned to care for others' bodies.

During my first year of medical school, I found a Sierra Club Service trip in California, where work fixing a hiking trail would defray the costs of my return to nature. On the first day, our crew from all over the United States hiked into the high mountains of the John Muir Wilderness and camped near Chalfant Lake. The water shimmered with fish popping through choppy waves like bursting soda bubbles.

Our crew worked a nearby trail—eight crouched heads, sixteen busy hands—kneading the earth. We gouged thick roots with a Pulaski, blasted a boulder, and rearranged the remnants. We diverted the flow of water while swapping ideas. Smashing rocks with a sledgehammer, I released my frustrations with school. I hacked. I pounded. I inhaled dirt. Our hands grew dry and cracked, our fingernails caked black. I relished the contrasts from our school crew of four bent over a dissecting table in anatomy lab inhaling formaldehyde.

On our lunch break sitting still in the sun, we were surrounded by movement: the beat and bump of the breeze, clouds marching in platoons overhead, and the sun dancing a jitterbug on the water. Afterward, our sunburns and high-altitude lassitude made it hard to resume work. At day's end we adventured over precipices, snowfields, boulders, forests, and streams, stopping at a high lake under a luminous pearl sky. Like the others, I removed my shirt, shorts, and socks and piled them by a rock before easing into the freezing water. We swam in deep blue translucence, the slopes of high peaks haloed by white slicing the sky.

Journal entry. June 5, 1986.

Up high, above the tree line, I hear the stillness, the searing sound of snow melting into creek. I must focus on this feeling of fullness I have been lacking in school. How to recreate it? Swimming in the lake, kicking our heels to the wind, we changed the blue of the water into shimmering crystal, and I felt a light silver energy protect us.

My cheeks were round with happiness, and red with the kiss of the sun. My scarf blew like a rippling flag again. My body, sturdy like a blaze on a map.

Having never camped out for a week before, I watched our group leaders prepare our food and became fast friends with Rob Dorival, a modern-day Paul Bunyan in charge of logistics. Crouching next to him as he cooked, I followed his eyes, focused on the fire his hands tended.

"How'd you come up with these recipes?" My mouth watered at the quesadillas sliding off his sizzling pan.

"We've been working on tasty camping menus for a long time." He flipped the pages of a pamphlet of recipes, showing me the lists of ingredients. "The spices are key."

After working together for a week, our group sang "Old Joe Has Gone Fishing" in rounds, immersed in harmony, as we sped away from the trees and back to our homes.

Saturday nights back in the South Bronx, I rushed people with gunshot wounds to the operating room. Sunday afternoons in the ER, I cared for sexual assault victims and for people with heart attacks or crack addictions.

My next low-cost vacation was at a yoga ashram in the Berkshire mountains of Massachusetts, long before yoga was accessible in every strip mall. There, I climbed to a top bunk in a dormitory-style room and tugged at the green nylon of my sleeping bag that had stored my dreams in a tight bundle. It felt slightly damp. Little crumbs of earth fell on the mattress. I buried my nose in the wrinkles, inhaled the staleness, and was flooded with memories of Nepal, California, Bruno, Mark, Irene, Robert, trees, rocks, and dust. I fell into the softest slumber when the sky was not yet black. We rose for 5:00 a.m. meditations, followed by yoga, more meditations, and more yoga.

In the dining room, we were required to eat our macrobiotic food in silence. People chewed forever on roughage and stared, either at their food, out the window, or at small photographs of the guru they carried to meals. From his picture he stared back, clad in white garb with a black beard. What was so hot about the guru? I had never seen a rabbi adored in this way. Everyone was excited he'd be leading a meditation that afternoon.

His deep slow voice led us through breathing and thoughts about nonattachment. Sitting cross-legged, I didn't feel the energy of his presence other participants had whispered about. But I liked his teaching, so I bought some cassette tapes of his lectures in the bookstore.

Next, I took a workshop in yogic breathing, intended to facilitate the desired emptiness of meditation. *Breathe in slowly: one, two, three, four, hold.* I remembered that the word "to breathe" in Hebrew, *linshom*, has the same root as the word for soul, *neshama*.

I lay down in the flotation tank, a container not much bigger than a coffin, filled with salt water. Immersed in the warm water, I watched the attendant close the lid, submerging me in blackness. My heart raced and I clenched my fists. A voice from outside explained where to find the emergency escape button. The only way to get through this was to use my new meditation skills. I took slow deep breaths, my muscles relaxed, and I floated to the surface.

My body melted away. I lost all sense of physical boundaries. My heartbeat swelled and resounded until it felt like a floating heart in the middle of a vast ocean with no separation between me and the world.

This compelling cadence communicated that it knew all and was a well of generosity. Instead of confined in a small container, I felt endless.

I had stumbled into this tank, into a consciousness that I had experienced only once before. One year earlier, I had departed the trail in the Everest region for no apparent reason and walked through trees, up a slope, to sit on a cliff. I told myself that I had veered sideways and upwards to acclimatize. A stream ran below me, and the great Himalayas towered around me. I thought about how I'd made it this far—both on my own and with others. The land was a part of me now.

The loud water and high mountains enveloped me in a simultaneous feeling of containment, safety, and expanse. I was keenly aware that no one in the world knew where I was at that moment, far from any expectations. The Himalayas accepted me wholly and connected me to a stillness so overwhelming, it had a sound. My heartbeat and the world's heartbeat were entwined in a way that felt both extraordinary, and like the most natural thing. I was off trail but somehow found. That day, I wrote "There is too much talking in our society. Too many letters, phones, everyone is accessible all the time." What would my twenty-two-year-old self think of our current world thrumming with email, cell phones, streaming news, and social media?

In the flotation tank I felt peace and unity between mind and body in a place other than the mountains. But I only had three days to spend at the ashram before returning to school.

That summer, I was assigned to do bench research in a lab, aligned with my interest in OB/GYN. A researcher taught me to bend glass into U-shaped probes and surgically implant them into rat brains to sample hormones from the ventro-medial thalamus while the rats performed specific behaviors. He showed me how to put on thick gloves, carry the rat to another room, carefully place its head in a trap, and release a razor-sharp, fatal guillotine. The problem was, I couldn't even kill a cockroach.

After murdering the rats, we dissected their brains.

One night in restless slumber I dreamed of rats, their tails going stiff under my ether, bloody holes oozing in their skulls and brown dead eyes. My no-nonsense boss appeared in her long white lab coat and curly bob saying to me, "Why are you working here? You seem removed," she glared. "You pretend to like this, but you're full of shit."

She was right. Everything I did felt like shit.

During that summer, I read an article in the *New York Review of Books* about Isak Dinesen that included a quote from her book *Out of Africa*: "Up in this air you breathed easily, drawing in a vital assurance and lightness of heart. In the highlands you woke up in the morning and thought: Here I am, where I ought to be."

I'd basked in that feeling in Nepal and in the flotation tank, but not in the present, not in school, and not in the lab.

A month later, in September 1986, I picked up Robert's letter from the mailroom and turned it over in my hand. I walked around my apartment with it. I smiled at it. I finally sat down and stared at it.

"Mimi, Will you be ready in 1988 to fix up climbers in need?"

"Ha Robert, I wish!" I yelped out loud to no one, tickled by his invitation to join an Everest expedition as "a member of the assault team as the doctor."

I was beginning my second year of medical school, the mnemonic for the bones of the hand still rattling through my head during a study break.

I grinned about how far we'd come. When we met, I assumed we'd never see each other again and attributed our connection to the spell of the mountains. But he showed up in New York within a month of my return from Nepal, and I'd visited him once in Colorado. If we weren't in a relationship with others, we coupled up when we saw each other.

Irene, my trekking partner from Nepal, had recently visited Robert in New Zealand. She wrote me: "You certainly need to teach me how you have this non-committal relationship with him," adding that she still liked and missed a climber she'd met in Nepal. From the moment Robert and I met, I'd placed our connection in a box, not letting my guard down about any relationship potential. My defunct relationship with Tom, my RMBL boyfriend, had convinced me that long-distance wouldn't work.

I mulled over Robert's question. Would I be "ready"? *Well Robert, no, I wouldn't.* I would be in my third year of medical school.

Reading on, he also asked me to "design a motivational eating program, plan a physical training program, and fundraise with corporate food and medical sponsors." He added, in a scribble, "I'll eat anything except walnuts, pecans, cashews."

My heart raced but then my head caught up.

What is he thinking? I'm not a doctor, nutritionist, physical trainer, or fundraiser. I was a student, sitting in my cramped bedroom in the Bronx, a striped cat named Sam in my lap, with a single window casting a trapezoidal amber glow on the hardwood floor. Attending classes all day, I spent the rest of my time studying. I was already immersed in a world foreign to me: new medical vocabularies, clinics, emergency rooms, procedures, protocols. Keeping up took every bit of my focus and energy. How would I enter the world of expedition planning? Train for my role? Convince people to financially support it? My mind raced with my mother's phrase: Who do you think you are? My parents did not seek adventure and risk, preferring to leave struggles for survival in the past.

Robert explained how he'd gotten a permit for Everest so quickly. Since securing permission from Nepal took years, he turned to China. The mountain straddles two countries, Nepal and Tibet, the border snaking through the peak. The once independent region of Tibet has been governed by China since an invasion in 1950. The political and spiritual leader of Tibet, His Holiness the Dalai Lama, fled to India in exile in 1959, and Tibetans seeking autonomy have been repressed ever since.

Robert didn't initially mention that his permit for the East Face, known as the Kangshung, was available only because no one else was interested. The East Face was considered too remote and treacherous to attempt. Steep and avalanche ridden, it had only been successfully climbed once before by a large American team. In contrast, Robert wanted to climb with a small team, using no supplemental oxygen or Sherpa support. He also wanted to attempt a new route, which was particularly audacious. As he wrote, "You are not taking on a challenge against others and asking yourself if you can do what others have done. You are taking on a challenge that you don't know is really possible at all."

But no matter which route or circumstance, the unpredictable weather and low oxygen at 29,035 feet make climbing Everest perilous and unpredictable. According to an analysis by Dr. Paul G. Firth and colleagues published in the *British Medical Journal* in 2008, on the occasions that a climb was successful between May 1975 and 2006, a death occurred on 31 percent of days when mountaineers reached the summit.

To convince me of the wisdom of his somewhat rogue approach, Robert wrote, "Everest from Tibet is far better than from Nepal. It looks like a real mountain there, not hidden away behind a few ridges." He added that the view of the mountain from China "looms . . . like a dragon in the background." *Hmmm, nice reference to Chinese mythology, Robert.*

He charged forward at full throttle, alight with lofty plans. Reading his words, I could almost see that spring in his step. He had more confidence in his pinky than I had in my whole person. As naive as I was, I doubt it would've made a difference if I'd known about the dangers of the East Face.

What if I could spend months sleeping under a Himalayan palette of stars again? "Look, Sam!" I waved the letter at my cat, and he looked at me, his tail sweeping the floor like a window washer. I leaned my forehead on the cool glass of my apartment's window, the moisture from my breath forming a film. I watched a bus roll to a stop and honk loudly for a man sitting hunched on a bench. A pigeon took flight, its gray wings flapping to escape the wheels and exhaust.

I sat down again, curled my legs under me, rubbed my dry eyes, and continued reading the letter.

"A week in China thoroughly convinced me of the value of this trip. It's a fascinating country. Tibet should prove a great place to spend a few months, and the mountains . . . well, we all know about those."

Yes, we did. A force as strong as gravity drew me to the accelerated rhythm of breath I'd experienced under those massive peaks. To inhale the fog and lose myself in the silence brushed by wind and the skies painted with unnamed colors. I wasn't drawn to this expedition to prove anything about myself, but rather to be myself. I wanted to wake up to fine blue mountain light, breathe in the wildness I loved, and live within vastness. Robert captured my feelings when he wrote: "The problem is after Nepal, or the Himalayas, it seems all downhill, bumps, hills and uninspiring-like."

Everest was identified as the highest mountain in the world by British surveyors and their Indian colleagues. In 1852, Radhanath Sikhdar, a brilliant Indian mathematician working for the survey of India, calculated Peak XV—as it was called then—to be 29,002 feet.

The Nepali name for the mountain is Sagarmatha, which means "Goddess of the Sky," while the Tibetan name, Chomolungma, means "Goddess Mother of the Earth." Both names express the awe and deep respect felt by the people living under its shadow. The English name, in contrast, honors a British geographer who held the post of India's surveyor general in the 1830s. Ironically, George Everest himself objected to using a Western name for the mountain, favoring the indigenous, more spiritual, versions.

In 1921, the first British reconnaissance expedition looking for routes up the mountain approached the East Face in Tibet, since Nepal was closed to foreigners. George Mallory and Guy Bullock described vertically hanging rock buttresses interspersed with avalanche-prone gullies and unsteady upper snow slopes with overhanging seracs. They were awed and humbled by thundering avalanches. Mallory's famous quote upon seeing the immense East Face was, "Other men, less wise, might attempt this way if they would, but, emphatically, it was not for us." His team moved on to attempt the North Face instead.

The Chinese closed access to Everest between 1950 and 1979 but achieved their own first ascent in 1960, via a northern approach. Once Tibet opened to foreigners again, the first ascents scaled northern routes. The East Face was not even attempted until 1981, when an American team was unsuccessful. They returned in 1983 as a siege-style large team using oxygen, and winches to ferry loads up the face, ultimately summiting six climbers. Siege-style expeditions use complicated logistics. Climbers advance the route, fixing ropes up the mountain, carrying loads and heavy oxygen canisters to stock camps, then return to lower camps to sleep.

By 1988, the planned year for Robert's climb and three and a half decades after the first successful climb, fewer than two hundred individuals had summited Everest. More recently, three and a half decades since our expedition, the mountain has become a bucket-list item, and has been portrayed as a circus, with more than 10,000 people having made the summit, half of those climbing as hired guides.

Climbers feel most alive and present when working at the knife-edge of their limitations, gripped in the present moment, finding quick solutions to problems both physical and mental. I'd experienced that while navigating cliffs in Nepal and longed to feel alive again in that singular way, my senses heightened and electric. I would certainly be working at the knife-edge of my limitations in my medical role. *Could I stretch myself that far?*

Although they had few choices, my grandmother, mother, and father had taken risks, adapted, and carried themselves to new places. Maybe I could too.

I wrote back to Robert: *I'm in.*

When Robert invited me, he'd already invited two climbers: Ed Webster, whom I'd met in Nepal, and Peter Hillary, the son of Sir Edmund Hillary, who, along with Tenzing Norgay was the first to summit Everest in 1953 as part of a British expedition in Nepal. Since Peter joined, Robert framed our expedition in 1988 as the thirty-fifth anniversary of the original successful climb to aid fundraising. Corporate sponsors donate to expeditions much as they do to other athletic events. Donations paid for expenses like gear, travel, and food but didn't support or pay individuals. Honoring the 1953 team, Robert also invited Norbu Tenzing, Norgay's oldest son, to join the support team, which consisted of people who would help to organize the expedition, trek with us to Base Camp, and then return home.

"(Climbing Everest) is basically the challenge between the individual and the mountain, and between the individual and himself," said Sir Edmund Hillary. "I think that everyone is battling a mountain like Everest, and the key to success is much the same." Assuming the role of medical officer, as Robert dubbed it, would be my personal Everest. Living beneath the sheer, exposed Kangshung Face meant no place to hide. I'd need to face my biggest fears.

As quickly as my excitement grew, so did my doubts. Pivoting from the expected path would entail more study and learning new domains.

Leafing through an Everest book in my Bronx bedroom, I rested my forehead on my palms. My mind raced with thoughts of disasters. Broken bones. Frostbite. Infections. I clenched my teeth thinking of medical school and the risks of being away in the middle of it. Would I miss rotations? Chance of a good residency?

My mind swerved to the ultimate risk, and my neck flushed with heat. The East Face had only been climbed once with a large team and more support. Robert's plan had never been done. Anything could happen. I might not return from this journey. *This idea is absurd. No. Gotta study.*

Then, I picked up Robert's letter again. *Well, maybe.* My head rushed with possibilities.

My mother's initial reaction to the expedition was to assume it would never take place because it was "ridiculous." Dad didn't say much.

I desperately wanted to work toward going but didn't feel courageous. Now I understand that courage is about moving forward despite fear. The allure is that "uncertainty is the essence of adventure," as said by Lincoln Hall, an intrepid Australian climber.

The only attribute I brought to the table was that I'd done relatively well hiking at high altitude in Nepal—acclimatizing without getting sick. But one of the mysteries of high altitude is that past success at acclimatization is no guarantee.

Since Robert was the expedition leader, and the creative director at several advertising agencies, he designed the plans to raise $250,000 and assigned tasks. His charisma drew people in.

Robert suggested I pitch an "Internship on Everest" idea, framing it as a public relations opportunity for the school. "Make them see it to their advantage," he said cheerfully. He advised me to phone the top person at the school ("heavyweights like big goals") and present a detailed plan. "Before you know it," he assured me, "you'll have the okay to go, and they'll be supporting it." In the meantime, he suggested I "focus on high-altitude nutrition and assisting in yak births."

Following Robert's advice, I met with the dean of students, wondering how I'd ask for three to four months away in the middle of my third year and still graduate on time. I sat across his large oak desk and took out our professional-looking expedition fundraising folder, complete with my business card and medical officer title. I expected him to laugh me out of the room—an automatic "no"—since requirements to graduate were tightly prescribed.

"My role is to advise the team in nutrition, training, prophylaxis of diseases in developing countries and altitude sickness. I will also attend to any medical emergencies that might arise." My voice quivered as I barely choked the words out. *I sound like a lunatic. No way he's sending me off to the wilds of Tibet.*

"I'm planning a research project. I'll observe, face-to-face, some of the physiological changes that occur with acclimatization and illness at high altitude." My voice steadied the longer I talked. I opened the brochure, showing him the details Robert had compiled.

"This is pretty gutsy," he said, leafing through the paperwork.

I was allotted one month of research in the school schedule, and I proposed combining that with vacation time from my third and fourth years.

The Dean leaned back in his chair, and a slow grin curled upward. "I love it," he said. "You can apply for an International Health Award to help fund you. But you can only go if you present your research and give a lecture on your experiences when you return."

"Yes, of course," I stood and shook his hand in disbelief.

"One more thing."

"Yes?"

"Bring me back a T-shirt."

I chuckled before turning to leave, then walked down the paneled hallway with framed photos of important men from the school's history.

I can go.

I wanted to call Robert right away, as I stepped out of the building into blinding daylight. I trembled with a potent dose of anxiety, sprinkled with a dash of pride and hope. My role had become official and sanctioned by the administration.

Now, there was no way out.

Climb High, Sleep Low

Hypoxia [hi-**POK**-see-uh]

noun

1. *Biology.* a very low level of oxygen, as in an organic environment

2. *Pathology.* an abnormally low amount of oxygen in the body tissues

Etymology: New Latin

First known use: 1941

Adjective: hypoxic

I shoved aside *Harrison's Internal Medicine* and opened *James Wilkerson's Medicine for Mountaineering,* my legs folded lotus style on my chair while studying in my favorite carrel in the medical library. Holding a hot coffee from the corner diner, I learned that without proper acclimatization, the low atmospheric pressure of high altitude, which results in low inspired oxygen—hypoxia—may cause acute mountain sickness (AMS). A low level of oxygen in the bloodstream affects the flow of blood and can cause edema, the swelling that occurs when fluid leaks from small blood vessels into the surrounding tissues. This contributes to symptoms of mild AMS: headache, nausea, loss of appetite, dizziness, sleeplessness, flu-like symptoms, or malaise, none of which is usually life-threatening. Hypoxia can also feel like anxiety.

With increasing edema and leakage, more serious conditions such as high-altitude pulmonary edema (HAPE) or high-altitude cerebral edema (HACE) may occur. HAPE starts as a dry cough and an unexpected degree of shortness of breath and can advance to a frothy or blood-tinged cough. At worst, this causes drowning in one's own fluids, killing roughly half of those affected, young people most at risk. HACE, a swelling of the brain, first appears like drunkenness: loss of balance, incoordination, and slurred speech. Memory loss and incontinence may occur, and progress to hallucinations and coma.

These conditions can cause death within six to eight hours. I buried my head in my hands as a group of students noisily whispered nearby. I imagined us, high on the frozen slopes of Everest, someone stumbling around, hypoxic and confused.

To further complicate matters, part of the body's acclimatization to high altitude is the production of more red blood cells, to deliver more oxygen to body tissues. While advantageous, this causes additional risks. The increased number of red blood cells, when combined with dehydration or immobility in tents due to bad weather, can cause life-threatening blood clots.

Slow ascent and acclimatization, with proper hydration, usually prevents AMS. I'd read about this in the trekking guide when I hiked in Nepal. If arriving at 8,000–10,000 feet, only moderate exercise is advised for the first one to two days. Above 10,000–12,000 feet, even if hiking to higher elevations, sleeping altitude should be increased by only about 1,000 feet per day, with scheduled rest days after gaining 2,000 feet. "Climb high/sleep low" is a common dictum for acclimatization, since it slows the pace of ascent, and allows climbers to inhale more oxygen during sleep which is beneficial.

AMS can resolve if a climber avoids further ascent. If symptoms don't resolve, or if they worsen, descent is imperative. Even with a severe condition such as HACE, a descent of only 2,000 feet often brings prompt, complete recovery.

The bright white pages of my new spiral notebook with "Everest" hand-lettered in pencil on the cover, filled quickly with scribbled notes about the indication for using acetazolamide, also known as Diamox, and its dosage. This mild diuretic aids acclimatization by acidification of the blood, prompting the body to increase respiratory rate, thereby increasing the inhalation of oxygen. Dosing is best when started prior to reaching altitude, but it can be used upon development of symptoms of AMS. After writing down additional advice about acclimatization such as drinking a lot of water and avoiding alcohol, I filed the library books back on the shelves. My first lesson on doctoring on Everest: completed.

I phoned Dr. Stefan Goldberg, whom I'd met at the high-altitude medical clinic in Nepal to tell him about my plans and ask for advice.

"Wow, Mimi. That's so cool," Stefan said when we finally connected by phone.

"I know, but scary. Will you help me?"

"Sure. I'm planning my first expedition right now. I'll be the doc for a climb up Makalu," he said, referring to Everest's neighbor, the world's fifth highest peak at 27,790 feet.

"How'd you get invited?" he asked, sounding a little jealous. When I explained, he became animated with excitement. "I'll share all my medication lists with you." His plan for assembling personal medical kits for the climbers was to minimize weight and bulk while still being complete. "Luckily," he added, "the team is limited to healthy climbers."

Expedition medicine requires being prepared for anything: dental problems, infections, orthopedic injuries, and surgical emergencies. *Could I yank a tooth? Set a limb? Do a tracheotomy? What if we had serious injuries or illness?* Thoughts of what could go wrong took me back to the gurney in Thailand, a patient in a foreign country, alone and near death with diarrhea. We'd be isolated and far away.

Stefan wrote a letter to help me request a funding grant to subsidize the Everest climb. "This project will be intellectually, physically, and emotionally challenging, and very exciting . . . a great exercise in responsibility and self-sufficiency."

Talk about understatements.

He continued. "Everything will have to be carried by yaks and porters into base camp, then by individual climbers up the mountain. There will be no plumbing, electricity or contact with the outside world except by foot messenger, and no chance for helicopter evacuation." While there was some chance for helicopters and other kinds of rescues in Nepal, there was to be none on the remote East Face.

Since I'd have to prepare for anything on the mountain, I'd have to soak up everything I could in school. For my first hospital rotation, I was assigned to shadow a medical resident in training. I spent hours trailing him down hallways, trying not to trip over my sneakers or drop my index cards scribbled with physiologic formulas.

I watched him from behind. His gait was awkward, consistent with someone who'd never done anything but study. Though I wasn't particularly attracted to him, I had a huge crush on him anyway. Perhaps it was the "crush" of finally practicing medicine and working in the hospital with its buzz of energy and meaningful work. I was happiest in action.

One morning at 2:00 a.m., Geeky Resident and I were on duty in Jacobi, the county hospital serving the indigent. We rushed from traumas to heart attacks. The hospital's artificial light kept us awake but couldn't offset the haunting dull green walls and the sad stories behind doorways. We were called to care for a man in his seventies with heart failure who needed his fluids carefully tracked and a urinary catheter replaced.

Technically, I didn't need to be at the hospital. Students were permitted to go home at midnight, but I thought if I stayed, I'd be showing the resident and our supervisors that I was a hard worker. I should have been home preparing my oral presentation scheduled for the following morning like the other students were. It never occurred to me that a good presentation made a better impression on my supervisors grading me than sweating in pursuit of the resident with the world's longest legs and even longer strides.

After eighteen months of endless study, that first month on the wards was thrilling. I was tired, stressed, and hungry *all* of the time, but I was doing amazing things with my resident's encouragement. Spinal tap? Check. Chest compressions for resuscitation? Check. Arterial blood gas? Check. These procedures quickly became routine.

We were on the internal medicine team. Here, the most cerebral instructors conducted rounds, discussing our patients for hours, quizzing us on minutia. "What else could your patient have?" they asked, expecting not an answer of five possibilities, but an entire list that included rare conditions we'd only read about in case reports. In this pre-Google era, we pored over textbooks and articles in the library after work.

When Geeky Resident and I reached the patient's bed, he asked, "Have you done a Foley yet?" referring to a urinary catheter.

"No."

"Okay—it's your turn. You've seen one, right? See one, do one, teach one. It's time for you to do one."

The unconscious patient lay between us on the thin hospital mattress. The resident pulled the patient's robe up, revealing his genitals. He handed me the package with the catheter and placed a sterile drape over the man's lap. I tried to remember the steps: open the package with non-sterile gloves but keep the catheter sterile, then change gloves. I quickly swabbed the penis with iodine. The resident already had sterile gloves on to assist me if needed.

"Pick it up with your left hand and insert the catheter with your right."

My forehead beaded with sweat. I needed to handle this penis, and do something to it, in front of a guy I fantasized about kissing in the broom closet. My hands trembled. *Why didn't I go home?*

The resident showed no outward reaction. This was routine.

I picked up the shrunken, wrinkled penis, momentarily turning my face away from its musty odor and clammy feel. The machines beeped, and I could see Geeky Resident standing with his hands held carefully in front of him to step in if *I screw up*. My left hand holding the penis shook as I raised the catheter with my right hand.

"Yup, just shove it in," he said. "You can push. You might feel a little resistance."

I pushed it through, snaking it deeper into the body. The end of the catheter, now inside the bladder, had a little balloon to keep it in place.

"That should do. Blow up the balloon."

I almost laughed, but it was clear the resident saw no puns or ironies here. I leaned over, hoping my glasses didn't fall into the sterile field, picked up the small syringe attached to the end of the Foley outside of the body, and inflated the internal balloon, securing it in the bladder.

"Good," he said, walking out of the room. I cleaned up the mess of supplies but couldn't erase the dark, damp circles of sweat staining the armpits of my peach button-down shirt.

On Everest there would be no resident to supervise or step in if I made a mistake.

I threw myself into preparation over the next year. Stefan's medical lists became an entire secondary curriculum I studied at night and on weekends, after days in the classroom and hospital. I researched and learned about each medication and condition, then contacted pharmaceutical companies and medical supply houses to inquire about donating supplies or sponsoring us financially.

Standing at the copy machine in my rumpled short white coat, I printed about forty medical articles to learn the latest theories about anything related to the extreme altitudes on Everest, including human physiology, red cell function, and nutritional considerations for peak performance.

My medical studies moved from "cadaver dead" to vibrantly alive.

Planning for my medical officer role required stratifying the most likely conditions and becoming an expert in those areas. For extreme conditions, I would stabilize and evacuate. The more likely conditions included heatstroke, snow blindness, frostbite, hypothermia, dehydration, acute complications like HAPE, HACE, or retinal hemorrhage, and hypercoagulable problems such as strokes and blood clots. At times I envied my fellow students only studying for exams and writing papers.

But my role didn't stop there. Robert had also assigned me to plan the food and physical training for the team. Food is essential fuel for an expedition. I wanted our team to be vegetarian for selfish reasons— because that's what I was familiar with. I also believed a vegetarian diet on the mountain to be more nutritious and digestible. High elevation kills appetite and makes food harder to digest, so we needed both variety and taste. Could I convince carnivorous climbers to forgo meat?

My idea was supported by the successful Australian Everest expedition led by Tim Macartney-Snape in 1984. They were the smallest team to chart a new route up Everest. They ascended the North Face in Tibet without porters or oxygen, just like we were planning to do on the East

Face. Their team had five climbers and two stood on the summit. Lincoln Hall wrote in his book about the climb, *White Limbo*: "The expedition's success is definitive proof that vegetarianism works in the toughest imaginable conditions."

"I think it's a good idea." Robert surprised me when he agreed. As a New Zealander, he held the Australians in high regard. We eventually included canned fish as a high-protein food.

In my first medical letter to the team, besides advising that everyone visit their doctor and check all the health boxes before our trip, I recommended a whole foods diet for training, and physical activity to include aerobic and strength training. I attached an article that explained yogic breathing, believing that training the respiratory muscles would benefit our exercise at altitude. Reading my letter now, I see insecurity and eagerness to gain the team's respect. "I will not have an MD at the time of the trip, something you should know, but I will contribute all that I can to keep everyone in good health and to restore those who have strayed."

Even though my research had led me to whole food diets, cross-training, and yogic breathing, it was a little out there of me to suggest these things considered fringe then. Later, I discovered that Stephen, one of our climbers, had described me as "earthy-crunchy" after we met.

His description might have had merit. I was twenty-one when I rode the Green Tortoise Bus cross-country, aka a hippie bus, the most affordable way to reach the Rocky Mountain Biological Lab in Colorado when I returned for a second summer. I didn't have money for a plane ticket, and for five dollars a day, we would cook on a charcoal grill and share our meals. Vegetarian, of course.

My mother and brother had taken me to the bus stop in Harlem. The bus driver wore a baseball cap with a fake arrow through it over long dreadlocks, while blasting Bob Marley onto 125th Street. Mom and Josh watched me climb the bus steps, and when I turned to wave goodbye, they both shook their heads.

I peered into the bus. People lounged on a massive foam sleeping platform that had replaced the seats.

"How does this work?" asked a doe-eyed young woman with long brown hair.

"I heard head to toe works best," someone responded.

I wasn't the only one who wondered how to sleep closely packed with strangers. I placed my daypack on the overhead rack and slid into a narrow spot at the corner of the mattress. *How am I going to get through five days and nights of this?* Within the first day, we figured out how to have fun passing the time listening to folk and rock music, playing card games, and engaging in endless massage trains. No bathroom was onboard, so no wafts of urine mixed with stale cigarette smoke, no sticky-stained cubicle where I'd have to hold my breath. The bus stopped for bathroom breaks every two hours.

The bus also stopped whenever the two drivers wanted. Before the first night was over, we were partying in a reggae bar in Chicago.

We covered ground at night and visited sites during the day. After hiking the sandy Black Hills of South Dakota, we gawked like aliens under the anomaly of Mount Rushmore, a tribute to US presidents and a stinging reminder of land stolen from indigenous people. One day, we hiked through a leafy forest and stopped at a stream. A guy threw off his clothes, jumped in, and covered his face with a thick layer of mud. More people joined, slinging mud at one another. They frolicked, so comfortable in their skins. Looking up through the leaves shimmering in the sky, I listened to the gleeful sounds of laughter and splashing. *I'm not missing this.*

I piled my clothes on a rock and jumped.

12

Labor and Delivery

"YOU CAN STILL CHOOSE SOMEONE ELSE—A REAL DOCTOR," I TOLD ROBert on the phone one year after I'd accepted his invitation.

"What good is the best doctor in the world if they decompensate at altitude?"

"You could have both! A doctor who has proven themselves at altitude!"

"They won't be so much fun or have that calming influence I'm counting on. Don't forget that you're also team psychologist. You'll have to remain chill and organized while the rest of us go crazy."

I laughed. *He met me while I was in the middle of a Zen-trekking experience in Nepal. Doesn't he realize a Jewish girl from New York City. is not typically seen as a calming influence?*

Robert pointed out that if we had a severe injury, there was no hope of helicopter evacuation, so even experienced doctors wouldn't be able to do much to save someone. Later, I'd realize many lightweight climbs didn't even take along a medical person because the teams were small. But I had to feel like my presence meant something. And it did. It meant everything. At least to me.

Luckily—and predictably—Robert had a plan to distract me.

"I'm contacting magazines to sell them the 'Mimi Gets Fit, Climbs Everest/Training' story," he said. This resulted in the *New York* magazine article that called me an "unlikely candidate for an assault team of any kind."

To get fit, I alternated running and weightlifting with climbing up and down the twenty-eight floors in my apartment building. I took the trusty maroon "beast" (unsurprisingly, the original owner hadn't wanted it back) and filled it with forty pounds of books to run up and down my stairwell. When I slipped it on my back, it felt like a hug from a long-lost friend.

I practiced rock climbing in the Catskills at "the Gunks," a popular climbing ridge, returning to the Country, where I'd first experienced wilderness. Ed Webster, whom I'd met in Nepal during the Shabbat dinner in the mountains, had taken me rock climbing for the first time during the previous year when I visited him in Colorado.

The med school gym smelled of sweat and iron when I picked up the smallest five-pound dumbbells, surrounded almost entirely by men grunting under heavy barbells. Gradually my strength increased, and I lifted ten pounds, then twenty. Completing repetitions was a concrete goal. For the first time, I had visible biceps.

When I wasn't in the weight room, I ran the track around the basketball court or down Morris Park Avenue, lined with trees. I rode my bike to City Island, a gem of a place with seafood shacks, near lapping waves on an eastern lip of the Bronx. Every night, instead of shuffling back from the hospital to my studio apartment and flopping on the couch, I ran. Being breathless with exertion relieved some anxieties.

Despite my research and physical training, I remained worried. Five months before the trip I sat in the tiny office of a student in the psychology doctoral program, part of the med school counseling service. My new psychotherapist didn't have much experience, and I didn't feel like I was in particularly able hands. How ironic.

I gripped the armrests of my chair, staring at the floor. "What if something bad happens? What if it's really serious? What if I freeze and don't remember what to do? What if the yak drops all the medicine and I have nothing to use?"

I was barely breathing when I looked up.

He looked at me perplexed. "It sounds like you have very real reasons to be anxious." *What?* Even he, the man who was supposed to be talking me through my fear, wondered whether going to Everest was a good idea. *I'm screwed.*

"You need to focus on what you've already done," he said. Focusing on what was in my control was my only remedy for the great uncertainty ahead.

I remembered John, the injured hiker at RMBL, whom I'd helped down the mountain. Unlike that sudden event, I'd had time to prepare for Everest, a slow, steady climb I worked on every weekend.

The culmination of my time in therapy was accepting uncertainty. We could be swept away by a big avalanche or some other unknown, but I shared the climbers' desire to do something that was calling to me—immersion in the mountains—despite the risk. This meshed with what I learned as a child hearing my father's story. Life could crumble in an instant no matter what. So I might as well live fiercely. Maybe the wilder the better. I didn't realize then that the real challenge is to figure out how to live fully and with uncertainty in everyday life.

Four months before our planned departure, I spent a six-week rotation on obstetrics and gynecology. I was finally taking care of women, and discovered I loved the fast pace of the labor and delivery unit and loved the thrill of delivering a baby. Throughout my career I would weep at deliveries, even when I hadn't met the mother in advance.

The rotation was even more exciting because I developed yet another crush, this time on my chief resident Steve. When I told my male buddies, who'd rotated through this ward earlier, James said, "Of course you have a crush on him. We all do. He's tall, handsome, a little wacky. We called him Hawkeye, like the doctor on *M*A*S*H*." A charming cowboy. Seems like I had a type.

One day, Steve pulled me out of a group of students and took me into a delivery room.

"You can do the entire delivery. I'll be here to help if you need me."

We gowned up, put masks, gloves, and paper booties on, and coached the patient through the pushing process. I trembled while following the steps I'd witnessed in other deliveries. I gently prepared the perineum and supported the baby's head to do the least damage. I suctioned the nos-trils, guided one shoulder then another, then caught the slippery wailing infant, holding on tight like a wide receiver with a football touchdown. Steve said, "Great job, Mimster."

I was smitten with OB. And with Steve.

The day after the rotation ended, he called me. "I couldn't ask you out while I was your superior," he laughed. "Are you free Saturday night?"

We dated until I left for the expedition. His nature was to leap in and get serious quickly. He'd already been married and divorced. Since dating didn't fit into my newfound acceptance of my Everest fate, which could include not returning, I was more guarded. But I loved spending time with him and appreciated his support while I prepared for the climb. I was also happy to be involved with him since Robert had a girlfriend, and this would prevent us from rekindling our interest in one another on the mountain.

One month before our departure, the climbing team had whittled down to four. A team that small had never completed a new route on Everest, unaided and without oxygen, let alone on the intimidating East Face, but it was too late to invite others. Several climbers had dropped out including Peter Hillary, Sir Edmund's son. Many said the plan was too dangerous.

Robert believed each of the remaining climbers added unique strengths to the team, and would hopefully be enough to get the job done. Ed Webster, thirty-two, was an expert at the hardest technical rock climbing. Paul Teare, twenty-eight, was an elite ice climber. Stephen Venables, thirty-four, and he, Robert Anderson, thirty, had both proven themselves adept at extremely high altitudes. Robert noted that his long spider legs were excellent for wading through snowfields high on the East Face.

Stephen was invited only a few months earlier. Robert had asked Lord John Hunt, the leader of the first successful Everest expedition in 1953, to be our honorary leader. Hunt said yes, on the condition a British climber be invited. He suggested Stephen.

We finalized the support team to help organize. They would trek with us to Base Camp, then go home. Rob Dorival, the chef I'd met on the Sierra Nevada trip, took over food planning, to my great relief. Norbu Tenzing worked on travel logistics. Miklos Pinther, the chief cartographer of the United Nations, planned to survey the height of Everest using new technology. Sandy Wylie, a friend of Robert's from New Zealand, served as treasurer. Wendy Davis was our PR specialist. A petite blonde whirlwind of energy, she darted enthusiastically between ideas. She became the most avid cheerleader of the team's goals, lining up corporate sponsors. Our photographer, Joseph Blackburn, was a genius at capturing nature, most notably as the official photographer for Yosemite National Park. He and I were the only nonclimbers on the assault team staying for the entire expedition.

Right before departure, I worked long hours on an orthopedics rotation. I spent my nights doing consults in the emergency rooms and admitting those who needed acute care. During morning pre-rounds at 5:00 a.m., I assessed patients room to room, my scrub pockets overflowing with scissors, gauze, and hydrogen peroxide, my white coat with index cards, pens, and a pocket flashlight. I changed dressings, scrubbed flesh that teemed with the colors and odors of both rot and renewal, removed stitches and staples, checked glucose levels, and reported the patients' status to my superiors. I leapt upstairs to the operating room like an Olympic hurdler—more stairs, more conditioning—all good. The orthopedic team, composed only of men, bantered about while banging on knees and screwing in hips. I remained silent, aiming the overhead light, retracting patient parts out of the operating field, flexing my new strong biceps, telling myself: *You'll soon be inhaling fresh air.*

Being busy prevented me from stressing about the trip, but also left me with little time to pack. On the day before our flight to Beijing, I ran to the drugstore to buy toothpaste and shampoo. I stayed up all night tossing things into my duffels.

Fortunately, while waiting outside the OR, I'd made lists. First, the lists of medical supplies we'd need on the climb, then packing lists which I now followed, black scribble on white, barely legible, smudged in pencil. I always only wrote in pencil—my internal doubt as marks on a page—erasable. Just before zippering my final duffel, I threw in my tap shoes.

I met most of my teammates in JFK airport. Watching Joe hug his wife and toddler daughter goodbye made me miss my family. Leaving for Tibet, the place that had called to me when I watched the slide show on acid rain, I thought of Amama, who'd returned to Germany every summer. And my mother, who returned yearly to Israel. Although my father only returned once to Latvia after his family was killed, he traveled to Europe every summer to lead psychology workshops. They were each drawn to different versions of home, not fully rooted where they lived. I was more like them than I'd understood. The mountains were my Germany, my Israel, my Latvia.

PART V

TO SURRENDER

Only to the extent that we expose ourselves over and over to annihilation can that which is indestructible be found in us.

—PEMA CHÖDRÖN

EVEREST 1988 KANGSHUNG FACE EXPEDITION MEMBERS:

ASSAULT TEAM—Name, nationality, age:

Robert Anderson, expedition leader and climber, United States, living in New Zealand, 30

Paul Teare, climber, Canadian living in United States, 28

Stephen Venables, climber, United Kingdom, 34

Edward Webster, climber, United States, 32

Joseph Blackburn, photographer, United States, 42

Mimi Zieman, medical officer, United States, 25

Pasang Norbu, cook and Base Camp manager, Nepal, 48

Kasang Tsering, assistant cook, Tibet, 22

SUPPORT TEAM—Name, nationality, age:

Wendy Davis, PR and fundraising, United States, 28

Robert Dorival, food planning, 33

Miklos Pinther, cartographer, United States, 50

Norbu Tenzing, logistics, India / United States, 24

Sandy Wylie, treasurer, New Zealand, 30

13

The Launch

"I toast the Leader of Everest '88—Robert!" Wendy held up a glass of white wine from her perch on the king-size bed, kicking off a long set of toasts to the Everest '88 Kangshung Face Expedition. Most of the team gathered in her hotel room in Beijing, while Ed, Paul, Stephen and Pasang, a Sherpa cook from Nepal, would meet us later in Tibet.

"I toast my good friend, Sandy, our accountant, who joined me from New Zealand!" Robert raised a glass.

"I toast the son of the first person to summit Everest—with his partner, a New Zealander!" replied Sandy, beaming at Norbu.

Surveying the room, I couldn't believe Robert had gathered this team, raised money, organized us, and I was a part of it. An ordinary person given an extraordinary opportunity. I reminded myself I was prepared. Prepared enough. *In any case, there's no turning back now.*

As if reading my mind, Wendy turned to me and said, "You'll do great. I have every confidence in you." She was only three years older, the trek to Base Camp a huge stretch for her, but she seemed so together.

The song "Dayenu," meaning "enough," from the Passover seder rang in my head. It celebrates a long list of God's miracles, saying each on its own would have been enough for the Jewish people to be thankful.

Had he given us the Torah, only given us the Torah, had he given us the Torah, Dayenu!

But in my mind, I thought not of the Jewish people and miracles but of a different list—where each thing on its own would *not* have been enough. The long list of random events that brought me to this hotel room:

If Dad hadn't forgotten to fill out the financial aid form for my favorite college, I wouldn't have gone to McGill.

If I hadn't gone to McGill, I wouldn't have seen the RMBL poster.

If I hadn't gone to RMBL, I wouldn't have seen the slide show about Tibet.

If Tibet wasn't closed to foreigners, I wouldn't have gone hiking in Nepal.

If my first trek around Annapurna hadn't been so cheap, I wouldn't have gone to Everest Base Camp.

If Dan hadn't invited Irene and me to the Everest party, I wouldn't have met Robert.

If Robert hadn't been so persistent, we wouldn't have grown to care for each other.

If the dean hadn't granted me time off, I wouldn't be here.

Tracing the dashed lines that placed me in that hotel room, so much seems random but feels like a symphony of the universe playing in the background. I was there, because of choices I made, while also recognizing I had few choices. Born in New York City to Sabina and Isaac, I had no input in that map. Yet they led me, somehow, to listen for opportunities, and to consider opportunities as possibilities.

We had gathered to get our donor-supplied gear: canvas boots, hats, T-shirts, hygiene packs, bibs, ski poles, shiny pink ice axes, huge mountain double boots for extreme conditions, and an ugly cap—"STUBAI" printed across it—which I would wear all the time. Thin and thick long underwear, double-layer gloves, gaiters, puffy light blue and pink down parkas, and a light blue fleece jacket that I wear to this day, our team's name, Everest '88, sewn onto the chest.

Rob Dorival, the chef, grinned. "It's like Christmas in February!" This gear was a big upgrade from my borrowed maroon backpack beast.

We pretended to be regular tourists in Beijing, as if our high-stakes purpose wasn't looming. After visiting the Forbidden City, we cruised in a bus through the soft, rounded Chinese hillside. In our protective bubble, we listened to lovely instrumental music while observing a curious world through the window. The dry, brown wintry landscape was full of bare trees standing en garde like thin soldiers, people traveling on old steam engine trains, pack animals, and many, many bicycles.

Our destination—the Great Wall—was rural, sunny, and still when we arrived, but we let loose like lab rats freed from their cages, balancing on the Wall as if on a tightrope. We paired off to get to know one another. Miklos, with thick, perfectly coiffed, swept-back hair, wearing tailored and ironed clothing, strolled with various teammates. Older, and with an important position at the UN, he lent our team gravitas. Norbu, closest to my age, was reserved while admiring the view. Joe busily caught everyone in candid shots.

Robert and Wendy chatted about ways to fulfill the needs of sponsors while devising more fundraising schemes. Watching the two of them, carefree and flirtatious, a pang of jealousy surprised me. Robert and I had come a long way. How were we going to interact on this trip? We'd barely exchanged a word so far, and I hoped we wouldn't continue to be this awkward. Maybe I wasn't as cool about our noncommittal relationship as Irene and I had thought. My heart always fluttered when I saw New Zealand stamps. His letters were full of charm and wit and even some feelings. Maybe I liked him more than I admitted.

On the bus back, I straddled the aisle, balancing each foot against the benches on either side, shy as I cleared my throat. "Everyone, I'm going to present some information about high altitude, and a medicine you can take before we fly to Lhasa in a few days. We're going to 12,000 feet. There's good evidence if you start Diamox today, it can prevent altitude sickness."

"Are there downsides?" asked Wendy.

"You could get tingling in the lips or fingertips, and you shouldn't take it if you're allergic to sulfa. The reason to consider it is our abrupt change in altitude."

"What if we don't take it?" Miklos asked.

"You might have more symptoms or take longer to adjust."

Everyone decided to take it. I successfully completed my first medical task. "Come to my room tonight for pills," I muttered like a drug dealer.

We flew to Chengdu, the capital of the Sichuan province and a required layover on the way to Tibet, and went straight to an enormous outdoor market to buy fresh food for the expedition. Woks of stir-fry stippled the air with the pungent scents of garlic and ginger, and tall pointed peaks of spices—red, gold, green—adorned the streets like gastronomic prayer flags. Vendors crouched over their fires. We purchased cooking staples: thick ginger root, garlic bulbs, and baskets of onions and potatoes.

At one herbal store, Joe held up a hairy hoof. "What do you think this is for?"

Swinging a dried seahorse, Norbu responded. "Maybe it's going to a dance with this?"

We stuck out in the crowds wearing our mountain clothes: big bright jackets and boots, cameras protruding like phalluses before us, shooting away, trying to capture what can never be conveyed in two dimensions. Magic in a frame.

Before our daybreak flight to Lhasa, the capital of Tibet and home of His Holiness the Dalai Lama before exile, I pulled Joe aside in the airport to sit next to me on a bench. I took out my research notebook to record the findings.

"Follow my finger with your eyes," I said in my most clinical voice. I feared they wouldn't respect me, since climbers tend to be "alpha" types, and Joe was a former Navy man.

"How often are you going to test us?"

"Each time we gain significant altitude. Your resting pulse is forty-five, like an athlete."

"Probably from running."

Joe seemed as fit as the climbers, and he had some climbing experience. Would I be able to keep up? Examining him made me feel empowered with a mission so unlike my travels in Nepal. We wouldn't have been able to enter Tibet if we weren't there in an official capacity, since it was closed to foreigners because of civil protests by Tibetans against the occupation. This was one year before the Tiananmen Square unrest when Chinese students protested for more freedoms. We had our Chinese Mountaineering Association permit and two assigned liaison officers.

Mr. Yang was our mountaineering liaison, an older man with hollowed cheeks, and Mr. Xi our interpreter, with chopped bangs who barely spoke English despite his role.

From the plane window, we welcomed our first view of snowy mountains jutting out of an endless brown plateau, like peaks of a meringue.

While still on the tarmac, I lined up the team. "Let's do some stretching," I suggested. They enthusiastically stood at attention. Facing them, I demonstrated, "Breathe in as you lift your arms overhead, breathe out as you fold your body towards the floor." I didn't restrain my woo-woo. "Imagine pushing the sparser oxygen molecules deep into your tissues." Who would have thought I'd lead dance stretches in Lhasa? Everyone loved inhaling the fresh mountain air and touching the Tibetan earth. We doubled over, laughing at ourselves.

Our first morning in Lhasa, we visited a Buddhist monastery near the main square, admiring women wearing fine turquoise jewelry and men dressed like warriors in knee-high boots and grand hats. I was in the place I had first seen in the slide show at RMBL. We sat cross-legged on the floor, surrounded by rows of gleaming candles. Monks chanted prayers while the sounds of cymbals and gongs vibrated through our bodies. Lining up after the service to meet the main monk in a sleeveless beige gown, we gave a slight nod with our hands in prayer position. The monk's eyes pierced into me. I eagerly practiced my Tibetan:

"*Keh-rang gi ming la kah-rey yin?*" I asked his name and told him mine: "*Nga Mimi yin.*" He nodded.

"*Sah-cha tsa-chen-po ray,*" I said. *This place is so powerful.*

The others left, but I stayed behind, feeling my heartbeat slow and my shoulders relax. I circled the altar in a line with Tibetans and admired the main statue of the Buddha at age seven, donated by a Nepali princess in the seventh century. I learned it had been shattered by the Chinese when they invaded but had since been restored. Many of the original statues were gold but had been reshaped from clay and covered in gold paint.

I didn't understand the meaning of the rituals since studying Tibetan Buddhism hadn't made it onto any of my lists. The most I could do was stand with my heart open.

"*Tashideleh*" was the greeting we exchanged. The monks poured me a mild yak butter tea. Sipping it felt like being invited under a blanket on a frosty day. Later, I watched seventy-five people wearing orange robes, young and old, praying in the beautifully ornamented courtyard of a nunnery. It wasn't important to attach a connection or meaning to these moments. What mattered was being fully present in them.

That night, we met our Tibetan liaison, Mr. Sonam, an energetic host who treated us to a lavish banquet featuring yak stomach and mutton burgers, while teaching us endless rounds of local songs. We had a remarkable introduction to the people and spirit of Tibet, but we couldn't avoid the undercurrent of oppression by the Chinese. One Tibetan man dressed in Western clothes approached with his hands cupped in front of him, "Please help us. Since the Chinese have crushed us, it is no freedom." It was difficult—impossible, even—for people to speak openly. A few tried but censored themselves and fell silent. Our government liaisons, Mr. Xi and Mr. Yang, watched these interactions. I wanted to know more but feared causing harm with questions.

The next morning, we rose in the dark to hike up back alleys to a rooftop overlooking the Potala palace, silently watching early sunrays seep through pink and orange clouds. The palace was the former home of the Dalai Lamas, where we'd later see worshippers file through rooms of elaborate carvings glittered with gold. The pilgrims recited mantras at the altars. They pinched anise and corn husks and tossed these offerings over their shoulders.

Mr. Sonam arranged for me to tour a local hospital. The administrator, Dawa, first showed me the pharmacy, where I was overwhelmed with the fresh fragrance of three hundred types of herbs, seeds, and nuts. People bustled to fill prescriptions, opening and closing intricately carved wooden drawers to mix formulations. Without prescription medicines doled out in plastic bags or the smell of bleach, this hospital had a soothing, airy feeling. The patients were greeted with hugs and not confined by intravenous tubes.

On the medicine ward, the doctor's eyes kindly welcomed me. "When I first meet a patient, I observe the face, noting color and structure. Then I read the pulse and take a history, including diet." The countenance was thought to hold more answers than anything Western medicine might have considered.

In the OB/GYN ward, a few women sat on single beds, the windows open, a brisk breeze flowing through simple white drapes. The doctor sat down on a chair near one of the patients and picked up her wrist, taking her pulse. "She lost her baby and then had monthly problems," Dawa interpreted.

"Do most women have regular cycles?"

The doctor nodded. "Most women have three to four babies."

"Do they have prenatal care?" He shook his head and made a *tsk* sound. Birth control was herbal. They didn't have access to the pill or even the diaphragm, like the grumpy gynecologist had provided me as a teenager. I couldn't understand the answers when I asked whether the Chinese imposed fertility regulations, and none of my further questions led to clarity. I wondered whether they were censoring themselves.

Dawa gave me a small pin, a magazine about the hospital, and the doctor's card. Just like the temples opened my heart to spirituality, seeing the radically different way medicine was practiced opened my mind. Who knew what treatment deemed "strange" by Westerners might be efficacious? This visit inspired me to do more. Later, I joined forces with a Tibetan man in New York to raise funds for this hospital.

I proudly attached the hospital pin to the lapel of my Patagonia windbreaker.

On our way to Everest, the sun beat down on our open-air truck as we crossed the highest plateau in the world, a flat unbroken expanse for miles in all directions. The landscape was rich with tones of red, brown, orange, tan, and blue, but the air was so dusty we had to wear face masks. Joe comically appeared in a gas mask.

Stopping for tea, we scavenged through rocks, discovering coal, quartz, and fossils of seashells. India and Eurasia had collided fifty million years earlier, bringing the seafloor up to this level of the earth, within reach of the sky. Locals approached, extending their hands caked with thick black grime. We shared our food. Two beautiful young girls gobbled tuna directly from the can with muddy fingers.

In Xegar, a large town in Western Tibet situated at 14,206 feet, the health of the team faltered. Tension developed from long hours of travel, high altitude, and stomach issues.

"I'm holding a clinic in my room," I announced.

People trickled in. "I just don't feel well. I have a headache and no energy," one of the support team members confided. The next two people had coughs. I placed my stethoscope on their chests, "Big breath in," I said. Their trust in me boosted my confidence, and I found management of these ailments routine.

Xegar was where we planned to meet Ed, Paul, Stephen, and Pasang, who were traveling overland from Nepal. We arrived at the main hotel, where we'd reserved rooms, only to find they'd been given away to a much larger Everest team. The proprietor told us we'd have to stay at the only other lodge in town. "You eat dinner here, then go," he said.

The Friendship Expedition consisted of a hundred Nepalese, Chinese, and Japanese climbers traveling with an additional 150 staff. They were planning the first live video feed from atop Everest, and the first traverse: Some would climb in Nepal and cross to Tibet and vice versa. Their Tibetan approach was from the usual northern side of the mountain, far from our East Face.

We sat in the corner of the dining room in our matching down parkas surrounded by the boisterous Friendship team wearing different color jackets: the Japanese wore yellow, the Chinese red, and the Nepalese orange. The meal was delayed because, like us, the Friendship Expedition was waiting for their Nepali climbers to arrive. When neither team arrived, we asked Mr. Xi to travel to the border and help with any problems.

We bunked four to a room in our dank lodge on the other side of town. Worried about our delayed teammates, Robert, Sandy, and some others stayed up drinking beers, and the rest of us went to sleep.

As we lay in our cots, Wendy asked me, "Are you getting into these sheets? It stinks of mold."

"Nah, I'm just using my sleeping bag. And wearing my shoes on the floor."

The following evening, we waited for our teammates to arrive in the main hotel during dinner. After a few hours, Paul, Ed, Stephen, and Pasang finally crossed the threshold. I jumped at Ed with a big hug.

"You made it!"

"We were stuck at the border."

"Did Mr. Xi help?"

"Nope, never saw him." He'd gotten lost along the way.

Paul crossed the dining room, bowlegged and bouncy, his arms swinging loosely, announcing to all of us, "The border was flooded." He dramatically crossed both arms, shaking the curls on his head wildly, flashing an arresting smile full of teeth. He had a California swagger, sprinkling his conversation with lots of "dudes" and "bros."

Pasang grinned hello, his gold tooth gleaming. His short stature, less than five feet, belied his solid strength. He was forty-nine, and had first visited Everest in 1962, as a "cookboy," but had become a successful businessman, running a lodge in Namche Bazaar. Composed, competent, and good humored, he knew the way things worked in these parts of the world. Our team was complete.

While acclimatizing in Xegar for a few days, Pasang took us to the *gompa* for a puja ceremony, a ritual blessing before a climb. The ancient monastery was stuffed with dusty, thick tapestries. Lining up one by one in front of the head monk, who sat at the altar, we bowed our heads as he gently draped a white prayer shawl around each of our necks. It was official. We were in the mountains, a team, receiving Buddhist blessings to keep us safe.

Vibrations from deep guttural chants pulsed through my body as I absorbed the gravity of the ritual. I closed my eyes and visualized each team member returning safely from the mountain. When the ceremony finished, the monks ate tsampa—barley flour the color of dirt and the consistency of cement—and served us yak butter tea. We accepted three servings each to be polite. The taste was growing on me.

The following day, Joe, Robert, Ed, Paul, Miklos, Norbu, and I hiked up a nearby mountain pass to acclimatize and see the views. On the hill, near a bush decorated with colorful prayer flags, Robert's telescope provided a magnified view of Everest, Makalu, and Cho Oyu, three of the world's tallest mountains. We would live in the shadow of that pyramidal rock for an entire season. At its mercy. We sat silently and humbly, in awe.

I heard "Mimi!" and turned to see two small boys, Tashi and Pasang Tsering, whom I'd met earlier in the morning, scampering along the path like playful goats. They grabbed each of my hands, and we skipped away from the group, up and down windy paths, counting to ten together in Tibetan: *Chik, Nyi, Sum, Shi, Ngah, Trook, Dun, Geh, Gu, Chu.*

We turned a corner and faced forceful gusts that made it hard to stay upright. Doubling back from the wind, we descended a different way, passing the gompa. There we met actual goats scattered among the ruins of the monastery. Goats and rocks blended into the feeling of *mountain*: of dry desert wind and endless brown.

Strolling down the trail, we passed houses built into cliffs and came upon a woman working a loom on her rooftop. She chased away a ferocious dog so I could visit with her. The boys fidgeted then left. I watched her weave an intricate tapestry of red and gold wool. I had only a hairband to gift her. She accepted it, and we exchanged grins. Tashi and Pasang Tsering appeared out of nowhere, and each took one of my hands to resume our jaunt down the mountain. We sang a Tibetan tune of high notes that floated on the wind through the cracks in the walls of the ruins and up to the prayer flags. I felt at one with Julie Andrews in *The Sound of Music*.

We departed Xegar in a pickup truck with a tarp cover for the daylong ride to our destination, where we'd start the trek to Base Camp. Stumbling out of the truck at a tea stop, where the burned juniper smoke competed with dust as the worst respiratory irritant, we escaped to a clearing for air. Locals crowded around us, touching our sleeves and begging. Stephen remarked, "Isn't this great we can all sit happily and stare at each other?" We couldn't help but be uncomfortable about all our stuff, among locals who had little, curious about the strangers in bright clothing.

We rode over more bumpy hills with dust grit scratching our eyes and reached the end of the road. Gesticulating wildly with local people, it took us twenty minutes to determine whether we had actually reached the village of Kharta.

This would prove to be an apropos start of the expedition. From that point on, we had no choice but to lean into confusion and surprise. As Wayne Dyer wrote, "Be open to everything and attached to nothing."

14

The Yaks Are Right Behind You

WE WOKE UP TO A CLOUDLESS, WARM DAY IN KHARTA. WE WERE PACKED and ready before breakfast for our five-day hike to Base Camp, after which the support team would leave, and we'd start the climb. The blue sky stretched like a tarp over us, with snowy peaks in the distance. We'd arranged for sixty yaks to haul our 120 barrels and duffels, and the local yak herders began weighing loads for even distribution.

The yaks took all day to trickle in, and we finally left at 3:00 p.m. After two hours on the trail, the herders unexpectedly quit for the day. Pasang coaxed them to continue but they refused. We dropped our backpacks, and each searched for spots to camp in a large meadow by a stream. Robert quickly staked his tent, then peeped his head out from inside.

He called me over. "You're staying with me, right?"

"What? No, I don't think that's a good idea." We'd barely spoken the whole trip. Despite all our planning, we'd never discussed our rules of engagement for the trip. "I don't want to make the other guys uncomfortable." I wanted to be on our usual friendly terms, instead of awkward. And, I didn't want anyone to feel uncomfortable about me being the only woman, once Wendy left, or resentful if there was a couple on the team.

"They won't care. If they do, we can change it up. This is a huge responsibility on me, and I could use your support," Robert persisted.

I sorted through my feelings. I'd felt jealous seeing him and Wendy together even though we'd both moved on and were dating others at home. I looked at his pitched tent and sleeping bag laid out. Then I looked at the meadow where I'd have to pitch my tent. Without thinking more, I swung my backpack inside, giggling and feeling naughty. Tenting with Robert was not a reasoned decision, and not something I thought would happen in any of my rehearsed scenarios for this trip.

That night, the team huddled around Pasang's fire, snowflakes falling around us.

"There's no way we can make Base Camp in five days at this rate," Paul said, shaking his head.

Pasang chimed in. "Herders saying too much snow for yaks to cross pass."

We needed to cross the Langma La pass, at 18,045 feet, from the Kharta valley to reach Everest in the Kama valley. Pasang had assumed the role of translator. Our Chinese liaison and translator had stayed back in Kharta and would stay there for the entire expedition. They were there in a symbolic role, or to intimidate us by representing the government's watchful eye. Not for real support.

"The yaks live here. Why would they be carrying loads if they can't cross the pass?" asked Joe. No one had an answer.

"Did you think it would be this freezing?" Wendy asked me. We wore every article of clothing we had, bouncing up and down and squeezing ourselves for warmth.

"Hell no!" I answered. "It's so annoying that the guys aren't as cold." In general, men have higher metabolic rates linked to larger muscle mass so they stay warmer and can eat more calories. We walked over to the fire and stretched out our gloved hands.

Standing and eating dinner in the snow that night was miserable, and it was near impossible for Pasang to cook. Since our luxurious three-room kitchen tent never cleared customs at JFK airport, Robert searched for an alternative and located an old canvas tent that appeared left over from the first Western expedition to this area in the 1920s. It was shaped like a teepee, and barely fit Pasang but it provided him with a workspace. The owner's condition for rental was that we hire her twenty-two-year-old son, Kasang, to work around camp. He had carried loads for the American expedition to this region five years earlier, so claimed to know the way up the valley. Robert agreed.

When the temperature dropped to twenty degrees below zero that night, Robert and I, freezing in our down bibs, inched closer to one another in the tent. It didn't take long for us to get physical, but we drew the line at public displays of affection.

In the morning we packed up camp, ready to leave early, while the herders lingered over a four-hour breakfast. Finally on the trail, I passed prayer flags, dusty and trampled, swaying like dandelions on the hilltops. My body's steps and breath united. Listening to the whistling wind and rushing water brought me totally into the present. My fingers brushed mani stones that celebrated Buddha with the prayer *om mani padme hum,* or "hail to the jewel in the lotus flower." Reciting the mantra is meant to promote compassion and help progress in core practices of Buddhism: generosity, ethics, tolerance and patience, perseverance, concentration, and wisdom. How fitting, given our inching pace and frustration with the herders.

After three hours, the herders announced they were done for the day. Pasang and Robert tried to motivate them but failed.

The following day, we packed camp, but the herders refused to leave in the pelting snow. Norbu and I did our best to motivate some movement, while the yaks circled.

"You yaks!" The herders sitting in the snow pointed at my boots, laughing. I guessed they thought it would be funny if I were a herder. I didn't yet know they picked on me because I was a woman.

"Stop it!" Norbu yelled, defending me. We both shivered as the wet snow fell on our necks. We bounced in place, discussing our frustration with the herders' lack of effort.

Then Norbu turned, spotting something down the hill.

"Look out!" he shouted. "The yaks are right behind you!" I turned around to see a herd of twenty or so charging toward me. I leapt out of the way, barely escaping them. Norbu and I collapsed in the snow, doubled over in laughter.

He looked over at me. "One of these days we'll be in NYC having coffee and remember this."

"Yes!" I screamed. "The yaks are right behind you!"

When we finally left camp that day, Ed, Paul, and I picked up the rear of the yak train, the rhythm of yak bells marking our steps. A light snow fell during the long, slow ramble across a huge valley scattered with juniper bushes. The herders stopped when we arrived at the last campsite before the pass, Lhatse, at 16,500 feet. They dropped their loads, said they could not go any farther in the snow, and demanded to be paid in full. While they haggled with Robert, I treated a long line of locals complaining of headaches, backaches, toothaches, and coughs, asking for medicine. They'd discovered my role.

Pasang spoke English and Tibetan as well as many other languages from his numerous expeditions. He worked hard to build rapport with the locals and learned that the American expeditions to the area in 1981 and 1983 were during autumn, before winter snows, which was why we hadn't heard about trouble with yaks crossing the pass. Now, we were stuck in deep drifts.

We had to switch gears. Robert and Pasang negotiated a plan to replace the yaks with human porters. We needed 120 people to carry the loads, one per person, to Base Camp, a three-day journey from Lhatse. The herders agreed to the plan and returned to their homes to recruit people.

Journal entry. March 11,1988, Lhatse.

The yaks descended, the lingering porters burn juniper as an offering to the gods, while the altitude weighs heavily on our bodies. We are slow and breathless. Things are out of our control, the elements and the people are steadfast. Sitting in this beautiful and remote place, admiring the peaks around us, Ed said this delay wasn't all bad since our bodies could take extra time to acclimatize.

Pasang taught Kasang everything about expedition work. He learned quickly and had a good sense of humor. One of the old British traditions, still a mainstay of Himalayan expedition life, is for the cooks to make hot morning tea and deliver it to the tents. This became Kasang's job.

The next morning, while it was still dark, we heard porters' footsteps approaching camp, so we packed up to leave. But the snow proved relentless, and our travel was called off. The porters left and we crawled back into our tents.

The following day, light snow was falling when porters reappeared. We packed up camp. The men fought for the lightest loads while the women watched. They'd carry whatever the men hadn't chosen. It devolved into a chaotic scene as wet snow fell sideways, and the porters abandoned their loads. We were perplexed that they lived in these lands but would not cross the pass in these conditions. Then we realized their gear was threadbare.

As the snow settled in tufts of white, our tents stowed and barrels packed, we sat on our duffels with nothing to do. The porters surrounded us, on strike. Paul unpacked our boom box and cranked up The Rolling Stones. We started singing and swaying, then Ed and I jumped up and danced wildly in the falling flurries. The porters created a circle around us, laughing uproariously as we bounced up and down in our mountain boots. Ed and I hammed it up, making faces, chicken wing moves, and twirling each other in do-si-dos. He dipped me, and the crowd clapped and cheered. Then one of the local Tibetan leaders, Jirmi, a handsome man with smiling eyes, approached me to dance, setting off howls of laughter and whooping. For one moment we were not warring strangers, stalled thigh-deep in snow, and hopeless. We were friends shimmying in the white, joyous, kicking our legs so high my climbing heels clapped the clouds.

The climbers opened a bottle of scotch, and there was no turning back. It was another memorable high-altitude rave.

The next morning a frightening boom echoed between the mountains. *An avalanche?* When I peered outside the tent, a blizzard and two feet of snow stared back. Sitting up in my sleeping bag, I heard footsteps: morning tea. But *tea makes pee*, and I dreaded leaving to pee. Unzip my sleeping bag, put on my coat, hat, gloves, gaiters, and boots. Wade into billowing snow and biting air to somewhere outside camp to bare my skin in the bitter cold. I glanced at Robert sleeping, packed in his down bag, wearing a goofy hat. Soon he'd start his morning routine: Kiehl's astringent and moisturizer, followed by sunblock and aftershave. Mine was wake up, drink tea, get dressed, leave to pee.

With these snow conditions, we wouldn't be able to cross the pass for days. I settled in to do my research on the climbers' adaptation to high altitude, which I'd promised the dean. A report came that Rob Dorival had "Ed's stomach disease." Several nights earlier, I'd treated Ed's vomiting and diarrhea with antiemetics and rehydration solution. I pulled on my gaiters and boots, grabbed the medical chest, and was on my way to a house call when I ran into Joe, who was breathless and needed his lungs checked. Then I got word Pasang had a sore throat. I triaged the reports and visited Rob D. first. He lay in his sleeping bag, his right arm stretched over his face.

"I vomited six times last night, feeling really weak." I took his temperature and pulse, examined his abdomen, and listened to his lungs, since he'd been fighting a cold and cough for weeks.

"I think you have what Ed had—a GI bug. Hopefully it will pass quickly, but we have to keep you hydrated."

I dug through the medical chest Stefan had recommended which functioned as my mobile clinic. Made for fishing tackle, it was four feet long with three shelves of compartments. Medications to treat everything were organized from A to Z, including four types of ophthalmic drops, seven different antibiotics, and eight dermatologic creams.

"I'm giving you something for vomiting, and rehydration solution."

"I'm nauseous." He grimaced. The wind battered the tent.

"You should feel better with the medicine, but I'm here with you. I'm giving you extra packets of Rehydrate. If it doesn't stay down, you gotta let me know."

I "rounded" on Joe and Pasang. Joe had malaise and felt weak, but it was nothing serious. I gave Pasang lozenges and Tylenol for his throat. I trudged from tent to tent in my double boots, getting wetter and wetter. I never thought of our Bronx hospitals as luxurious, but a ceiling over my head would have felt deluxe. Despite the poor conditions, I felt full of purpose: a doctor in the mountains, just as I'd imagined. So far, I could handle everything.

We ate breakfast standing in the snowfall. As soon as a pancake fell on the plate, it was covered with a layer of frost. One bite of pancake, breathe hard from chewing at altitude, another layer of frost.

"We're going to leave today," Miklos crossed his arms in front of his chest, bouncing for warmth. "The support team has had enough snow."

"We'll never reach Base Camp at this slow-as-snail rate. Might as well leave," added Wendy.

Miklos, Norbu, Wendy, Sandy, and Rob D. planned to pack and head for home within a few hours. Since the storm could worsen, I was concerned about Rob D. hiking. He was weak and barely able to sit up after a sleepless night, so I went to his tent to pack his gear. He lay on the ground. "I don't want to be a burden. I hate that you're having to do this," he said.

"That's what I'm here for. I hate that you guys are going to miss Base Camp. This snow is ridiculous."

Since the porters had all left, the climbers planned to escort the support team down the valley, carrying their gear. Pasang and Joe were both sick and in no position to help.

"I feel good, so I'm going to carry gear and go with you," I told Robert.

"I don't want you coming. It'll be a long hard day, and we'll be returning at night. You need to stay here and stay healthy for everyone else."

"I need to be with Rob D. more than anyone."

"Honestly, I don't want you slowing us down."

What? "I'm going. I want to be there for Rob!"

Before the support team left, we met in Norbu's tent for a goodbye ceremony. Norbu read from his father's memoir, *Tiger of the Snows*.

"The world is too small, Everest too great, for anything but tolerance and understanding. That is the most important of all things I have learned from my climbing and traveling. Whatever the difference between East and West, they are nothing compared to our common humanity."

Norbu's voice was gentle and calm. "My father's footsteps mean so much to me."

His words reminded me of my father's messages about unity between people. We both had fathers whose journeys inspired awe. We both were given opportunities because of what our fathers had been through and achieved. Tenzing Norgay's message about tolerance was particularly relevant, given our current disconnect with the locals. The message had an extra resonance for Norbu, who had not come here to trace his ancestry but was surprised to learn his father was from this valley and some of the locals were relatives.

After taking in the moment quietly, the support team stood up to go. I pulled Wendy aside by her hand. "Don't leave me alone with all these guys—I need you."

"I'm rooting for you. Make us women proud!" She gave me a big squeeze.

Packing everyone took time, and we didn't get going until afternoon. Paul broke trail in thigh-deep snow. I followed him, second, panting. Even though I knew Robert was right—I *was* slow—his comment infuriated me. I was determined to prove him wrong and use all my power to keep up.

We waddled down the valley in a whiteout. I checked on Rob D. periodically, and he appeared better—at least he wasn't vomiting. Robert patiently held him by the arm. When we reached the site of our last camp, the snow stopped falling, and a dazzling, rapid choreography of moving clouds overhead introduced the first sight of sun we'd seen in days. We met five porters prepared to carry loads; word had somehow traveled that we were coming, which meant we could start back sooner than we'd anticipated.

"Rob, here's some extra medicine." I hugged him, then Norbu. A warm tear dropped down my cheek.

After our goodbyes, we turned around and faced uphill, becoming a consolidated group nearing our purpose. Remaining on the team were the four climbers—Robert, Stephen, Paul, and Ed—Pasang, Kasang, Joe, and me. We waded up the slopes, and I did indeed fall to the last position. I watched four fierce bodies climbing the slopes ahead. I kept them in sight, wasn't slowing them down and was fine to be alone, going at my own pace.

At one point, I couldn't put it off anymore. *If only they knew I have to deal with this crap.* It was tricky, pulling my pants down in snow up to my underwear—to change my tampon. I'd come a long way from that first GYN appointment when I'd asked about trouble inserting tampons. *Ha!* And that rude doctor who'd inspired me to become a kinder doctor. *Ha!* If she could see me now.

When I finished, I ran uphill to stay in line of sight of the climbers. The sky cleared and an eerie light of dusk surrounded us. I kept up, even if no one else noticed. I was behind them—separate—but still part of the team. At the same time, I was proud to be a woman dealing with womanly things and able to hold her own. Capable and strong.

The first morning after our support team left, we woke to bright sunlight. The men threw off their shirts to soak up the rays and slathered on Kiehl's sunscreen. They revealed their lean bodies, flat stomachs and forearms divided into reams of muscle, while I kept on my thermal underwear covered with a long flannel lumberjack shirt. Without snowfall, breakfast was civilized. We sat at a table, eating omelets and muesli. The boom box played, and people did their laundry, which could now be dried in the sun. I spent the day doing physical exams on Stephen and Paul and reading medical texts. At 4:15, the sun set, and the wind chill rose.

Now that we'd regrouped, the climbers focused on Everest. That night was the first of many when they bonded by telling and retelling the stories of every climb they'd ever completed. They described how they traveled, who they knew in common, girlfriends who came and went. Even when they repeated stories, the listening climbers were riveted and reacted with oohs and ahs. The climbers were wisecracking swashbucklers with muscles and testosterone. Joe fit in as a former Navy man. I did not. I couldn't throw my shirt off either. This was not much different than standing to the side at the operating table with the all-male orthopedics team. No one seemed to notice me.

I tried not to drink too much tea at night because I dreaded exiting the tent for the midnight pee, but it came no matter what. At least the sky glittered with stars now that we had good weather, but I needed a solution. The men all used pee bottles inside their tents. I hadn't considered this an option.

"Heidi used a pee bottle on the Everest West Ridge expedition," Ed remarked with a daring face.

"Tell me more, Ed. You're holding out on me."

"I don't know much more, but I know it was a big deal when she figured it out."

The challenge was set. I needed to find a water bottle with a wide enough opening to avoid spilling on our fluffy down sleeping bags and avoid pee stage-fright with Robert sleeping close by.

The next morning, we hiked up to the pass and got a close-up and humbling view of Everest. The gargantuan East Face glared at us, impassive but also defiant, its prominent plume within reach. We would gauge the winds on Everest by the size and stretch of this flag of snow trailing from the peak. We were disappointed that the support team were missing this clear weather and magnificent view. Eating lunch at 18,000 feet was difficult, and digestion was uncomfortably stalled. I descended from the pass like a turtle. Robert was right about how slow I was. And now he was being kind, waiting for me, but—unfairly on my part—that also irritated me.

I wasn't slow because of my gender, but because I wasn't a climber or an athlete. Or maybe it was just my natural rhythm. Joe was also slower than the climbers, but he could blame his heavy photography gear. Ed, the slowest of the climbers, admitted he'd been given a nickname of "turtle" on other climbs. But as the only woman, I was particularly motivated to keep up, never complain, and have a positive spirit. To represent my gender well.

We were still stuck at Lhatse the next day, our sixth day there, waiting for 120 porters. Each day some porters trickled in, then left when the weather deteriorated. This day was overcast and chilly with a light snow drizzle. Ed quoted from a biography of Hemingway he was reading. "Three sports make a real man: bull fighting, rock climbing, and speed racing." So, the climbers decided this would be a good day to break out the rock-climbing gear. They had yet to climb with one another.

With boyish excitement, they laid out climbing racks, ropes, pitons, and carabiners in front of a steep gray cliff. The metal of the gear reflected the glare in the sky, while the pink and orange ropes graced the ground with color. Stephen threw a rack over his torso, loaded with clanking metal pieces like a staple gun, and marched to the rock.

They stood beneath the crag analyzing possible routes up a small buttress. Jaunty as usual, Stephen raced up the cliff.

"Ishteamy is a steamy one," Paul remarked. "Better watch out for him." Ishteamy was Stephen's new nickname, along with the variation "Steamy," based on how Kasang pronounced his name.

"You Yanks spend too much time yakking," Stephen called back.

"We Yanks might be yakking, but we could use some real yaks right now," added Joe.

"The porters better come soon," Robert said. "Looks like the weather is better. We're wasting another day." He bore the brunt of our delays.

"Never a waste if we get to rock climb," Ed said. He had gracefully set up another route next to Stephen's during all the yakking.

Despite my training climbs at the Gunks in New York, and in Boulder with Ed, my skills were rudimentary. They all climbed up Ed's route and deemed it elegant and difficult with a 5.10b rating in climbing parlance. They christened the route, *Free Tibet*. I sat on the ground cross-legged, admiring their skills.

"Mim, you want to climb? I can set up an easier route for you."

"Of course, Ed—thanks!"

He came down his route, then created another adjacent one. He fixed a few pitons in the middle of the rock face and threw the rope down to me from the top of the cliff. Robert and Joe came down, and Robert checked that I had threaded the rope properly through my harness.

A scavenger bird circled in the white sky. Ed belayed me from above, and Robert and Joe watched from the ground. I reached up to find a handhold, trying to place my right foot on the rock and couldn't seem to transfer my body to the rock. I tried again, and my foot slipped, unable to get a purchase. My hands were no help hoisting me to find a position on the rock. I tried with my left foot and that didn't work either.

I was stuck before I even started.

A red wave of embarrassment flooded my body.

Robert couldn't stand waiting anymore, and palmed my right buttock, pushing me up into the first move. "That's why climbers are so skinny. The gluteus maximus is hard to wing over and pull up."

Really? As if I'm not self-conscious enough with my ass framed by harness straps!

After Robert got me on the rock, it wasn't that hard to inch up to the top, especially with Ed providing a "tight belay," pulling hard on the rope to make me feel supported. They categorized it as a 5.7 climb, not completely basic, making me feel somewhat better. Later, I learned they named the route *Mimi's Crack*. Clever.

Out of nowhere, our original, luxurious kitchen tent, stalled at JFK, arrived on the back of a beautiful young Tibetan woman, named Sonam Putti, who routinely detoured to visit me for aspirin. No wonder she had headaches. She was always carrying sixty-pound loads. The support team had located the tent in Kharta and sent it to us, along with a letter for me from Wendy. "Your concern for everyone's well-being, mentally & physically is clear in the care and attention you've shown us all." My eyes welled up. She didn't need to say that but she knew how stretched I felt. I would miss her.

That night the BBC radio played a St. Patrick's Day special. We weren't talking about our delay, although we'd been stuck in this camp for a week. The climbers were in a singular space of mental preparation, focusing on finding a route up the East Face. While they bantered on about what route they could create, I thought about everything that was anomalous in that moment: listening to Irish brogue in Tibet, how proud we were to be awake at 8:00 p.m., and how the simple pleasure of no snowfall meant the world to us.

15

How to Ride an Avalanche

ON OUR EIGHTH MORNING OF CAMPING AT LHATSE, WAITING FOR POR-
ters to help us cross the pass, I wrapped the blood pressure cuff around
Robert's arm and pumped, then slowly released the air, noting the num-
bers on the gauge. I placed two fingers on his radial artery and counted
the thumps while looking at the second hand of my new Rolex watch.

Before we'd left New York, Rolex had given each of us a watch during
a ceremony at the Explorers Club, in addition to providing financial support for the expedition. The men received large adventure-style GMT
models, and I got a small feminine model. The following day, I called
Rolex and traded mine in for the men's version. Now, I looked at that
clunky thing on my wrist, meant to remind me I was a fierce adventurer
like the guys, and admitted it didn't suit me at all.

Blood pressure and pulse normal. Robert swallowed a nifedipine pill,
and we waited. A case report in the literature indicated that this medication, normally used to lower blood pressure, might help with altitude
sickness.

"Okay, now stand up and I'll take your vitals again," I said, measuring
his blood pressure and pulse at various time intervals and positions.

"I have a great feeling about this!" Robert sang in a chipper voice.
He had done an ad campaign for the manufacturer, secured a bottle of
pills, and sold himself on the idea of using them. But before he ingested
nifedipine on the mountain, we wanted to make sure he didn't have an
adverse reaction such as dizziness, headache, or a drop in blood pressure.

None of the other climbers wanted to experiment with their bodies high on Everest, but Robert did.

Our experiment was completed without adverse effects. Robert planned to use nifedipine only in dire circumstances, specifically with symptoms of pulmonary edema. I didn't know if this was a good idea, but I considered my role to provide information and let people make their own decisions. Robert added the pills to his first aid kit along with the fizzy vitamins that made him even bouncier. He'd gotten those from another advertising client. It turns out Robert had foresight. Nifedipine is now used routinely for prevention and treatment of high-altitude pulmonary edema.

Returning to my sleeping bag for a midmorning snuggle, I flipped the pages of *White Limbo*, the book about the Australian Everest expedition most like ours, the success of which convinced us to go vegetarian. In the prologue, Lincoln Hall, the author and one of the climbers, addressed the question of why mountaineers climb: "Part of my mind dismissed the question as irrelevant. My existence was irrevocably bound with the challenge, the friendships, and the lack of confusion which makes mountaineering separate from the illusions and pretensions of everyday living. It did not matter that there was no pot of gold at the top. It was enough to climb the rainbow."

His words spoke to me. We were living with singular focus, and friendships were developing from our intense life together. Scanning our tent, seven feet long and four feet wide, I was amazed Robert and I and all our stuff could share this space and be okay. More than okay, cozy. I shut the book, reached for my Walkman, popped in a meditation tape by the guru from the ashram I'd visited, and closed my eyes. Next, Joni Mitchell piped through my headphones, my favorite female guru and source of feminine energy and inspiration. I related to her words about skating to a faraway place. Wishing her feet could fly. Yes.

The overnight snow landed in a smooth layer of infinite crystals, piled high and soft, filling in the contours of the rocks surrounding camp. The first one up, I shoveled around everyone's tent while Kasang delivered morning tea. We spent dinner huddled in Ed's tent. Nepal radio reported fierce winds—120 kph—in Kathmandu. The dinner conversation droned on endlessly about climbing. Into our second week camped in the same spot, I began to feel captive in a snowy mess, our activities on a continuous loop of sameness.

"What do you do for a living? Go to the Himalayas and fart for two months," Paul joked. Stephen farted, and Kasang laughed. Sometimes "Steamy" was especially polite and ran up from the table to do it. This condition is now comically named HAFE, or high-altitude flatus emission.

"What am I doing here?" I yelped. High in the mountains was the place I was free to be myself. Bravado talk of climbing and farting wasn't what I had in mind.

"Christina felt the same way," Ed said, referring to his girlfriend on a previous Everest expedition. "She hated all the macho stuff." I skipped dessert, huffed back to my tent, put my headphones on, and melted into the soothing sounds of Joan Armatrading. Another female musical antidote to my immersion in this camp of masculinity.

That night, the temperature dropped. Robert prepared for bedtime by massaging moisturizer into his forehead. He leaned over to me. "You need to put astringent on your face, then use some of this amazing Kiehl's cream." He followed with upbeat chatter about his advertising ideas and other dreams, but I wasn't in the mood to listen.

I was thinking about the county hospitals I'd been working in where I took care of patients with addictions, AIDS, gunshot wounds, misery. *How do I juxtapose my life there with this?* There I was useful but not happy. Here I might be useful—I wasn't sure yet—but happy, for the most part. *If I feel miserable here, I have only myself to blame.* These thoughts cycled back to one of my usual worries. I'd worked hard to secure time away. *What if I don't get back to school on time?* We were behind schedule. This lesson played on repeat: take a deep breath and don't worry about what you can't control.

I wore a hat, gloves, and all my down layers to sleep, but the guys told me they slept bare. Pressure in my bladder woke me at 2:00 a.m. Robert faced away from me, exhaling with long slow breaths of deep sleep. I unzipped my sleeping bag and felt a waft of cold air. Shivering, I slipped off my down bib, grabbed the widemouthed Nalgene bottle I'd found in our supplies, and inched over to the corner of the tent in the dark, shoving my sleeping bag away with my foot. I turned on my battery-operated reading light and aimed it at the corner away from Robert, my breath visible in the cold.

Robert stretched his legs and stirred. *Shit! Stay sleeping!* I crouched low in a small ball and pulled down my thermal underwear, trying to get the bottle beneath me. It was a little too tall to fit, so I put the opening under me, with the bottle at an angle, waited, and took a deep breath to relax. A trickle dropped on my fingers. I adjusted the opening of the bottle under me and waited again. The bottom became warm as liquid dripped in. I exhaled in relief. When I finished, I secured the top, hid it under a pile of clothes, got dressed and snuggled back into my bag.

The urine was frozen by morning.

On the first day of spring, the sky was blue, and we gathered for breakfast in the newly erected "sheik" tent which had room for a table.

"Happy Birthday Ed!" I handed him a card I'd painted with watercolors I'd tucked into my duffel before we left. We were sipping tea and feeling luxurious, sitting upright, and protected from the elements. *If only we had a copy of the* New York Times, I thought. You can't take the City out of the girl.

"Guess what?" I added, "We have another reason to celebrate. I christened the pee bottle!"

"I knew you had it in you!" Ed smiled.

"Robert, watch your stuff!" Paul teased.

Just when I thought life couldn't get better, Ed hung the solar shower—since we finally had sun—and I washed my hair for the first time in two weeks.

I wanted to expose my skin, aching to breathe after being buried under heavy layers for weeks, just like the guys had. I hiked up to the pass alone. Halfway there, I disrobed, and romped upward in my underwear.

At night, we had a birthday party for Ed with Mexican food, Glenlivet, and a huge carrot cake that Pasang baked, somehow, without an oven. If I didn't take food on my plate initially, it would be quickly usurped by hungry men. What would my girlfriends at home do?

The whole evening was dominated by the gift Ed unwrapped from *his* girlfriend—a silk nighty. The other guys were terribly jealous and teased him endlessly. Stephen said, "I'm paranoid about losing too much weight. The worst would be going home, sleeping with a woman, and she says, 'Ow your bones are hurting me.'"

"Your ribs are pointy sk-yoooo-wers," Paul mimicked a hypothetical woman of the future.

How maddening that Stephen, who ate every meal as if it would be his last, was worried about being too skinny. Although I no longer had an eating disorder, I still carried with me a fear of fat.

Back in the tent, Robert tenderly leaned over and cinched the collar on my sleeping bag. "Don't forget to cream your cuticles." I had never done that even at home. "I promised your mother I would take good care of you," he added.

"Wow, I had no idea you two talked. Okay, pass me the Kiehl's cream."

"Yeah, on the phone before leaving."

"Are you afraid of her?" Maybe she'd yelled and scared him.

"No, she and I have an understanding." I wondered how he achieved something that had been so hard for me. But, knowing they'd discussed me surprised and warmed me.

"Tell me about your girlfriend." I hoped for more connection.

"No, no, no."

I wanted to discuss our intimacy, though undefined. It was a betrayal we weren't addressing. We'd shared a tent for two weeks now, but he made it clear that, with the risks facing us, we should not whisper of emotion under the penumbra of the plumed mountain, so near now we were breathless in her shadow.

We searched for ways to set up a candle in the tent and figured out how to secure it inside a shoe, balanced, so as not to burn anything. We tucked in for the night, comfortable and warm.

The next day, the climbers and I walked up to the pass. I wished I could bottle the light, fresh air. To feel healthy, fully acclimatized *and* enjoying good weather amounted to a high for all of us.

That night Robert opened some pockets in his duffel.

"Here's where I keep my passport, money, and papers, and my family contact information."

"Stop. You'll be fine," I said, with a jolt of panic. Robert was such a force that I couldn't imagine him not returning from the mountain. I also couldn't picture my life with him gone.

"No." His face was serious. "It's important for you to know."

I didn't want to talk about it. All I wanted at that moment was the warmth of his arm around me in this cold cocoon. When we closed our eyes to sleep or opened them upon awakening, we envisioned only the mountain and what we would be doing there. With the developing intimacy of our group, even if I didn't want to think about terrible possible outcomes, I periodically took out my medical binder and quizzed myself on how to handle emergencies. I reviewed the temperature of water needed to thaw frostbitten fingers, the dose of epinephrine to revive a stopped heart. Seeing the East Face at the pass, I couldn't ignore the high stakes riding on my shoulders.

On March 24 a light snow fell when porters trickled into camp at 4:00 a.m. We distributed loads and were short thirty-five people. We'd planned for yaks to carry our stuff. But now, people of all ages bent under the weight of our blue barrels, a troubling image of the disparities in our fortunes and privilege. We paid the wages set by the Chinese, but was it enough? I'd been so focused on preparing for my medical role, I hadn't thought about the impact of us being here. About my relationship with the locals, medical interactions with them, or being a foreign woman in this remote valley.

We were unsure how to handle our conflicts with the Tibetans. We had come to a business agreement, but there was a mismatch of power. We had resources and were interlopers in their space which got few visitors. We had an agenda, goals, and a timeline. Although we were grateful people agreed to carry our loads, we were also frustrated with the short workdays, and uncomfortable with how much the locals stared at us because of our foreign ways.

We needed the patience and tolerance Norbu's father had written about. Pasang did his best to bridge our two cultures, talking calmly, ensuring fairness, and outfitting the Tibetans with proper equipment. He insisted the porters who joined us were eager participants, happy to earn income they sorely needed. This disparity was a known source of conflict for mountaineering expeditions then, and the struggle to bridge cultures and ensure fair treatment and wages of locals continues today.

Robert set the plan for the day: "Stephen and Joe, you go out front. Mimi, you go next. Once more porters come, Ed and Pasang will leave with them. Paul and I will pick up the rear." I carried my own pack to assuage some of my guilt.

I was alone all day with a throng of porters. They each hauled a blue barrel or a gray duffel, slightly stooped, inching up the slopes in a long line, like rungs on a ladder to the sky. Sometimes moving and sometimes still. They took long, frequent rest stops and swigs of *chang*. After each stop, I gesticulated wildly, "We're all leaving now!" To generate enthusiasm, I smiled and pumped my fists in the air, saying "*Tashideleh!*"

On a steep hill, I came across a man lying face down. I tapped him on the shoulder. No movement. *Uh oh. Dead.* Just like me to race to the worst possible scenario. I leaned in closer and saw his chest faintly moving up and down, while his friends mimicked that he had enjoyed too much chang at the rest stop. I managed to rouse him and nudge him along, but he stopped every three steps. Eventually I left him, knowing Ed and Pasang weren't far behind.

I encountered a slight man with a gray goatee, slumped over and carrying the number thirteen duffel, which was my medical chest. I walked behind him, so I could keep track of him and the medicine. I didn't let anyone else fall behind me to ensure we'd all make it over, waiting for stragglers who stopped to relieve themselves.

Around midday, I was on the crest of a hill, surrounded by a large crowd of porters taking a break. A middle-aged man with full facial hair, flanked by two friends, approached, and leaned in close to my face. He exchanged some words with his friends then stuck his middle finger through a hole made with the fingers of his other hand while making moaning sounds. My feet tingled and my face burned. I waved my arms and yelled, "Don't you ever do that again! I am giving you NO medicine. Get away from me. AWAY!" One after another, people turned and left.

I ran to catch up with Joe. We waited at the crest of the pass for the porters to organize and descend with us to the campsite Stephen had chosen near the bottom of the slope. When we couldn't get them to move, Joe and I gave up and ran down the hill. We looked behind us and watched the porters lining up on top of the pass. There was some inching forward and stopping. We were yelling at them and waving arms to join us, but nothing.

Suddenly, and for no apparent reason, close to a hundred porters trampled down the steep slope, yelling and whooping. The earth trembled. We delighted in their glee.

I settled into Joe's tent for the night and grabbed a towel to dry my soaking feet. "I know I'm an idiot. I wore my canvas boots," I said. I couldn't decide which was worse—getting wet from sweating in my heavy high-altitude mountain boots or wet from snow seeping through canvas. I was still a city girl, one who loved nature, but who hadn't yet mastered mountain life.

Nightfall brought a clear and shining sky with a crescent moon like a crooked smile flanked by bright star dimple. Joe's tent was roomier, and I was thrilled to successfully use the pee bottle despite him sleeping nearby. Robert and Paul didn't catch up to us that night.

Upon awakening, a dull light suffused the tent. I leaned outside to watch my first sunrise over Everest's East Face. First the summit was illuminated in oranges and pinks, then the Face was slowly revealed, followed by the high peak of Lhotse, the fourth highest mountain in the world, to the left. By the time the sun reached our camp an hour later, around fifteen porters lined up seeking treatment for snow blindness. The sun's reflection off the snow can burn the corneas, and these porters had crossed the pass without the protection of good sunglasses. One by one, I administered eye drops and aspirin, while Stephen constructed makeshift sunglasses from cardboard, with a narrow slit to see through.

While hiking the next day, I was periodically stopped by Tibetans showing me wounds and asking for medicine. Mid-afternoon, three men surrounded me, laughing, and making lewd hand gestures again. One of them pulled on my arm, jerking me toward the ground. My heart raced, and knees wobbled. I raised my ski pole, and shouted, "Go away." While

I yelled, several women stood about twenty feet away, watching but not helping me. I was disappointed there wasn't more of a sisterhood to speak up for me.

Joe approached. "What's going on? Back off!" he yelled as he leaned his tall body into the group and waved his ski pole, dispersing the crowd.

"Back off!" I echoed.

How was I to handle my conflicting emotions about wanting to treat anyone with a medical need but feeling vulnerable? I resented needing a man to protect me. I decided to provide medical aid to the porters only when we were in camp, when I wasn't alone.

Robert and Paul caught up with us. At night in our tent Robert warned, "I don't want you to be scared, but this slope is pretty steep, the snow is deep and wet, and it could avalanche or there could be a rockslide, so let's run through an avalanche drill."

When a sentence starts with "Don't be scared but . . ." and you are on a remote Himalayan slope, what did he expect? I was terrified, of course.

"Keep your boots, headlamp, and ice axe nearby. Remember how to ride an avalanche, feet pointing downhill, arms close to your body."

I arranged my gear nearby as instructed, willing myself to remember the rule that if such a crisis were to strike, to point my feet down, arms tucked in. I didn't sleep at all, listening to the winds howl and the snow patter on the tent. At one point I heard rocks falling and woke Robert up in a panic. He listened and reassured me that it was far away, that no avalanche was barreling toward us. He rolled over and resumed snoring. I kept one eye open and my ears on high alert.

In the morning, a Tibetan teenager showed me a deep cut in his finger. I recognized him as one of the guys who'd harassed me the day before.

"Bug off!" I yelled. Then I called Pasang over. "Please explain to him that I will not help him because he disrespected me yesterday." Pasang spoke softly in Tibetan. The young man nodded his head and turned to walk away.

"Okay, Pasang, tell him I'll help this one last time but no more bullshit."

The cut could have used a suture, but I cleaned it and approximated the edges with narrow adhesive strips because digging out suture supplies would take too long. "Come back if it gets worse," I said, then applied salve to Kasang's kitchen burn, and bandaged blisters on Robert's feet, the most routine of conditions amidst my personal tempest.

Two days later, the porters went on strike again. We woke up at 5:30 a.m. to a perfectly clear day, but they refused to move. Robert strutted around shirtless and hatless with his hair smoothed back, black wraparound goggles and green long underwear hugging his muscular legs. He waved a ski pole. "You will get paid when we reach base camp. The sooner we get there, the sooner you'll get paid!" While the men protested, the women sat farther back on the hillside, whispering and giggling.

They finally hiked a short distance to a camp on lower ground without snow where we would stay that night. On the way there, I rounded a ridge and saw the gargantuan East Face close by. My eyes teared with relief.

Just before reaching camp, a man made the "screw sign" with me again. I complained to Robert, who dramatically threw off his pack and towered over the guy in threat. The man retreated with his head bowed. I was drained by the behavior of the Tibetan men, feeling singled out and violated. At times when they said *tashideleh*, I didn't respond, because I didn't want to be friendly and invite attention. But if I didn't respond, they made fun of my haughtiness. When they snickered and jeered, I felt exposed, like a wild, naked, Western woman, despite wearing huge baggy pants and a long flannel shirt reaching halfway down my thighs because I didn't want to draw attention. This was a clash of mores, of us in their space, of misunderstanding. And yet, harassing women—harassing *me*—was as acceptable in Tibet as it was at home.

Our final day trekking was long. I shuffled like an old lady. Although I left with Stephen, I soon lagged far behind, searching the snow for his footprints. *Just keep dragging and you'll get there.* My arm burned from the pressure of leaning on my ski pole, my backpack weighed heavy on my hips. My feet sweat in my heavy double boots.

Ed walked down a hill toward me. "Mim, Base Camp is just five minutes away. Let me take your pack." It slid off my back before he got his words out.

I was close to my destination yet a long way from the Versailles, where I'd dreamed of what was out there in the world. I was a long way from RMBL and the first time I hiked into the sky. A long way from slinging on a suitcase-backpack to see Nepal. And a long way from the Bronx, from medical rounds and trailing residents, studying late into the night. All of this was loaded in my pack as I straggled into Base Camp at close to 17,000 feet. The imposing mountain at the head of the Kang-shung valley was a symbol of the tall duties before me. Medical needs might escalate at higher altitudes.

I spotted Robert sitting in the grass, doling out wads of cash to porters who were lined up sporting huge grins. My teammates raced to assemble loads to ferry to Advanced Base Camp because we needed porters to help with this task before they left us.

We had finally reached our home for the next few months: a grassy spot abutting the 11,000-foot icy wall of the East Face of Everest.

It was supposed to take us five days to reach Base Camp. It took twenty-two.

16

Kangshung Life

ROBERT AND PASANG CHOSE THE LOCATION FOR BASE CAMP AS AN ideal way station between the lower Kama valley, from which we got mail, and the mountain. Our new home was a flat moraine with a ridge of hills on one side abutting the Kangshung glacier.

"Ed and I are going up the glacier with two porters to find a site for Advanced Base Camp," Robert said, slinging his pack on his shoulders. Twenty porters had agreed to work one additional day ferrying loads once a safe spot for Advanced Base was selected. There, we would fashion a second home on rocks, ice, and snow.

"Good luck!" I waved, while a deafening wind whipped my hair across my face. Shivering, I dug out two hats, a scarf, and mittens from my duffel. Thick flakes of snow fell, making us worry the porters would quit.

"Mim, let's do the food." Stephen's British accent elevated the mundane task. He laid out a huge blue tarp and pointed. "We'll pile food here for Base Camp, here for Advanced Base, and here for the mountain." We dumped blue barrels to sort. I tucked my chin away from the wind, and tossed boxes of crackers, soups, noodles, and drinks into piles.

"I'm working on the climbing gear," Paul shouted from the outskirts of camp, where he sat hunched over on a rock, repairing a mini stove.

Joe organized photography equipment, and later I divided medicines for the three locations while Stephen, Pasang, and Kasang erected the cook tent and built a pantry.

"It's just four hours from Base Camp," Robert explained when they returned.

"We marked the route with cairns," added Ed.

During our first dinner in the sheik tent at Base Camp, Pasang announced "Kasang and me, we stay in Base Camp full-time, not camping on glacier."

"Why?" I asked.

"Too dangerous. Too cold." I searched Robert's face wondering whether this had been worked out in advance.

"I make Base Camp great place for rest. You come, I cook, you feel good," Pasang said.

That Pasang considered Advanced Base unfit for himself, but fine for Joe and me, came as a surprise. I didn't fully grasp it at the time, but this meant Joe and I were to be tasked with the cooking since the climbers would be busy climbing. That wasn't a role I'd prepared for. When no one was sick or injured, I'd be "support," which might include anything. Now cooking was high on the list.

We'd mostly stay at Advanced Base Camp, but anyone had the option to return to Base Camp for a break from glacial living. At almost 18,000 feet, Advanced Base was near enough to the East Face to reach rapidly on climbing days, but far enough away to avoid crushing avalanches. The climbers would slowly advance the route up the mountain and descend to sleep at Advanced Base. Eventually, they'd build other camps on the mountain, and stay in them, as they created a line to the South Col, a flat saddle of the mountain that connects the East Face to the Nepali South ridge. The South Col was to be their final campsite before the summit attempt. There, the climbers planned to join the most popular route to the summit from the Nepali side.

The following morning, Robert and I walked Stephen, Paul, and twenty porters hauling gear to the edge of the moraine where it intersected with active ice.

"Be safe, guys!" I waved as they set off.

I called Ed into an empty tent and faced him holding my medical binder and pen. "Let's complete your Base Camp physical." I sat upright, all-business, to minimize any discomfort over undressing in front of me. I treated these encounters like any clinical visit but felt like Lucy from *Peanuts*—only pretending to be a professional.

"Owwwww," Ed exaggerated when my cold stethoscope touched his bare skin.

"Everything okay, Ed?" Robert yelled sarcastically from outside.

"Don't worry, mister. You're next!" I barked back.

In private, the guys were open and trusting, but as a group, they teased me. After the physical, I administered the fifteen-question mental status exam I repeated at different elevations. *What's today's date? I'm going to state three words I need you to repeat back to me. Copy these shapes.*

That afternoon, we had another Tibetan puja ceremony. Pasang draped prayer flags from our sheik tent to two rock altars he'd built, binding us to this spot of earth with colorful squares of luck and peace. He recited prayers for a safe climb and burned juniper, instructing us to toss rice over our right shoulders. Our wishes wafted upward in the whirlwind of herbal-scented smoke to flutter overhead with the flags.

As it had in Nepal, the full moon that night reminded me it was Passover. I foraged around the pantry for ingredients to host a spontaneous seder, the ritual meal. I cooked a hard-boiled egg, used potatoes for the vegetable, and looked for something to use in place of matzah. Moving packages around, I spotted sea toast crackers and picked one out of the box. The resemblance was uncanny. I made charoset, a sticky dish meant to symbolize the cement used by slaves, with dates, dried peaches, and nuts. Smelling the sweet fruit reminded me of Passover in the Versailles. There, after Josh and I moved to Orthodox schools, we'd scrubbed the apartment, and exchanged all our dishes, pots, and cutlery for a Passover set to conform with kashruth laws. One particularly memorable experience occurred when I was eight. Mom had returned from the fishmonger.

"Did you get everything?" Amama asked. "It's not right unless we have carp, pike, and whitefish."

"Yes, Mutti, of course." Mom unwrapped the fish from the brown butcher paper, releasing a pungent smell. I screwed the clamp of the metal meat grinder, the same gadget they used for chopped liver, to the edge of the table, "You know, Ma, we can buy prepared gefilte fish these days," Mom said.

"It's not the same and you know it. Besides, Pushkin loves my fish." Amama would do anything for Josh.

Cranking the handle made me tired. Amama set a huge pot on the stove to boil onions and carrots while Mom took over rotating the crank. They dropped oval-shaped patties of fish into the pot, and a mouthwatering scent of sea billowed in a cloud of steam. The following morning, I learned that Amama and Mom fell asleep, and the fish disintegrated in the simmering stew. Instead of abandoning the mission, they scrambled to start from scratch.

As I set the table in our tent, I thought they would appreciate that I'd assembled something, even if it was a simple seder plate with sea toast crackers.

From the head of the table, I lit two candles to start the ceremony.

"The theme of the Passover story is freedom, as when the Jews were freed from slavery in Egypt and set out to wander in the desert," I said to the guys seated around the table in down parkas.

Once again, as when I'd camped near the waterfall in Nepal, I was in the Himalayas at the start of a journey and connecting to my ancestors who'd set out to wander, some by choice and others by necessity. My father had moved from slavery in Siberia to freedom. He loved to sit like a king at the head of the Passover table leading songs and stories. Despite the divorce and their ongoing battles, my parents came together for the seder. Even my mother's eyes flashed proud when my father sang. Jewish wisdom holds that the righteous pass on the eve of a holiday. Nineteen years after this impromptu mountain seder, on the eve of Passover, my father would die.

Once again, in Base Camp, I was immersed in freedom within nature but also a fear of the unknown. Perhaps, part of my birthright was to wander. Was I always to feel the most freedom—or most like myself—in places that tested my limits and abilities in ways they were rarely tested in my regular life? Would the humdrum of "normal" life always pale in comparison to these mountain moments?

I demonstrated to my teammates dipping potatoes into salted water. "The vegetables represent spring and the salted water tears of bondage."

I asked the central seder question: "How does this night differ from all others?"

Robert said, "I'm relieved we are finally getting to the climb."

"I was very moved today by the puja ceremony." The flickering flames of the candles danced black in Ed's blue eyes.

Joe said, "It's breathtaking here, I can't wait to photograph it all."

"We're almost rid of the gawkers!" Paul's wide grin beamed. We all laughed.

I explained that the Haggadah, the book of the seder, discusses how to tell the Passover story differently to four distinct kinds of sons. "Or daughters," I added, wishing the text acknowledged girls.

I turned to Stephen. "There's the wise son," I said, since he was an Oxford graduate. Then I mentioned the "bad son," and glared at Paul. His face lit up with a smile full of teeth. "Nah, me?"

We leaned in around the table, the sleeves of our parkas touching. Everest loomed large in the cauldron of cold outside, but we warmed connecting through a ritual that brought a sense of home to me. Here my Jewish practice was far from a box, but rather an opening that made me feel closer to my teammates, connected to my family, and more accepted for who I was. The men delighted in the ritual.

Stephen poured whiskey shots, and we toasted to safety on our final night before moving to the mountain.

After we cleared dishes, I held my teacup in mittened hands, waiting for the liquid to warm my chest. "Since we're going to Advanced Base tomorrow, can we talk about high altitude for a minute? Situations can deteriorate quickly. You guys need to watch out for each other because altitude can impair judgment and the affected person may be unaware of his condition."

They nodded silently. They were experienced climbers who knew this information better than I did, but I thought it important to review, even if I was taking my role too seriously.

I retreated to my tent and wondered what their greatest protection would be. Pasang's chants and prayer flags? Their camaraderie and brotherhood? Anything I did medically?

I hurried to write a letter to my mother for the porters to take with them down the valley the next day, detailing our long trek to Base Camp and our seder. I rummaged through my pack outside for stamps, and my fingers quickly went numb. The sky was so bright I could almost read, and the entire East Face was illuminated as if theater spotlights were positioned directly above us. How lucky to be in this extraordinary place. Just like Isak Dinesen wrote in *Out of Africa*, I was in the right place here.

That night, while I piled on layer after layer of thermals, I asked Robert, "Do you think it will always be this freezing?" My voice quivered through chattering teeth.

"I think we're camped in a wind tunnel. That's why the snow on the ground cleared so quickly."

Robert tucked into his sleeping bag. "This is what we've been waiting for."

"Yeah, I can't believe we're here."

"Let's not share a tent at Advanced Base," he said. I recognized this mood of his. He was intently focused on the climb.

"Good idea." Everyone would stay in their own tent, and nobody would feel left out.

The tent flapped against my head all night, and the wind gusts roared like jet planes taking off. Decades later my kids would mock my need for a sweater in the air-conditioning of a hot Atlanta day. "I can't believe you were on Everest," they'd tease, and roll their eyes.

I woke up groggy and didn't hear Kasang bringing tea. "Mimi," he repeated until I stirred and grunted. He leaned into the tent with his smiling face. "Goo Mornu, Mimi," he repeated.

"Thank you, Kasang."

I forced myself up on my elbows, then sat slumped in my sleeping bag, slowly sipping one cup of tea after another, to clear my mouth of dried cotton. Outside, Robert chirped, "It's a beautiful day in the neighborhood." Dehydration, so insidious at altitude, made it hard to think, my neurons parched like kindling. A cool breeze wafted through the yellow tent flaps, and swept through my brain, helping to unstick my thoughts. I needed to pack for Advanced Base. The effort to choose what to bring and then bury it deep into my pack was immense, inordinate. I had predicted the weeks hiking in would be all the acclimatization I'd need, but sluggishness overcame me at this altitude.

We left Base Camp as a group. For the first time, Joe and I stepped onto the Kangshung glacier, the direct flowing ice tail that drained

Everest, a contiguous mass of ice, rocks, and ponds. The Face—stoic and towering—dominated the view. Before long, I looked up from my feet and noticed I was walking alone. *Damn Robert! I know I'm slow!* I yelled at his voice in my head. When I hiked, I imagined myself as my Capricorn sign, a goat, slow but persistent, able to climb any mountain. The more I stumbled over flinty rocks, not wanting to twist an ankle, I remembered something about the goat having a fish tail too. Then I imagined the glacier as a huge pond of water to swim and skate across.

I looked back down to focus on my feet since walking on uneven rocks required concentration. It was easy to become disoriented on the glacier as the gray landscape was dull and the light flat, so the rocks didn't emerge as separate from one another. The climbers had made a rule that no one was to travel the glacier alone. Technically, I wasn't alone since we'd all left together. The team had created a safe route and marked it well. I was unlikely to fall into a deep crevasse covered by a trapdoor of snow crust. I lumbered along and searched for tracks in the snow, trying to find the next cairn. The continuous soundtrack of flowing ice and loose rocks teetering on their perches reminded me that the ground could shift at any moment, yet this would become our new home away from home.

My pack weighed heavy on my shoulders, and I labored to breathe as I passed ponds of stark navy blue and crystalline teal. Lots of gray and black rock in all directions and of all sizes: mountains, hills, boulders, rocks, pebbles. This remote place was so surreal, so alien and foreboding, with the creaking, the constant creaking, and gurgling like walking on a different planet. One moment I pinched myself, grateful I was at Everest with the steep Face in front of me. The next moment brought trepidation: I was responsible for all things medical. Mostly I felt lonely and tired slogging along, picking out the route through the confusing landscape.

After six hours, Stephen walked toward me.

"Mimi, camp's only twenty minutes' walk. Want me to carry your pack there?"

"Hell yeah!" I unbuckled my hip strap. *God it would be nice to have Stephen's energy!* His lanky body glided effortlessly, as if hovering a few inches above the ground. As he pranced away, I could barely hear him muttering under his breath, his custom while hiking. He could've been saying anything. Sometimes he cursed "those bloody bastards," which could refer to anyone who annoyed him at that moment.

I crept into Advanced Base Camp where the guys sat on blue barrels. Joe and Ed were, surprisingly, behind me. A thundering crash pierced the air followed by a deep guttural rumble. The earth reverberated underfoot as an enormous maelstrom of snow and ice descended the East Face and careened toward us.

"What!?!" I screamed. My voice was no match for the deafening explosion *So, this is what Pasang was talking about*, I thought, awestruck by the danger. The wave tumbled along the stretch of our potential route the guys had already named "Big Al Gully." Seconds later, the air cracked—*boom, boom, boom*—and another colossal burst of snow thrust toward us from Lhotse, the towering face to the left of our route.

"Other men LESS WISE . . ." Paul quoted the words Mallory had said upon seeing the East Face, which had become our motto. "Other men less wise might attempt this way if they would but it was emphatically not for us." We soon learned that Big Al was not only a menacing brute, but also an ill consumptive, overcome with paroxysms, spasming with unpredictable regularity. During this avalanche, the snow didn't reach us at camp. We were reassured by the care Robert and Ed had applied to choosing this spot.

Robert handed me a cup of tea. "You can put yourself in my tent."

This was familiar.

No time for pros and cons. I threw my pack inside, grateful to not pitch a tent. At our new altitude, I was beat. Our team was getting along great, and no one seemed to care we were sharing a tent. Maybe this was growth for me to not retreat to solitude in my usual stubborn way, and at the same time, maybe I failed as a feminist in these moments.

Life at Advanced Base was like occupying the orchestra seats of an amphitheater. We faced a stage of towering steep slopes draped by curtains of wispy snow. As spectators, we watched the natural elements sing and dance in a dramatic showcase. Each day, Act One was the changing cones and shafts of sunrise, the lifting veil of night revealing pink and orange and yellow spotlights. Act Two was the main act of the day, the longest act, an act showering us with the brightness of whites—and some grays and sprays of clouds—until the swift fall of shadows enveloped us in the chill of twilight. Avalanches dominated the score in surround sound with syncopated rhythms (swing, percussive, tympanic), accented by the cracks, gurgles, and groans of the rivers of ice beneath our feet.

Act Three, the finale, shined with the twinkle and swoosh of star and moon. This wild beauty is what enticed me to face my fears and join the team, the waning sun spraying golden on the peaks, the white caps shimmering under a final dust of blue before black.

Frequent avalanches careened down the Face each day. Despite this, or maybe because of this, Advanced Base was magnificent. The faces of Lhotse and Everest rose 11,000 feet straight above us, into the purest air I'd ever inhaled. Chilled, weightless air I could barely feel.

The climbers named features of the Face. "Big Al Gully," was directly below "Big Al," an overhanging block of ice that was the source of most of the avalanches, although the face of Lhotse contributed a fair share.

Finding the best way up a mountain takes days, weeks, or months when creating a new route. As they advanced, the climbers secured ropes to the steepest slopes to hold them if they were to fall and to help them descend quickly. Once a camp was established, they stocked it with food and gear to use while they stayed there, and to bring farther up the mountain to the next camp.

The route they created from Advanced Base to the South Col required crossing the Kangshung glacier for about one mile to an icefall at the base of the Face. Snow ledges led to a headwall they rock climbed toward the Scottish Gully, a steep snow chute regularly prone to avalanche. Then, a rock and snow traverse of the Cauliflower Ridge toward Camp One, followed by upper snow ledges to the South Col, the saddle connecting to the Nepali side of the mountain. (Less than a decade later, the South Col is where the physician and climber Beck Weathers would lie in the cold, presumed dead, in the infamous 1996 Everest storm disaster that became the subject of many books, including Jon Krakauer's *Into Thin Air*.)

The climbers christened our team's route the "Neverest Buttress," a callout to having no Sherpa support and no oxygen.

They rotated partners and took turns lead climbing, which they considered the most challenging and fun part of climbing. "Fun" is debatable, as Jon Krakauer writes about a climbing partner in *Eiger Dreams*. "He tends to confuse things like life-or-death climbing with fun."

The lead figured the way up, fixed protective anchors to the mountain, and attached his rope to the anchors. Picking out a new route, rare on Everest, required the mental nimbleness of a chess master, the physicality of an Olympian, and the fearlessness of an astronaut.

On the first day, the climbers set out in two teams: Stephen and Robert left at 7:00 a.m. and reached the Scottish Gully. The weather was warm and windless when they returned around 3:00 p.m., but by the time the second team, Ed and Paul, arrived back at camp, we were engulfed in a wet vortex of snow. Ed crept into camp, his beard bejeweled with icicle ornaments. Each ascent to new heights took a toll on the climbers' bodies and required time to acclimatize.

While the four of them braved a new route, I did chores all day. I took a blue barrel, ice axe, and bucket down a small slope to a frozen pool. Raising the axe high in the air and throwing it down, I cracked the ice layer on top. Then, I scooped water with the bucket to fill the barrel two-thirds full, stopping to catch my breath and wipe sweat from my brow. Six people at high altitude had significant water needs. But this water did more than refill our tanks: It made us feel at one with the glacier, tasting pure as sky. I scrambled up slippery rocks back to camp with my heavy haul balanced on my shoulder. This became my daily routine. I loved doing something physically demanding, since life at Advanced Base had limited opportunities for movement. No one was permitted to travel alone beyond camp, which was only about three acres wide, the risk of falling into a crevasse too great.

I approached Joe sitting on a rock, flipping through pictures.

"Look at this cutie." His blonde toddler, Claire, in a plaid velvet Christmas dress clutched a teddy bear. Next, he showed me a photo of his wife.

"Ellen is stunning," I nodded. A working model, tall and blonde, she and Joe were a picture-perfect couple—he, the epitome of tall, dark, and handsome. The only married teammate, he missed his family terribly.

I boiled water for the climbers' arrival back at camp. Because of the thinner, drier air, water evaporates faster and boils at lower temperatures (177°F at our elevation vs. 212°F at sea level), so it took much longer to cook. If pasta water takes ten minutes to boil at sea level, it took over thirty minutes at our elevation because of the lower water temperature. I didn't account for this when I began cooking dinner, and as darkness fell, I was still standing over a pot of pea soup with ramen, steam fogging my glasses. Unable to see, I poured in an embarrassment of oregano. Tired, and hunched over on barrels in frozen night air, the guys dredged the muck in their dinner bowls searching for palatable bites.

As soon as the sun set at around 6:00 p.m., the bitter air besieged us like the blasting breath of a dragon. It was impossible to remain outside without shivering wildly. We ate early, retreated to our tents, read books, listened to music, wrote letters or in our journals, and fell asleep by eight or nine. We endured unbearably long nights, our sleep restless from high-altitude hypoxia. This schedule was best for the climbers who left in the middle of the night to climb, when the snow crust was hard. Increasing sunlight brought two problems: The sun reflecting off the snow made the climbing hot, and avalanches intensified.

My first night, I awakened at midnight and used the pee bottle, unable to get back to sleep. Earlier, Robert sat up and snacked. He was tall and lean and expended much energy climbing, so he sometimes ate at night. I certainly didn't need to eat but I thought *maybe it'll warm me*, so I snacked on gorp and switched on my mini book lamp, nestled deep into my sleeping bag so as not to wake Robert, and opened *The Razor's Edge* by Somerset Maugham. The story resonated, detailing the protagonist's search for spirituality and meaning. An eerie moan then a crack and a belch pierced the air. I held my breath. *It's just the glacier moving,* I inhaled deeply. *We're in a safe spot.*

Day after day, night after night, I would reassure myself during each terrifying clap of ice breaking off the mountain, imagining them pummeling toward us. I got two hours of sleep here and there, did some reading, and stared at the tent nylon, listening to the wind and avalanches.

The next day, Joe and I tracked the climbers through the telescope.

"They're moving well," Joe said. Robert was flinging his two ice axes into the snowy, sixty-degree slope of the Scottish Gully.

"Ha! I can barely cross the glacier," I said. Their physical abilities were extraordinary and humbling.

"Think about it. They have almost a hundred years of climbing between them," Joe said.

"They are so different from one another, too." Robert took his role as leader seriously, Stephen was singularly focused and fast, Paul corralled everyone with his spirit and humor, and Ed was pensive and romantic.

Kasang and Pasang arrived at 2:30 p.m. exhausted from carrying loads from Base Camp, having left at 9:00 a.m. Even they moved more slowly than the climbers. After they left, a huge powder cloud swirled off the mountain and cratered down the valley toward us. Joe and I rushed into his tent, zippered the flap, huddled, and braced for the avalanche. Two blasts of strong wind and a light snowfall engulfed our tent. We giggled like kids on a roller-coaster ride.

When the climbers returned, they expected me to have warm drinks ready. I had boiled water but used it for the tea I gave Pasang and Kasang. I resented that traditionally female chores like cooking were expected more of me than Joe. But I had to admit that Joe contributed in other ways, like building things around camp.

I remembered Steve's advice and got a warm feeling thinking about this man I'd been dating. "You need to do everything possible to support the team." He'd made me think more deeply about what a supporting role meant, not only with his advice but also because he was so supportive of me. "I'm so proud of you, Mimster," he'd say. Thinking about him egged me on now. *I need to do whatever is needed for this climb.* I felt guilty being with Robert while dating Steve, but I hadn't completely opened my heart to Steve. With him, I'd behaved the way Robert was now with me, "focused on the mountain."

Books were my way of getting through the long days and nights, and I needed to go to Base Camp for more. How ironic that my love of reading had grown out of a need to be transported at a young age to all those great adventures waiting for me in the world, yet here on my biggest adventure, I needed books again. Reading was connection, and companionship, and it reached the core of my thoughts and imagination. Books had even strengthened my physical core, when I used them to fill the maroon beast and hauled it up and down the stairs of my apartment building in training.

Joe joined me on the trek to Base Camp, and we slogged for almost seven hours, arriving at nightfall. The air, palpably thicker with oxygen, was a rich and sultry heaviness passing through my nostrils. Pasang treated us to dumpling soup—the work of a real cook.

I had packed *The Merck Manual*, a comprehensive medical reference that wasn't too big or heavy. As I read it that night—part of my continual review of medicine—something evoked the memory of my surgery rotation and my first oral exam. I had mixed up the anatomic anomalies of omphalocele and gastroschisis, which both involve defects of a newborn's abdominal wall. I passed the exam but felt exposed and judged by my mistake. Simply recalling this error, my heart pounded, and my face tingled. Here I was, in the Kangshung Valley of Tibet, still feeling bad about that exam. As students, we were expected to be perfect and fit a mold. But why did I still care about that test? I had a long way to go before accepting my mistakes and fallibility.

I placed *The Merck Manual* atop my medical notebooks and sifted through my stack of novels. I picked up Robertson Davies's *Fifth Business*, which Ed had lent me. Reading novels again ventilated my brain, allowing me to think about the human condition from an existential perspective as opposed to the physical. I enjoyed this extra time to breathe, fed by glacial water and blueness. I remembered how I'd felt trapped in medical school and now feared returning for residency training. But then I admitted the obvious: The privilege of studying medicine was the only reason I was there. Changing professions was impossible because I'd taken out large student loans for medical school. How would I pay them back if I didn't continue?

Journal entry. April 9, 1988, Base Camp.

I had a vivid dream of being buried underground, choking. I gasped and yelled for help; I turned around and saw Joe beside me, also breathless and mute. I woke up in a sweat, gulping for air. I stared at the tent ceiling, catching my breath. I checked on Joe. He was fine. I think my dream is related to thoughts about school and feeling trapped.

After dinner, feeling lightheaded, I realized I was getting my period exactly twenty-eight days after the last one, which I'd had when the support team left. Fortunately, with Robert at Advanced Base, I was tenting alone like a queen, my things spread out all over, enjoying an amazing sunset, with all the privacy I needed to take care of myself.

Snow fell heavily all night, and I awakened to white fog in the morning. While sitting quietly at breakfast, I couldn't catch my breath, and remembered the feeling of choking in my dream. The climbers joined us in Base Camp that evening, thwarted by the storm. They also mentioned feeling suffocated and explained the breathlessness was caused by the low-pressure storm system which delivers fewer oxygen molecules per breath. They named our crazy storms "the Kangshung Microclimate."

So maybe I wasn't choking because of medical school.

Although the nights at Base Camp were as long and endless as at Advanced Base, the days were much better. I walked the solid ground of the moraine with no fear of falling. But I was at risk from a different danger: my thoughts cloaking me with the fear of returning to New York. I didn't know then that whenever I felt confined, my thoughts were the trap. I was filled with chronic self-doubt having nothing to do with where I was or what I did. My unease was part of my inheritance from my father, prompted by his story I'd first heard at age six that turned my life around in an instant. The story that made my breath stall, changed my matter, altered my sense of self. The story that had led me to feel insecure, that had trained my stomach to knot and my mind to churn. The story that had propelled me from somewhere deep toward Base Camp.

The story, a haunting that did not let me rest.

17

Nothing Out of the Ordinary

IN MID-APRIL, ALMOST TWO MONTHS AFTER WE'D LEFT NEW YORK, the grass covering the windswept earth of Base Camp was mostly brown, with spots of soft yellow and a hint of green. During rest days, we looked for things to do, and one day Robert and I hiked up the ridge behind camp to fly a paraglider he'd brought. The wind wasn't strong enough to lift off, but our high vantage point made Base Camp look like a narrow airstrip nestled between peaks.

A few days later, the climbers and I returned to Advanced Base. On the trail, I sang nearly the entire *Wizard of Oz* soundtrack but couldn't remember the Munchkin song. That night, I startled awake at 2:30 a.m., lilting words announcing Dorothy's fall to earth playing in my head.

Although Joe and I got bored at Advanced Base, the climbers returned from the "Neverest Buttress" in the afternoons with astonishing stories of climbing feats and near-fatal misses. One day Robert and Ed stumbled into camp late in the afternoon.

"We reached a huge crevasse with no way around," Robert stretched his arms wide. "Big Al Gully was on the right"—with enormous blocks of ice capable of crushing them in an instant—and no way to maneuver on the left.

"Before I knew it, Ed had climbed down a hundred feet."

"*Into* the crevasse?" Joe dropped his jaw.

Robert nodded. "I followed him. It was so freaky—we were inside the bowels of Everest." While Ed was investigating whether he could climb up the other side, he hammered a screw into the ice, attaching it by rope to his harness for protection in case he fell.

"We heard an atomic blast sound," Robert said. "The hammer made a hyoooooge block of ice explode." Robert stretched his hands wide in the air. "It shattered into giant boulders, right where Ed was." He paused, then choked up. "I thought I'd lost him." He paused again. "I didn't realize Ed was right next to me. He'd flown back in an instant."

"Yeah, so what did Robert do?" Ed interjected. "He said 'go back there so I can take a picture of where I thought I lost you.'"

They climbed up the opposite side of the crevasse and fixed a rope across the top. For the rest of the climb, when they went up and down the route, they crossed the crevasse by hanging upside down and pulling themselves across the rope.

"I hadn't done a Tyrolean traverse since Outward Bound," Robert said.

"No one ever has at this altitude," Ed said, flipping mentally through his encyclopedic knowledge of climbing. They christened the crevasse that had almost derailed the expedition the "Jaws of Doom."

I whispered to Joe, "Please remind me never to complain about being bored."

Stephen knew I was stir-crazy at Advanced Base, eating early, going to bed early, dealing with the insufferable cold. One day he turned to me and said, "Shall we do it?" He had promised to take me ice climbing on one of his rest days, so I grabbed my ice axes, and clomped behind him in my crampons, loving the grip and tinny sound of sharp metal on blue ice. Stephen searched for an ice cliff, then leapt onto an ice wall that rose from a lake for my first ice climbing lesson.

"When your axe gets a purchase, you can then move your feet. You kick the toe point in, and when it sticks, you can move your other axe."

Sounded like a dance move.

He glided up the wall like Spider-Man, alternating axes, and crampons. I followed him: axe, axe, foot, foot. Halfway up, hanging by my arms, I harnessed all my strength and grunted while kicking my crampons into the ice.

"You're making a lot of orgasmic noises." He laughed from above.

I couldn't laugh. I was too busy concentrating on being aggressive, stabbing in the axes and crampons to ascend. *Like dancing, maybe, but much harder.* I rammed in my right axe, then left, gasping, my right foot, grunt, grunt, then left, one, two, counting, breathing hard. Finally, I flung my body across the top of the ledge, panting.

Stephen wasted no time moving on to another pitch.

"Bloody hell. See how the ice shatters every time I try to get a purchase? It's called dinner plating."

"The ice shattering like a plate would?"

"Exactly. Now you try."

I tried. I grunted. I couldn't. My arms were Jell-O.

"Do the first cliff again. It's good practice," Stephen instructed.

We climbed down the back of the cliff, and I went back to the first pitch. I couldn't move. My muscles quivered like a blown electric fuse. Stephen, on the other hand, climbed upwards, traversed sideways, and down-climbed effortlessly using only one axe. I was humbled. And exhilarated. I loved everything about it.

Heavy snowfall that night made us grateful to have dinner under Joe's new shelter, a blue tarp strung over rocks he'd fashioned into seats. I got antsy, singing, dancing, and complaining because no one wanted to put on Broadway shows. The guys smiled and buried their heads in their rehydrated meals.

A massive overnight dump of snow created another depressing delay because of avalanche risk. By afternoon, our amphitheater's curtain of clouds cleared to reveal a radiant sky. The thin atmosphere of our high elevation didn't absorb much of the sun's radiation, so on a sunny day, we could wear T-shirts, even if we'd been wearing two hats and down bibs at night.

The warmth of the sun on my face inspired me to let loose. I slid into our tent and rummaged through my backpack to find something fun to wear. After slipping off my long underwear, I rolled on tie-dyed tights with concentric circles of pink, yellow, and blue, the most feminine thing I'd worn in months. I didn't remember packing them or why I did. I put on a royal blue long-sleeved top that hit mid-thigh, strapped on my tap shoes, and grabbed an umbrella.

Outside, my legs felt chilly in tights. I used my hands to climb up a mound of rocks topped with a flat surface, the East Face a spectacular backdrop. The men were lounging outside their tents.

I shouted, "Guys—look here—the show must go on!" One by one, they looked up. Paul's eyes opened wide with a huge grin. Ed looked over at Robert and chuckled. When they looked at me, a rush of adrenaline moved through me. I started singing, "One" from *A Chorus Line*, clicking my metal taps against the boulder. The guys cheered and my voice rose. I threw off my ugly Stubai mountain cap, tipped my head back and looked at the sky, the sun hot on my cheeks. I turned to the side and kicked my right leg high, then faced the guys and stretched my arms out wide with jazz hands. I swayed my hips side to side, pirouetted, used my umbrella like a cane, and then popped it open for a dramatic finish.

"She's gone full-on bonkers," Stephen said.

"Yeah, but let's join her!" Ed ran to his tent to change clothes.

"Why don't you put on your Kiehl's stuff for sponsor shots?" Joe said. Robert had inspired everyone to wash and cream with Kiehl's, so we happily complied.

The climbers and I dressed up in ski bibs given to us by Kiehl's and posed for pictures, me in tap shoes. They put their hands on their hips, jutted out their chests, and, holding ice axes, imitated my jazz hands.

This time, they followed my lead.

I called it my Guinness-World-Record-Breaking-Highest-Altitude Tap Dance. Doing my favorite thing, in my favorite place, wholly myself and unabashed.

A photo of the climbers looking silly on the glacier is still on display in many Kiehl's stores.

The next day, the sun shimmered off the bright white snow, tiny crystals gleaming, a perfect day for the climbers to carry loads to Camp One, which they'd established a few days earlier. They needed only a few more carries of supplies to store at the higher camps before the final summit attempt—the moment we'd been waiting for.

Ed turned to me and said, "I can't climb today. My knee's throbbing." I leaned in close, gently palpating an inflamed, red nodule, while he winced. "It's a small abscess, Ed. Maybe an ingrown hair." I cleaned it with hydrogen peroxide, dressed it with gauze, and canceled my plans to return to Base Camp in case Ed needed me. Stephen and Paul left for Camp One, and Robert hung back with Ed.

Robert and I chatted on the "stoop"—boulders facing the mountain.

"You're less hard-edged than you used to be." He stared straight ahead.

"What does that mean?" I tilted my head to the side.

"Your whole New York thing. You were so cautious when we met. You didn't trust how we felt about each other." I'd been focused on the ways Robert wasn't opening up, not recognizing that I was just as guarded.

"Okay. So, let's talk. Tell me about your girlfriend."

He shook his head. "No, it's not relevant."

"Why not?"

"Because we're here now, and I don't want to talk about it."

"Okay. So, let's talk about New York pizza. I can take you out to the best place when you visit!" I reverted to our usual banter instead of discussing what the hell we were doing rooming together with significant others at home.

"No. I can't talk about pizza—it's too hard," he smiled. Almost three months in, everything was hard about missing the comforts of normal life, food, communication with the outside world.

After a pause he said, "I'm humble when I meet people." That thought came out of nowhere, but he was opening up.

"I beg to differ based on our first meeting."

"It's obvious I knew you already."

That night, Robert and I read quietly in our respective cocoons by the light of a diminishing candle. When it blew out, the smell of smoke smoldered in silence. As I lay awake, listening to the sounds of snowfall in night, the faithful drop, drop, drop, a piercing avalanche from Lhotse boomed. Startled, I wondered if this one was serious, so I woke Robert up. We listened to the fall, the flow, the timber, the cadence, the tumble of rolling acoustic waves, one after another. "It's nothing out of the ordinary," Robert whispered. But on that mountain, everything was out of the ordinary for me.

The whole team returned to Base Camp for R & R, and I walked behind Robert. He pulled far ahead, and I passed a heart he'd drawn in the snow next to the trail. My whole body filled with a warm tingle. I thought of Blondie's "Heart of Glass," and how inaccessible he felt, despite his rare endearing comments and our infrequent moments of genuine connection.

Journal entry. April 23, 1988, 7:30 a.m. bed tea at Base Camp.

Joe shouts from his tent, "My pulse is 48!" [proud he was well adapted to the altitude]. Robert yells, "No wonder your toes are cold." Robert is wearing a hat that can only honestly be called a bonnet. With his tweed knee-length knickers, I doubt he would dress this way in real life. We are all a bit ridiculous, tipsy from isolation.

Snow continued all day. Paul said, "The day at altitude goes so quickly because the brain moves so slowly."

One afternoon, while Kasang fetched water, he observed a hawk attack a small pheasant, killing it instantly with a bite to its neck. He swept in and proudly brought the pheasant back to cook.

"You're not thinking of eating that?" I shouted, as the guys' mouths watered. "You're going to get sick," I warned. "Maybe it has diseases. Also, you haven't been eating meat, so your digestion will be screwed."

They ignored me and devoured "Charlie," as they named the bird. I boycotted the meal, joining them after Charlie was cleared, in time to see them licking their fingers. Even as I suffered the effects of their indigestion, I doubted they would heed my warnings about eating meat if another "Charlie" were captured.

One day, Robert, Joe, and I walked to the site of the previous American expedition's Base Camp farther up the moraine. Robert started bouldering, climbing rocks low to the ground, while Joe photographed him. I picked out a trail behind them toward a pointy brown summit. The weather cycled rapidly between a misty breeze of hail, and clear blue warmth with a lingering aroma of petrichor. I hesitated. *Will they be pissed at me for climbing alone?* The summit was alluring, so I forged ahead. I squeezed my body around huge boulders, slippery with snow, navigated gaping holes between rocks, and reached a dip below the peak, panting heavily. I didn't want them to worry so I ran back, deciding to return another time, but I was emboldened to physically challenge myself. I wanted to chart my own course, different from the guys but strong in my own way.

The following morning was gray, and at breakfast, everyone laughed at my hair, greasy spikes pointing every which way. I crossed my arms in front of my chest and frowned, but they just laughed more. Finally, I joined them laughing, which morphed into crying. I huffed out of the tent and returned wearing Joe's gas mask. "I may look like shit, but you guys stink!"

In the afternoon, I returned alone to my previous day's peak and summitted, setting my high-altitude record around 21,000 feet. I sang during my descent to keep myself company. Words from The Who's *Tommy* album and Joni Mitchell's *Blue* sailed into the Tibetan sky.

My moods, like my steps, cycled from down to up and back down again.

The afternoon before the climbers and Joe returned to Advanced Base, I conducted research, examining their eyes for signs of retinal hemorrhage, a risk at high altitude. I decided to stay longer in Base Camp before the looming summit bid, when I'd be needed full-time at Advanced Base in case of illness or injury.

Walking back to the tent after dinner, Robert said, "We're getting along so well."

"Yeah," I joked, "you'd think we'd be divorcing by now, in separate tents, fighting over who gets the dog."

He draped his puffy down jacket arm around my shoulder, and I knew in that moment I wouldn't return to dating Steve. I cared for him, but we had an energy mismatch—his felt frenetic. I couldn't read when he was in the room without feeling like he needed something from me, and I realized my measure of who I'd date going forward was whether we could read peacefully in the same room—or tent—together.

The next day, when the climbers and Joe left for Advanced Base, I challenged myself to a lovely flat jog in the valley. Being able to run at 17,000 feet perked me up. That night was bright, but with a heavy cloud layer portending another storm. I had my first moment of doubt whether they'd complete the route. The monsoon season, beginning late spring, was closing in, and I was skeptical about the Kangshung microclimate.

Pasang summoned me to dinner. Entering the warm orange tent, I was surprised to smell dal bhat and encounter a large group: Pasang, Kasang, AngChu (one of the Tibetan leaders from our trek in), and his brother, Angkya.

Pasang relished being the "big boss," while Kasang pranced proudly from stove to table, his stringy long braids bouncing. He'd transformed since we first met near Kharta, now wearing our team's clothing, fully one of us. Beaming with pride, he showed off to the visitors how much he'd learned under Pasang's tutelage.

Kasang made me laugh until I cried again. He imitated the slow walkers: Pasang, Ed, Joe, and me, bent over, shuffling, huffing, and puffing and holding out our hands asking for tea. Then the fast walkers: Robert, Stephen, Paul and Kasang, standing erect and briskly covering ground, smiling. His mimic made me think of my father, "the fastest walker in Latvia." I wished I'd gotten those genes.

The next morning, I challenged myself to hike up another peak. On the summit, I was as high as the *Neverest Buttress*, close to 22,000 feet, with a clear 360-degree view: Tibet to the east, Khartse to the north, Everest to the west, and Makalu/Pethangste to the south. Raising my arms, pumping the sky, I yelped out loud: *Woohoo!*

I built a small cairn and sat cross-legged, admiring the view, rubbing my hands together for warmth and listening to the breeze. Suddenly a loud noise thundered, *pop, pop, pop,* and the earth shook. The pops set off a small hurricane of snow from a spot on the ground in front of me. Round balls of ice whirled upwards in a foot-high twister. Another *pop* boomed. I ran as fast as possible to get out of there. I feared an earthquake, another risk in the Himalayas.

At dinner, I questioned whether the others had felt a quake, but no one noticed anything besides the routine avalanches. As we cleaned up,

Pasang hummed a tune and stomped his feet in rhythm to show our guests he knew Tibetan dance. We all joined in, then shuffled to the melodies of Nepal radio. Kasang promised that after the climbers made the summit, "Big party in Kharta with chang and dance." After I left, the laughter and stomping continued. I watched their shadows sway in the tent, grateful for the understanding and relationship we now had with the Tibetans, instead of the tension we'd had during the walk in. I didn't feel singled out or like an outsider. I felt friendship.

On May 1, all four climbers broke trail and carried loads to a new height on the mountain, establishing Camp Two. Situated under an overhanging ice cliff at 24,442 feet, they called it "The Flying Wing." They stashed loads and returned to Camp One to sleep. The following day they spent a rest day at Camp One while the weather deteriorated. Again.

Our team's plan for the summit bid had involved reaching Camp One on the first day of climbing, well stocked with tents and food rations from earlier load carries. The second day they'd go to Camp Two, The Flying Wing. On the third day they planned to cover new ground up the Face and reach the South Col, the saddle between the East Face and the Nepali south side of the mountain, completing their new route on Everest. There, they hoped to join the standard route from Nepal, also called the "yak route" for its popularity, pitch tents on the South Col, rest, and leave for the summit bid late on the evening of that third day. The fourth day they would continue to the summit, then return to the South Col. On the fifth day they'd descend back to us. While reaching the South Col would take three days, descending could be accomplished in a single day, gravity in their favor. For this plan, they needed five straight days of decent weather. That felt like wishful thinking.

Pasang, Kasang, and I cranked the dial on the radio in Base Camp past the fuzz to hear news from Nepal. "The Friendship expedition plans to summit Everest on May 5th." The team who bumped us out of our hotel rooms in Xegar were four days away from attempting to reach the top from other sides of the mountain. I told Pasang I'd leave for Advanced Base in the morning since our guys might also be close to a summit bid.

When I reached Advanced Base, all the climbers were on the mountain. Without a radio to communicate, Joe and I wondered if they were going for the summit bid, but in the afternoon, their voices approached from the distance.

They'd descended because of bad weather.

Joe and I were growing impatient. He missed his family, and I was nervous about returning late for school. We needed to be supportive, but each time they came back down the mountain, it lengthened the trip. We slipped into his tent.

"Why do they keep returning? The weather's not that bad," he whispered.

I nodded. "Maybe they don't really want to go up. Maybe they're terrified."

I'd be terrified. Whispering these thoughts was a huge betrayal, and we confessed how guilty we felt second-guessing their decisions. We knew it wasn't our place to do so. It was our lowest moment. But venting with each other brought comfort in the face of powerlessness. Weather, and the climbers' decisions, were out of our control.

On May 5, the day of the scheduled summit bid for the Friendship Expedition, the weather was gorgeous. Everest's iconic plume, waving like a flag on windy days, was barely visible, the expanse of blue sky unbroken.

But our team was separated. It had been snowing heavily with multiple avalanches the day before, so Ed and Paul had gone to Base Camp to rest. Waking up to glorious weather they quickly returned to Advanced Base.

The air was crisp as steel and the sky blue and clear when the climbers lined up for a picture, dressed in their gear to leave again for a summit bid. No ominous clouds gathering, no whirling flakes of snow.

Stephen shouted, "Come on, Yanks! This time we'll bloody make it!" He darted across the glacier, always the quickest to depart.

"It's a beautiful day in the neighborhood," Robert sang in his cheery voice as he slung his large red pack onto his shoulders, climbing ropes draped around his torso, ready for an Everest rodeo. He hugged me. "See you when I'm home from the office!" His long legs bounced away as if on springs.

"We're coming! Hold your British hawwwwwses," Paul yelled at Stephen, feigning an English accent as he lumbered away with his lovable bowlegged gait. He waved to Joe and me. "Bye dudes!"

Falling in line, Ed turned for a final look at camp, as if taking measure of what he was leaving. When his eyes met mine, I was struck by the significance of this moment we had waited so long for. They were finally leaving for the summit, moving into uncharted territory, and anything might happen. I was never far from my fear of the worst happening to one of these guys I'd bonded with. I was also never far from the fear of being forced to address a serious injury. What if I failed? I reminded myself confidence is key, and so is faith. Ed waved his red oversized mittens, "See you guys, love you!"

Joe and I waved back and watched them march off in colorful gear, across the rubble and the white, their crampons cracking the ice.

"Woohoo!" yelled Joe.

"Stay safe!" I whooped, waving my arms wildly, as they moved farther into the white.

Joe said under his breath with a smirk, "See you for dinner!"

Indeed, snow rolled in at dusk, and we heard the climbers' voices as they returned to camp, defeated by bad weather. I felt so frustrated that I didn't join the discussion about what to do.

Moods were grim all around.

The glacier was melting under our feet in the spring warmth. Whereas before I'd been sleeping on a mattress of snow, I now slept on lumpy rock. As Robert neared our tent, his foot plunged into a pool of water. We needed to find a different spot, and soon. Another sign we needed to get this summit bid done and dusted.

Stephen brought his whiskey to dinner. After one sip, I picked up a package of Rehydrate drink mix and quizzed Joe, "How many carbohydrates per package? How much sugar?" At times when I had nothing to read or do, I memorized food packages. I turned to Stephen, the Oxford graduate, and said, "Okay, wise guy, tell me how much protein in our mixed rice and beans box?" I picked up packages, one by one, and quizzed them on the nutritional information.

"She's bonkers again," Stephen observed.

"Classic tent fever," added Joe. We laughed under the tarp until 8:30, a late and raucous evening.

After another few false starts, on the evening of May 7, Joe and I delivered dinner to the climbers' tents and filled water bottles, hoping they might rest and get a fresh start in the morning. The night cleared and the moon shone brilliantly. At 1:00 a.m., when I had to pee, the temperature was warm enough to go outside. In the bright moonlight, the mountain's face was clear, its ridges defined as if by black marker. I woke up again at 4:00 a.m. to check the weather and found an impeccably clear day. We were behind schedule. I wondered: *Will they ever leave for the summit?*

18

Lost in the Sky

"Robert, what do you think of the weather?" Ed shouted from his tent the morning of May 8. "There's fog in the valley, and every time there's been fog, it snowed." The pit in my stomach churned at the thought of another delay when I looked outside at a cloudless dawn.

"We have to go for it," Robert said. "Not many more days of the season to try." With the short window of fine weather in May, it was now or never.

Yes! I ran to the stove to start breakfast.

After the climbers left, Joe and I watched them through the telescope. We were relieved to see them reach Camp One to sleep, with no storm brewing to turn them back.

The East Face up to the Col was a massive white wall, completely visible to us. The next day, we watched the climbers wading in thigh-deep snow, in steady snowfall, to reach Camp Two at dusk.

On the third day of May 10, Joe and I were thrilled by the morning's crystal-clear sky. We watched the climbers get a slow start, occasionally seeing a head pop up in the viewfinder, figuring they were exhausted from the long slog to Camp Two. They finally left at 7:30 a.m. We knew their plan was to reach the South Col in four hours and rest there before starting their summit bid at 10:00 that evening. By midmorning the temperature was warm enough that Joe and I wore T-shirts to air out our bodies in the sunshine. We sang and danced around camp, composing a skit to surprise the guys called "Support Team Dudes."

In the late afternoon, massive winds howled. The glacier cracked emphatically beneath us. An avalanche scuffed the side of the route and gushed down Big Al. Everything smelled raw and rotting as the snow-melt unearthed rock, silt, and decomposing matter that had been buried for months of winter.

We watched the climbers' inching pace, noting how much effort each step took. Then, clouds shifted obscuring the top of the mountain and we lost sight of them. We figured since they'd never climbed this slope before, the combination of steep terrain, extreme elevation and no supplemental oxygen, must have been extremely challenging. Just before nightfall, we thought we spotted tracks all the way to the Col. That would mean they'd accomplished an amazing feat: a new route on Everest, without oxygen or porter support.

But it also meant a grueling, twelve-hour day for them. Much longer than anticipated.

Joe and I bunked together to watch the summit bid. We scrutinized the mountain at 11:00 p.m., midnight, and 2:00 a.m., hoping to spot headlights. We stayed up until the chill of morning, when we watched a spectacular sunrise fanning over the Face.

At 7:40 a.m., Joe spotted someone descending the route with a wide gait. Soon we recognized Paul. No one else followed. We anxiously awaited his arrival, concerned about an accident or injury. Confused because he moved speedily, we watched him glissade, or ride on his ass, most of the way down the snowy slopes. He reached Camp One before noon. When he reached the flat of the glacier, Joe and I hurried to meet him.

"Dudes, I was hammered," Paul said. "My head felt like it was in a vise. I was close to jinjiput! (our team's word for *dead*). I was up all night vomiting, coughing up blood. Dudes, there was no question. I almost bit it." Paul looked pale, his hair matted, the corners of his eyes tight. I was eager to get him to the tent and assess him.

"Why did you descend alone?" I asked. "You sound like you were in pretty bad shape."

"No, they wanted to come with me. But I left before they could get ready. I got better quickly. By the time I reached Camp Two I was already feeling like myself."

Paul's symptoms suggested severe altitude sickness, including cerebral and pulmonary edema. We laid him down. Joe put water on for tea, and I examined him. He was coherent and his vital signs were good. Judging by his appearance, descending had cured him. He had a touch of frostnip on the tips of his fingers but otherwise seemed healthy and unscathed. When I beamed the ophthalmoscope in his eyes, his eyes bounded side to side in a tiny involuntary movement—nystagmus—a symptom of brain disturbance but not dangerous on its own.

"Dude, you completed a new route on Everest. Congratulations!" Joe beamed hearing the good news about the climb's progress. "It's amazing how fast you made it down in the shape you were in."

"You got down the whole route in half a day!" I added.

Paul's severe symptoms resolved quickly because he descended a whopping 8,000 feet. We spent the rest of the day pumping Paul with food and liquids, surprised at his rapid improvement.

Paul had accomplished a heroic and ultimately selfless feat. He not only completed a new route but descended on his own so as not to disrupt his teammates' climb. That he'd been astute enough to decide to descend was impressive proof that small decisions can make the difference between life and death. Yet he was not with the others on his way to Everest's summit. Did I detect some disappointment in his eyes, in addition to the nystagmus? In true Paul fashion, if he felt badly, he didn't let on. Although I was thrilled about his physical well-being, I couldn't help feeling a little disappointed for him, too.

Paul explained the others would be delayed by a day. Since it had taken so long to get to the Col, Robert, Stephen, and Ed were resting and intended to start for the summit that night. They'd return to the Col by the end of the following day, May 12, spending an extra day in the Death Zone.

Joe and I got a 4:00 a.m. start the next day and glued our eyes to the telescope. The peak was clear but soon clouds rolled in. There was no sign of the climbers. We stared at the Face, mesmerized by waterfalls of spindrift and drapes of snow dangling from the triangular buttress. Pasang and AngChu came from Base Camp, wondering if we needed help since they, too, saw nothing on the route.

"AngChu wants to show you something," Pasang said. AngChu lifted his left pant leg and removed his sock. Overwhelmed by the odor, I asked him to wash his foot before leaning in for a closer look, which revealed a bright circular red mark and some swelling.

"I've never seen anything like it," I said. They explained he had twisted his ankle and had gone to a Tibetan doctor, who did "cupping" on it, leaving that mark. I cleaned and wrapped his ankle with an ACE bandage. "AngChu, come back if it's not getting better."

We scrutinized the clear Col for a long time, our faces turned upwards, and saw no sign of Robert, Ed, and Stephen all morning. Sometimes we looked so hard, we imagined movement when there was none.

"Maybe they got back to the Col very late and crashed," I offered hopefully.

Joe kept his eyes glued to the scope. "Maybe they met climbers from the Friendship Team and decided to descend a different route into Tibet or Nepal."

I prayed he was right.

As it darkened, our feet numbed, so we retreated to Joe's tent, and sang songs from *West Side Story*. He became weary, and I was wired, so finally he announced, "Dude, I'm going to sleep."

We watched for three more days. One day, the South Col was foggy, suggesting snow. One night there was snow and lightning. Another night, monsoon snows, and still no sign of the climbers. When all I wanted was a sign from the mountain, I received a packet of mail. My father had written about a recent bout with the flu. I thought of his losses in the storm of war, helpless to save those he loved. Here, I stared into a different storm, helpless to rescue my teammates.

He also wrote me that Josh, who worked in the music industry, was away touring with a band. I thought of the contrast of Josh in movement and me in waiting. We'd both found ways to be transported to other worlds, both in improbable places that our parents had no languages for. Places with distinct beats, pulses, soundtracks, and possibilities.

Staring up at the East Face, missing our lost climbers, my thoughts scoured the past for the moments of warmth and tenderness we'd shared. I'd first met Robert at the expedition party and Ed the following night at the Shabbat dinner in Nepal.

Ed had told us during the hike to Base Camp about how he'd lost his girlfriend, Lauren, years earlier in a tragic climbing accident. They were together when she fell off a cliff in Colorado. He had also been deeply affected by the loss of the climber Roger Marshall, who he'd been to Everest with on a prior expedition. Now, I feared I'd lost Ed, along with Robert, and Stephen.

Ed was the first to teach me rock climbing, in Eldorado Canyon near Boulder, before I'd been invited to join the team. I visited him during my first winter break of medical school, relieved to escape the pace and workload. The day was cold, but the sun shined like a neon lemon. Ed explained knots and safety, clipped the rope into my harness, then patiently guided me up the rock while I stretched my double-jointed, dancer-trained limbs to reach distant handholds and cling to slippery cracks. I was breathless with all sorts of fears: slipping, falling, instability, heights. At one point, I couldn't figure out how to move and froze. My legs shook violently.

"That's called 'sewing machine legs,'" Ed yelled down.

Ed taught me the importance of trust in a climbing partner. I later learned that day together was also a test to see if I'd be a good candidate to join them on Everest.

Next, I spent time with Robert, who was in Colorado visiting family.

"I'm surprised you can ski," Robert called to me through a huge grin on a slope at Keystone, the rest of his face hidden behind goggles and a helmet.

"I love it!" I shouted back, giddy to be sharing a new mountain experience with him.

My skiing was mediocre, but whenever I got the chance to ski, I was the first on the lift in the morning and the last off at the end of the day. That afternoon, the chairlift that connected two hubs of the resort broke down, while snow fell sideways in heavy sheets. We needed to find another way back to the main parking lot three miles away. Cross-country skiing in our downhill skis translated to a miserable mess. Robert spotted a snowcat loading skiers for the drive back. All the seats were taken.

"Grab on!" he yelled. I didn't have time to think since the vehicle was moving. A long rope was rigged to the back. I struggled to sidestep, wobbling in skis to grab the rope trailing on the ground. I picked it up and clung for dear life, shivering, wet, and terrified I'd lose my grip and wipe out. Robert, in contrast, barely hung on with one arm while using the other to pull additional skiers onto the rope. Effortlessly taking charge, he laughed, enjoying every moment of this precarious and prescient adventure.

Thinking about Robert and Ed while I waited beneath the East Face, I almost heard Robert's laughter. Being tethered to rocks and gliding down snowy slopes was their natural place in the world. *At least they're doing what they love more than anything else.*

That we'd been through this much together and now they were missing, and likely dead was unfathomable. As unfathomable as it was for me to comprehend the deaths of my grandparents, aunts, and uncle I'd never met, or my father surviving it all.

My throat felt thick, and my eyes welled thinking about Dad. Perhaps he was staving off more devastation by staying remote, as if behind a wall of glass. I'd always felt sad for him for having endured such loss. Maybe I'd understand him more now, knowing how it felt to want to escape the pain of connection that would ultimately cause grief.

Shivering in my sleeping bag, the blizzard pelting the tent, my friends gone, I wondered if I'd made a huge mistake coming here. Forming intense bonds—being vulnerable together—then losing them. No answers came, just the wind thrashing the tent and the taste of salty tears trailing into my mouth, reminding me of my first yak butter tea in Nepal.

The first morning of my trek in the Everest region, I attended a special blessing ceremony in a wealthy villager's home near Namche Bazaar. Women bent over vats, churning salty butter tea in the kitchen, stencils of steam floating upward. Brewed with dark leaves, lots of salt and yak butter, the mixture tasted like drinking barn. I spent all day there with

LOST IN THE SKY

several other climbers I'd met, being fed steamed doughballs, yak stew, Tibetan fried doughnuts, and endless salty tea. Monks sculpted and painted statuettes out of butter and molded 150 cones of tsampa, with red pinnacles to represent the 150 families in the village blessed that day.

An older monk with a goatee and glasses said, "When the light leaves your eyes, it will be replaced by water." So it was, because when I left the monks and sat in the dim kitchen by the light of the fire, barely seeing but listening to the low pitch of vibrating chants, my eyes filled and ran over from a feeling of spiritual fullness, a certain oneness. At the end of the day, the monks wrapped their books in white lace and red cloth, placed them in a big stack, and clapped a rhythm with final prayers.

The monks were deliberate, calm, in the present. I was reminded of my training for this trip, those long runs, pacing my breath as I ran, calming with the effort. This was another lesson from the mountains, and I tried to hold on tightly to it now, even if it offered only the smallest comfort: Every breath is a breath. Nobody controls the future. Not every misstep can be predicted, even if you wished and worked for it to be otherwise.

Taking a deep breath, the cold air in my nostrils, exhaling, with my shoulders releasing, I swallowed my fear. There was nowhere to hide and no way to quit. Maybe our teammates were on the mountain facing their biggest fears at this very moment. Maybe we were connected.

Before I drifted off to sleep, I remembered how the day of blessings had ended in the village. The donkeys outside floated through flurries, their collar bells singing a love song in the storm. I hummed into the air sending strength and love to Robert, Ed, and Stephen. *Be strong. Come back.*

Nine days after their departure, we gave up hope that Stephen, Robert, and Ed were still alive on our route.

Their time in the Death Zone was beyond the limits of survival.

I'd never see Robert again. Even without a defined relationship, I had thought he'd be in my life forever as a friend. We were going to celebrate in Lhasa and Hong Kong on the way home. We had more pizza places to try. We would meet at a café in Paris. We would climb other mountains.

There was nothing to do but pull up camp. We threw food and gear into our big blue barrels. I dragged my leaden limbs from barrel to barrel, as if wading through thick sludge. My head exploded with what-ifs. I didn't want to touch anyone's personal stuff.

I looked for a book in Robert's duffel. I handled his quirky woolen knickers and furry Russian hat and fell to my knees. Seeing the things that made Robert unique and lovable, I doubled over and heaved.

Just in case, Joe descended to Base Camp to send questions with a mail runner, who would take five days to reach the valley floor: Did our climbers join another team? Has anyone seen or heard from them?

Paul and I would leave the next morning. We bunked together in the last tent standing on the melting glacier of Advanced Base Camp, the dripping sound of thawing ice a constant backdrop of dissolution. We curled up in our sleeping bags, and repeated possibilities and scenarios.

"They must have taken another route. They're tough," Paul whispered. After a deep sigh, he added "They would have found a way."

"They're amazing climbers," I said.

In the eerie silence, I heard their voices in my head, coming up the glacier the way they did at the end of a typical day of climbing. I heard their voices, and I heard the never-ending avalanches, as if nothing had changed.

The wind rattled the tent. Paul stroked my hair as I wept into the down of my sleeping bag. I turned to look at him and recognized his despair as my own. We embraced—then quickly separated. He reached out his hand to hold mine in comfort. Shock and loss had unbound my mind from my body, creating a separate hovering observer, one able to escape pain. From above, I saw us facing away from each other, alone in our separate bags. We hated ourselves for being alive and needed to simmer in our separate sadness.

We'd been using our routine sleeping pills to get through the last few nights but that night I dug into my medical kit for a stronger sedative, one we'd never taken before. We melted into the deepest darkness available, the only relief available from the endless white.

Paul bolted uprightly a few hours later. "I hear voices."

"What?" I said groggily.

"Listen." He held his hand out to shush me.

I inched up on one elbow. I heard the tent flap rattling. Nothing else.

I sat up fully and wrapped my arms around my body, straining to listen. It was 4:00 a.m. and still dark. The wind abated for a moment.

"Hey!" Someone said. "Hey! Joe! Mimi! Paul!"

I sat for a second, alarmed, thinking I might still be dreaming. The voice came again.

"Hey!" It was Stephen. A voice we hadn't heard in ten days.

I gasped. "Oh my God!" While my words were rolling out, Paul had already darted outside, my brain a beat behind. I pulled on my boots, my heart pounding in my ears, and ran after him, loose laces tripping me on the rocks in the blackness.

Faint voices shouted again.

Could it be?

I barely saw the outline of Paul guiding Stephen up the hill that led to our camp, Ed not far behind. I ran to the stove to put water on to boil—they would surely need fluids—then back to the tent. My feet moved automatically but my numb, cold brain couldn't keep up. Paul gently laid Stephen's gaunt body down in the tent.

"Stephen!" I kneeled, my hands on his chest, gasping.

"Orange," he said through closed eyes. *Shit, he wants orange Rehydrate and we're out.*

"Dude, what happened?" Paul asked while I ran a few yards away to get the grapefruit mix, already packed in a barrel.

"We saw no signs of you! We packed up Camp!" I handed him the drink.

"We made it. The summit." Stephen's eyelids fluttered, swallowed by desperate fatigue. I grabbed Paul's sleeping bag, piled it on top of Stephen, and rubbed his torso. "I shouldn't have left Robert." He opened his eyes and looked at me. "He's still on the mountain." I'd assumed Robert was a few steps behind. Stephen felt guilty about leaving him. *Why? Is he injured?*

Paul ran outside to help Ed.

I grabbed my medical instruments from my sleeping bag where I kept them warm and ready for use. I took Stephen's blood pressure, pulse, and temperature. He was dehydrated and mildly hypothermic with a temperature of 96°F. His nose was white, and he was shivering. We warmed him up by removing all his clothing, wet from snow and sweat, and dressed him in fresh dry clothes, layering our sleeping bags back on top of him.

"Stephen, is it okay if I remove your gloves? I need to look at your fingers."

"Yeah, okay."

I peeled off his gloves. Underneath were pale fingertips, no longer frozen and about to experience the heat of daytime.

"Stephen, I'm going to give your fingers a warm bath. Looks like there's some frostbite."

Frostbite results from exposure to extreme cold when the body shuts off the blood flow to the most distal tips of extremities to conserve important flow to the internal organs. The decreased blood flow also deprives the tissues of oxygen. Warming treatment baths for frostbite are supposed to be given when extremities are frozen, have not yet thawed, and are not at risk of refreezing which can cause damage.

Stephen's fingers might have frozen and thawed several times during his descent. Since I didn't know what they'd been through, I proceeded with the treatment. At least his fingers were no longer at risk of freezing, and the bath would allow the tissue to be thoroughly and rapidly rewarmed and cleaned. I boiled water for the rewarming protocol and waited for it to cool. At 100°F, I added antiseptic and carried the bowl quickly and carefully to the tent. I placed Stephen's fingers in the warm liquid. He moved, barely, but his eyes remained closed. He seemed far away.

In the meantime, Paul had helped Ed to Camp, and laid him beside Stephen in the tent. Ed's eyes had a wild look, and his hair stood straight up like a troll doll. Noting his blood pressure as good, his pulse rapid, I found him also mildly hypothermic. Paul undressed and warmed him, while I rubbed the stethoscope between my palms before pressing the metal onto his chest. His breath sounds were clear.

I moved on to his hands, gently pulling back his mittens. My heart stopped. The skin of most of his fingers was completely denuded, hanging from the middle of his fingers like unraveled yarn. When Paul saw Ed's fingers, he got out our single emergency oxygen canister and hooked Ed up with a nasal cannula. His condition was severe, his tissues starved of blood flow and oxygen.

Ed looked at me. "Is it bad?"

"Guys, what happened?" I asked, changing the subject. "We didn't think we'd see you again."

"We were too wiped to move," Stephen whispered.

"He made the summit." Ed tipped his head toward Stephen.

"He got us down." Stephen nodded at Ed, his voice cracking. "But we needed to get here so badly we left Robert."

"Robert's behind us on the route," Ed said.

I sprinted to put up more water to boil for Ed's finger bath. We had only one small burner. The water baths had to be twenty minutes long and required carefully adding hotter water to keep the temperature right. Paul kept the water boiling, then carried it over and helped me administer the baths. While I opened packages of gauze and cut strips of tape for dressings, Ed and Stephen described a long summit day during which they had all struggled in the Death Zone.

They had climbed as individuals, unroped, each man for himself. Stephen pulled ahead, the only one to make the summit (29,035 feet), but it was too late in the day to return to the South Col. He sat in the snow all night, around 28,000 feet, shivering and hallucinating from hypoxia. His enormous strength of body and mind allowed him to survive.

Robert and Ed made the South Summit, around three hundred feet short of their goal, before turning around. They spent the night in an empty tent that had been abandoned by the Friendship expedition.

The following day, the three were reunited, a day they wasted lying in their tents at the South Col. Another extra day in the Death Zone—too tired to descend.

Once they left the Col, Robert, Ed, and Stephen spent two nights in extreme lethargy at Camp Two, below the Death Zone, unable to harness the strength to move and get down. They were hypoxic, dehydrated and starving, with little food or gas to melt snow for water. On the morning of the third day there, Ed left, warning, "Don't wait long, Stephen. You've got to get up and move. If you don't get down alive, you won't be able to enjoy being famous." Eventually Stephen caught up with Ed, but Robert lagged, and they pulled away from him above Camp One. Once Ed and Stephen got their momentum, they didn't stop for anything, digging out sections of rope in the dark, their headlamp bulbs burned out. They had hardly eaten in five days and were fighting through what would be a nineteen-hour day with no water.

Stephen lifted his head. "We were screaming for you!"

"We didn't hear you." I bit my lower lip. "We took sleeping pills. I'm so sorry." My throat swelled nearly shut. We could have helped them sooner.

"We thought you were dead." My eyes watered again, and my chest tightened. All those days I'd thought they were gone, and now they were back. We'd been so certain, otherwise we wouldn't have packed up camp.

From our place on the glacier, Paul spotted movement on the mountain. A dark figure moving below Camp One. He ran to the telescope.

"Robert's coming down the ropes." Paul ran back to me. "I'm going up to help him." I took a deep breath. Robert would be back soon.

I turned my focus on Ed, dipping his fingers in the tepid water. He cried out in pain. I dug out some Tylenol with codeine and held a cup up to his lips.

"I took pictures of sunrise the morning of the summit bid," Ed said, staring at his fingers.

"So, that's when your fingers froze?"

"Yes," Ed whispered, and hung his head. "I took my mittens off."

He explained he'd only worn liner gloves and his fingers froze to the camera's metal while he shot about twenty pictures. Joe and I had watched that sunrise.

"Is it bad?" he asked again through half-closed eyes.

I looked up at him to answer but he'd fallen asleep. I dressed each finger separately with gauze, sterilized the bowl again, and repeated the process for his and Stephen's badly frostbitten toes. In between baths I filled a barrel with new snow to melt and woke them to feed them an endless amount of tea and soup.

A few hours later, I bumped into Kasang while running to the stove to sterilize the bowl. "Happy," he said while knocking his heart, his eyes smiling. He, Joe, and Pasang were setting up camp again. AngChu and Sonam were stringing a tarp to work under in the snow. Joe had a good view of Robert through the scope. "He's moving down steadily."

By afternoon, Paul had returned from up the glacier without Robert but with a knee injury. He had twisted it on the uneven rubble. The severe stress did not help his balance. I wrapped it with an Ace bandage, and he descended to Base Camp with the Tibetans, dejected that he couldn't help. Joe went up the glacier to find Robert.

I had been crouching for much of the day and now stood up in falling wet snow, my bones stiff, chilled, and creaking like the glacier. Robert still wasn't back, and I didn't know what kind of shape he was in, why he was this delayed. I looked at Stephen and Ed sleeping side by side, men who had endured the liminal border of blackness and had defied the odds. Their battle with the mountain was over, but as with many traumas, the struggle was just beginning.

While sterilizing instruments several hours later, I heard something and looked around camp. Searching the glacier, I saw a speck in the distance. *Is it Robert?* The speck got closer and bigger. It had to be. He was a few hundred yards away, lumbering up the glacier, leaning on Joe. I raced toward them. I squeezed Robert in a big hug, but his hands hung stiffly by his sides. "Hey," he said.

"I was afraid I'd never see you again." My eyes welled up as I held his two mittens in mine. His eyes were vacant, his face gaunt. I bolted back to camp to set up for his care.

Joe patiently guided Robert back and settled him into our tent, resurrected by the Tibetans. I repeated the same medical processes: examining, warming, and hydrating him, and water baths for his fingers and toes. His fingers were frozen and mottled, pink at the bases and mostly white and woody at the tips. The skin was intact, but the frostbite looked severe. Three of his toes were also white.

"Hey, we made it," he said with a small smile. His unguided team had created a new route and had gotten one man to the summit. His eyes closed, and he whispered something unintelligible.

In the evening, when I finished dressing Robert's hands and feet, I reached into a barrel for a box of noodles to cook dinner, and the light went dark. My headlamp was blown. Feeling my way around, touching lined-up barrels, I bumped into the stove and knocked over a pan of heated water. *Dammit! Wasted water and propane.* I sucked in air through flaring nostrils, crumbled onto a rock, and buried my head in my hands, my entire body shaking. This was no time to lose it. I put another pot on.

Joe was in Ed and Stephen's tent, attending to them. It was late when I brought them noodles and went to feed Robert. When I lifted a forkful into his mouth, he became agitated and stammered, "Did you see that?" *No*, I thought, *there's nothing here.*

Robert insisted people had spoken to him in the tent, had moved around him. "I saw a lot of things on the mountain," he said, mumbling and muttering while his eyes grew heavy. His body melted into the layers of down and his breathing calmed with the slow rhythm of sleep.

When I finished boiling water for drinks, I sat down again on a rock, and looked up at the ashen dawn sky. I replayed the past twenty-four hours. We'd drugged ourselves to sleep thinking our friends gone. We'd heard their voices, then worked nonstop. Now I wondered: *Did I forget anything? Did I follow the protocols correctly? Is there anything else I should be doing?* My stomach seized with the memory of images from Maurice Herzog's *Annapurna*, of frostbite that turned gangrenous and required amputation.

I took a deep breath. Our guys seemed okay. I'd worked all day under snowfall, which made it impossible to keep things organized and sterile, but they were improving. Most importantly, they were home and alive.

At the moment that I remembered how quickly everyone had rushed to pitch in, my body surrendered to swelling sobs. I rocked back and forth on the cold rocks, crossed my arms, and squeezed myself, thanking God, the universe, Pasang, Kasang, Joe, Paul, and our Tibetan visitors. For the past few days, I'd been using sleeping pills to escape the pain of losing them, but now I felt thankful to be fully present in the crisp air.

Some change is slow, even invisible, what might be called *glacial*. But Stephen, Ed, and Robert returning after we'd thought them dead was sudden. The climbers had gained safety but remained shaken, with physical and emotional fissures gaping like the Jaws of Doom. Our ground had literally shifted underfoot. We would need to search for new balance, land on a new dashed line, one we could find on no map.

I returned to the tent and collapsed into a deep sleep.

19

Mind over Mountain

Journal entry. May 18, 1988. The day after the climbers' return.

Things continue to be stressful. Soaked and bandaged Robert's fingers and toes. He stayed in the tent all day and is occasionally still hearing voices. Soaked and bandaged Stephen and Ed's toes, and Ed's fingers. Stephen's fingers are in good shape and will not need more care. They are doing well but are "less themselves." Stephen's nose turned black today and we are still working in the ever-present snowfall.

Two days after they returned, Joe and I packed everyone's things, took down the tents, and dressed Ed, Stephen, and Robert to return to Base Camp. We gave them a head start on the trail. Ideally, they would have been carried on stretchers and not walking on injured toes, but we didn't have such resources. Before leaving, I looked at the bare glacier, our life at Advanced Base Camp packed away. I waved to Joe as he left camp. "I'll catch up!"

My chin trembling, my back aching from crouching during the climbers' treatments, my tears flowed. Overcome with relief about their return, fear that their wounded bodies were vulnerable, and sadness about leaving a place I'd dreamed about, I searched the ground to make sure I wasn't forgetting something. Scraps of gauze littered the rubble, specks of blood, the story of where we'd been. Dashed lines in red.

I still had some cleaning to do.

I took down the prayer flags we'd strung on rocks and wrapped them around my shoulders and over my pack, the colorful square cloths an embrace. Facing the mountain, I folded my body forward for a stretch and a prayer, a touch of toes and rock with my fingers. After seventeen straight days in the confines of this camp, I stood up and turned my back on Everest. But the Face did not notice. Whether white and avalanching or gray and gurgling, it never shed tears.

Walking away at a brisk pace in light snow, I caught up with Joe and Robert. After a few minutes together, we found Ed on the ground, face up with his eyes closed. I patted his shoulder and he shuddered with a chill. "I sat down to rest. I guess I fell asleep," he explained. The three of us picked him up and walked with him, snow crunching under our boots, the only sound during our long, slow amble.

Back in the warm sheik tent at Base Camp, with a lantern, table, and chairs, we sat like sultans. My eyes fluttered with fatigue. Joe leaned over to me. "You were so bored before and now you're working nonstop."

In the middle of the night, I helped Robert outside to pee. The fingers that had helped him scale Everest were not up to this basic task. At sunrise, he barraged me with snide comments. Although I can't remember them, his words added to the hurt I already felt that he hadn't mentioned thinking of me at all during his torturous descent. No feelings that he missed me or wanted to return to me. Now, I bit my lips, wanting to feel empathy for him and why he may be taking his stress out on me, but instead I folded inward, drained.

I left him, stomped up the moraine, sat on the frosty hillside, and cried.

I sobbed about the climbers and their injuries, hoping I'd done the right things to treat them. I sobbed knowing they were still vulnerable, that evacuating them was going to take time, that their conditions could worsen. I sobbed because Robert was being a jerk. Still crying, I stormed farther up the moraine, sat down again, and listened to the glacial drip of ice in the morning sun.

I charged up the ridge to the farthest cairns we'd set up, for a last look at Everest in the morning clouds. The mountain that had enticed me, made me feel more alive than ever, challenged me in ways I'd never expected, and then imperiled my team. The mountain that had kept the climbers from us, then barely let them return. The mountain I'd stared at for what felt like thousands of hours. The mountain I thought had stolen the climbers' bodies, and that still held our emotions in its grip. I was furious at that mountain, even though I'd wanted more than anything to live in its shadow.

Standing, I turned away from Everest again, then jogged back to face the day.

I took over the pantry, setting up supplies: disinfectant, packages of gauze, tape, scissors, gloves, basins for bathing. I visited the climbers in their tents to check on them and collect urine samples to assess dehydration. Pasang cooked a large breakfast with pancakes, and everyone withdrew into their own thoughts.

I went outside to gather extra supplies and was startled by two Western-looking men in bright parkas approaching. In nearly three months, we had not seen anyone who wasn't Tibetan or greeted new people in English. I mustered a "Hello," then after jumbled thoughts, asked "Who are you?"

They didn't respond. They might have been equally confused seeing me, in long underwear, a neck warmer wrapped around my head, untied mountain boots, a flowy Indian scarf, and surgical gloves on my hands.

Finally, I blurted, "You're not the famous French trekkers, are you?" We had a running joke about imaginary French trekkers who were going to show up when we least expected.

"No, we're Americans." The taller of the two men took off his sunglasses, while the other man turned his head to survey camp. Paul and Joe heard me talking and came outside.

"We're on a tour of nine trekkers," the other American added.

I stretched my latex-gloved hands to show our visitors. "We have injured climbers."

"We have two surgeons in our group," the tall one said.

"What kind?" I asked.

"A vascular surgeon and an orthopedist."

I turned to Paul and Joe. "Those are frostbite experts!"

After seeing no one for months I was shocked we had real doctors—surgeons no less—nearby. Paul and Kasang brought our table outside and offered them tea. I was excited to hear the group also had two women, hopeful they'd visit. Too busy to join the tea party, I pleaded, "Can you ask the surgeons to come here? We could really use their help. We have injured climbers. Please!"

On my way to the sheik tent, I turned around to say *please* one more time, then entered the kitchen to boil pots of water for frostbite treatments. I led Robert to our shower tent and helped him to wash and dress. We didn't talk about what had happened between us. I brought him into my pantry medical suite to soak, mobilize, and clean his fingers, bandaging them loosely, hoping the surgeons would examine them. I tended to his feet similarly, then sterilized the basin and called Ed in.

I suggested Ed look away and tipped his hat over his eyes, then removed the bandage from his first finger. A shrunken black stub of a distal phalanx—the whole tip of his finger—stared back. He turned toward me, lifted his hat, saw his finger, and looked up at me with wide eyes. Then he rounded his back away from me, an animal curled up in defense, more unwrapping, more fingers, more rocking with sobs, digit after digit, dead, inch-long black fingertips like shriveled prunes, wailing, shaking his head, sobs piercing my heart. I wished I could protect him from this pain. He looked at me incredulously, but I had no answers. I, too, was surprised at how rapidly his shredded fingers had turned to coal.

"Will I be able to climb?" he asked. The gauze adhered to his final two fingers. The fingers that weren't black were raw, weeping with serous fluid, or perhaps infected.

I didn't have an answer.

"Goddammit," he said, turning away.

I handed him two Tylenol with codeine and, allowing time for the medicine to take effect, left the tent to get someone to help me distract him. Paul came, and threw his arm around Ed's shoulder, enveloping him tightly in his grip, diverting his head so he couldn't watch me while I resumed working. Ed shouted in agony as I carefully unstuck each layer of gauze from his last two fingers. My stomach filled with nausea knowing he was in pain.

Paul had no reaction to the gore and was even able to joke. "Dude, look on the bright side. We're getting out of here and you don't need to lift a finger."

At this tender moment, men's voices outside the tent headed in our direction. Hoping it was the surgeons, I grabbed some packs of sterile surgical gloves, and walked outside, waving them in the air. "Hello! I need a consult!"

Dr. Nas Eftekhar and Dr. Fero Sadeghian were middle-aged, bearded, affable adventurers from New York, enjoying a trek in the Himalayas. As a vascular surgeon, Fero was an expert in understanding the cause and treatment of frostbite injuries. Nas, an orthopedist from Columbia University, treated bones and joints. He was the type of surgeon who did amputations. They joined me to walk back to the tent.

"We were surprised to hear you wanted medical help," Nas said. They took inventory of our supplies and my setup for treatment.

"You did all this?" Fero asked.

"Yes. I'm so glad you're here. I need you to examine the climbers." I explained the climbers' delays on the descent, their condition upon return, and the treatment I'd given so far. I removed the gauze covering Ed's fingers.

They examined Ed, Robert, and Stephen in successive private consultations. They were thorough and deliberate, carefully examining the skin, where the injuries were, where the healthy tissue remained. Nearly all of Stephen's left toes were frostbitten. His fingers looked good now, but his nose was black. I'd covered it with a large gauze bandage.

Robert had nine blackened fingertips and three frostbitten toes on his left foot. "It's severe frostbite but these may recover, since there's no blisters or torn skin," Nas said. Ed had eight shriveled fingertips and three frostbitten left toes. Strangely, all three climbers had frozen left toes and normal right toes. Nas and Fero conversed quietly with each other.

"You have supplies with you? Do you have antibiotics? Enough gauze?"

"Yes."

"Look," Nas said. "You've done everything you could. With frostbite, it's a waiting game. You can't know the ultimate outcome until time passes."

"But please tell me anything else I should think of, anything else I should do. Should I have done anything differently? I was planning to start Ed on antibiotics today." I needed reassurance. Craved direction. Supervision. Help.

They advised building stretchers to carry Stephen and Ed to minimize the impact of walking. Robert's feet weren't as bad, and they assured me he would be okay to walk. The doctors agreed I should start Ed on antibiotics.

"I'm planning to continue these water baths to clean and wrap them every day. Do you agree?"

"Yes."

"I know the gauze looks bulky on each finger. I thought it best to keep them separate—is there a better way to dress them?"

Nas gently picked up Ed's hand. "No. I'm not sure everyone would have done it this way, maybe they would wrap the whole hand together, but this way is better."

"Mimi, I can't believe you are a medical student," Fero said. They asked me several questions about how I prepared, where I was from, and why I was there.

Nas removed his glasses and looked me in the eyes. "You need to go into orthopedics. You have a guaranteed spot in my residency at Columbia," he said. "I'm not kidding. You should come train with me. Please get in touch when you get back to New York."

My face felt impossibly hot. I was so relieved I hadn't screwed up and stunned to have a top-notch medical consult in remote Tibet, but Nas offering me a job was over the top. The guys would tease me about this endlessly.

After holding my breath for days and trembling with the fate of Robert's, Ed's, and Stephen's limbs in my hands, I exhaled. I'd come far from hiding under my covers reading about Florence Nightingale caring for injured soldiers to being here caring for injured climbers. As a child, I'd chanted the Jewish psalm 118, *Min Ha-Meitzar*, but didn't understand how it might apply in my life. "From a narrow place I called out . . . God answered me with the expanse." I had journeyed from my boxes toward the expanse of place, but also encountered expanses of body, mind, spirit. And here, now, of breath. Of release of fear.

Despite my unlikeliness, my body—my map—had proved reliable. I was grateful for its strength, for not getting sick or injured. I would need to remember to value my body's abilities, and not dwell on its shortcomings and its imprinted shame.

After the doctors left, I was alone again to manage things. No more visits from specialists. No more hope I'd get a visit from the women trekking with them.

Years later, Fero published *They Call Me Fero*, a book in which he recalled visiting us at Base Camp: "The cost of this success was also high. All members of the team suffered from varying degrees of frostbite and physical and psychological injuries. . . . The sense of gloom, thickly palpable in their camp, was much improved after our visit."

I was surprised and touched that he'd saved this note and included it in his book:

"I received the following . . . delivered by a Tibetan mail runner:

May 20, 8:00 pm—Everest Base Camp

Endless thanks for your support and encouragement today. It was quite an unbelievable vision to see your companions this morning after three months of isolated company, but to find out that two surgeons were on their way down was very reassuring for both the climbers and myself. It was very generous of you to help and advise me. The past few days were exasperating, and it was a great relief for me to have you here. Needless to say, the climbers enjoyed your care and expertise and felt better after your consultation. Sincerely, Miriam Zieman"

Ever since the climbers descended, Paul and Pasang had been sending word to our Chinese liaisons, pleading for emergency evacuation, preferably by helicopter. They explained we had severe injuries and lives and limbs were at stake. The Chinese answered repeatedly: "It is not possible."

Early on the second day in Base Camp, I walked up the hill behind camp to get some air and space. Sharp shafts of morning sun spotlighted the hill sideways. The breeze cold on my face, I sat thinking about the day ahead, twisting shoots of grass. Paul walked toward me.

"I know how stressed you are." His crinkly eyes met mine while he pulled his hands out from behind his back and presented me with a small bouquet of yellow buttercups.

"But you're stressed, too. You're running camp!" I choked out the words through heaving sobs.

Paul had become the de facto leader. He joked and cajoled us through the wearying tasks of caring for the climbers and breaking down camp. During most of the trip, Paul and I hadn't spent much one-on-one time, but for the past week we'd worried together, then worked side by side.

I was learning to let go of the notion I had to tough it out on my own, what Robert might have meant by my "New York edge," formed by city life, but also by my family. As a Holocaust survivor's daughter, I'd lost trust in people and decided not to burden or depend on my father. He'd been through enough. All the while, my mother and grandmother's voices in my head: *Never depend on a man.*

I hadn't learned how to let people in. I was the obstruction to the love I craved.

During the next day's bath treatments, Robert, Stephen, and Ed each shared their worries with me.

Ed's saucer blue eyes bored into my heart, "What's my life going to be like?"

"I don't know Ed, but I think things will work out."

"I can't believe I took those pictures. Was it worth it?" he questioned. "Was climbing worth it? Will I be able to climb again?" His eyes glistened with tears. Maybe climbing had been worth it, but taking the pictures was a mistake anyone could have made but he'd have to live with.

It would be a long time before I'd understand everything we'd been through on that glacier, that I'd experienced the greatest emptiness and the greatest strength there. Now I realize that living and loving while knowing all could be lost is the essence of the greatest aliveness.

During the next few days, Joe, Paul, and several local Tibetans built stretchers while I did medical work. Stephen, Robert, and Ed were weak and subdued, resting in their tents, processing what they'd been through. Joe moved into Ed's tent to care for him full-time, helping him dress, eat, and pee, exercising deep compassion and patience.

I moved too and pitched my own tent to create distance from Robert.

He was processing a devastating near-death experience and had been hallucinating just days before, accounting for his uncharacteristically mean behavior. But I was processing the other side of this near-death experience—thinking him and the others dead—and the realization he didn't seem to return my feelings. I needed peace to focus on the injured.

Joe, Pasang, Paul, and I carried the weight of the injured together and comforted one another. In our ensemble, one person's gears kicked in when another's faltered. A shared dream had lifted us here, and now we shared the gravity of that dream. We—and the injured—were all at the knife-edge of our limits.

More often than not, mountaineering expeditions are rife with conflicts. Climbers argue over who gets to tackle the greatest climbing challenges. People get edgy and irritable living at high altitude. Completing even simple tasks is hard. Insomnia causes restlessness. Fatigue and lethargy are the default, yet it's expected that everyone shares the workload. Weather can be wearying. Teammates get on each other's nerves. We experienced some of that, but our camaraderie deepened with time. The intimacy of physically caring for one another—Joe and Paul helping Robert, Stephen, and Ed to clothe, pee, and bathe, me treating their wounds—entwined us like a tree with tangled roots.

The night before we left Base Camp, Robert raised a glass of whiskey. "To Stephen: the first British man to summit Everest without oxygen!" Sitting safely in our sheik tent, he kicked off a series of toasts bookending our toasts from our seder night.

"To our honorary leader: Lord John Hunt who suggested I join the team." Stephen threw back a gulp of amber. "And, to the Yanks, who have become such good friends during an unusually happy expedition!"

"And to *The Woman*," Stephen continued, "dare I say she didn't only tolerate our insufferable male company but took pleasure in it and her special status."

I felt my cheeks redden and smiled. He was right. For most of the trip, I'd felt lonely as the only woman, different, wanting to prove myself on behalf of all women. But now, they respected me as a person, regardless of my gender. They *did* treat me in a special way. I felt seen. This makeshift family had developed the mutual trust I'd always craved. Now, they, too, would be forever stitched into the seams of my pack.

The following morning, Paul and Kasang dug a huge pit farther up the moraine and filled it with combustible garbage. Thorough in their intent to leave the ground as pristine as we'd found it, they even burned or buried trash from the previous American expeditions. The three of us stood over the open fire, smoke graying the view of the East Face behind the pit, dots of ash peppering the wind. I turned around to see Stephen and Ed being lifted off the ground, each man with four porters, one at each corner of his stretcher. *If only it were as easy to burn away the pain.*

As we descended the valley, a soft wind carried the fragrance of wet earth. Wildflowers dotted the grassy landscape. After teetering on rocks and sinking in melting ice, I appreciated the solid earth underfoot. How important each step forward was.

The first afternoon, when we reached a big yak-grazing meadow where we'd camped on the way up, Paul waved his ski poles, trying to convince the porters to continue farther down to the river. He didn't succeed.

That night, Robert developed a fever. On exam I found a tracking red line from one frostbitten toe up his leg. It was warm to the touch—a classic cellulitis—exactly what I'd been fearing. Infections can spread and develop complications like gangrene and sepsis. I administered antibiotics and stayed in his tent to monitor his condition. He was grateful for my care, and some of his warmth toward me returned. In the middle of the night, his fever broke. Afterward, I trekked beside him in case his condition worsened, his daypack layered atop my backpack. The infection slowly dissipated.

Each night, we set up camp and unpacked their belongings before laying the injured climbers down to rest. I soaked three pairs of feet and two sets of fingers, put on fresh bandages, and sterilized the bowl between each treatment. Raw in the elements—dirt, wind, snow—I was concerned about more infections. Herzog's story of amputations during his team's retreat still haunted me.

The following day, I admired the change in the valleys, now snowless and full of budding trees. The air felt thick, luxuriously rich with oxygen, like breathing cake. But along with the beauty of movement and the hopefulness of spring, a heavy helplessness depressed us. Robert, Ed, and Stephen were suffering. At dinner on the third night, we stared into our congealed couscous, when Ed stumbled toward us moaning loudly.

"Paul, can you please help me pee?" Tears streamed down his cheeks.

Paul stood up and said with mock severity, "Ed, this is the last time I'm holding it. You've got to learn to do it yourself!"

We all released the tension with a huge laugh, Ed joining in.

On the fourth night, after we crossed the pass that had thwarted us on the way in, Kasang hosted the party he'd promised in AngChu's house. A huge pot of fermented barley—*thongba*—studded with many straws, lay on the floor between all the members of our team and the Tibetans. As we sucked the thongba, more boiling water was added, creating an endless amount of fermented drink. In between sips I got up and shuffle-danced with the Tibetans, braced arms, swayed and relaxed, knowing we were only one day's walk from the trailhead. After dancing to songs from *Saturday Night Fever* and other disco hits, we stumbled back to our tents. It was another Himalayan rave, of sorts.

My head thrummed when Kasang woke me up, summoning me back to AngChu's house where a crowd of Tibetans gathered for a medical visit. They wanted me to drink chang. At 9:00 in the morning. I politely declined. I treated an assortment of headaches, backaches, and coughs, then joined everyone back on the trail.

In the late afternoon, I spotted the teahouse in Kharta and ran the last bit there. Our Chinese liaisons stood at the threshold. My steps quickened as I neared, dropping my pack in the courtyard. Pasang shook his head, and I soon understood that the vans we'd requested to evacuate the injured weren't there. We'd sent word ten days earlier that we needed immediate evacuation and assumed transportation to Lhasa would be waiting for us, and the injured would be whisked away to proper medical care.

Entering the teahouse, my eyes adjusted to the darkness. A black film of thick grime coated every surface, topped with a layer of rolling dust. What I'd hoped would be a place of healing was the filthiest place we'd been in months.

"Let's do your water baths," I called to the guys as I walked past the Chinese officials and Pasang in deep conversation. I tore open packages of sterile gauze as the climbers entered the squalid room. Pasang had already boiled water on the stove, and I laid out supplies. Emotions bubbled from deep inside me. My heart pounded and heat rose from my chest. My hands trembled as I walked to the threshold.

"We need to get out of here!" I screamed at Mr. Xi. "Where is our transport? You know we have injured—why isn't it here?"

"No trucks. Many days," he shook his head.

"What? NO! We need them now! We need to get the climbers out of here NOW!" I stomped my feet, and my voice overran the room and rang through the wooden walls, loud and rage-filled like my mother's. I leaned forward at the threshold, spittle on my lips. "We have injured! We need to leave now!" I shouted, "pulling an Amama." Two defiant women with big mouths and feet, voices ringing between my ears, the words catapulting from my throat.

Pasang held his palm out like a stop sign to quiet me, worried I'd anger the Chinese. He led them away, speaking in hushed, calm tones.

At various times that day, everyone took turns pleading with the Chinese but received the same response: It would take several days. We set up tents on the dusty ground in the courtyard because it was cleaner than the lodge.

It wouldn't do much good this time, but I had claimed my voice.

I understand now that I couldn't fully embrace my family—their legacy of pain, their expectations, the way their words overwhelmed mine—until I found my own voice and learned to trust it. My voice guided me to the wilderness, and there, in that silence and effort and pure mountain air,

I lost myself and found myself again and again, sometimes several times a day. In that place of refuge and in the white nothingness, in reaching those moments of despair and darkness, a shift occurred. A shift, then a crack, then a shaft of light slanting into the crevasse deep inside my body.

I was now more myself than I could have hoped for. There would be no more hiding. Quitting would be reserved for things that didn't align with my heart and soul, not for things that were simply hard. I felt a great privilege to have the skills to help my teammates, increasing my purpose and confidence with my choice of a life in medicine.

I didn't yet know that my voice, discovered by following my own path, infused with Amama's courage, grounded in my father's sense of justice, steeped within Mom's outrage, would empower my lifelong mission to advocate for all women's rights to self-determination, having had the privilege to achieve my own. There had been no map to follow for what I'd just been through, but I would use what I learned—and was yet to learn—for this mission.

After three nights in Kharta, two vans arrived on a crisp blue-sky morning. I stepped outside and inhaled wet soil, wild roses, and abandon. We took turns hugging Kasang goodbye and each hopped into one of the vans. My driver flashed a toothless, joyful grin, his bare left elbow pointed outside his open window as he revved up the car and popped a cassette into the dash. I sat behind him, rolled down my window, and smelled the grassy wind as the car jerked into first gear and a flock of birds speckled the sky.

John Denver's "Rocky Mountain High" rang through the car. Robert turned around to face me from the passenger's seat next to the driver, and we grinned at each other. Ed looked at me from his seat near the window behind Robert, the sunlight a white trapezoid on his cheek, his shining blue eyes ethereal. Paul leaned over and beamed as the breeze tousled his curls. While a medley of Western tunes blasted, we each absorbed the moment quietly. We were riding into the future, a new unknown, carrying fresh scars, proud and raw.

I would pause at the next blank space, the next in-between, before landing on a new dashed line, and I would cope with my choice. It wouldn't be easy. I've since understood that I don't choose easy; but I can also choose to not feel weighted. I'd need to learn to free myself from my own judgments. I'd need to grant myself permission to make mistakes, to move forward with uncertainty, and to make room for lightness. I'd need to believe in my rise to the edge of the cliff through the power of my own hands and feet.

After a few minutes, a familiar beat boomed from the radio. I looked at the guys seated in the van, their faces creased from the sun. One of my favorite disco songs, "Funky Town," was playing. It's a song that always got my hips and feet moving, that always made me smile and twirl with joy. I tapped the driver's shoulder, "Can you please turn it up?" He turned to me, his face beaming, while he cranked up the volume. We sped across the brown plains.

We were soon to be home, with colors, cadence, and conversation beyond our little group, out of the shadow of the mountain, and into a world rushing to embrace us.

As I danced in my seat, the guys laughed and shimmied. We were fragmented and whole. Uniquely ourselves, yet together.

I tilted up on my toes in my hard mountain boots and leaned my body out the window, my long messy hair blowing freely in the Tibetan wind, my fingers sweeping the sky.

Epilogue

From the front row of an auditorium in London's Royal Geographic Society, I watched my teammates lecture about our expedition. Twenty-five years had passed, and Stephen had organized an anniversary gala to support a charity helping people with brain cancer. His beautiful son, Ollie, had died of this disease. Instead of our matching fleece team jackets, we wore black-tie apparel along with the wrinkles we'd gained since our youthful adventure.

"We need to get down!" Ed was on the stage reenacting their harrowing descent from the East Face. He pantomimed taking huge gulps of air, then turned toward the audience with wild bulging blue eyes. "Stephen, we need to move!" He stooped over and hyperventilated.

Ed's hammed-up performance mesmerized me. He, Robert, and Stephen took turns speaking. Paul was, as ever, content to stay out of the limelight.

Ed had faced eighteen surgeries, and a few tough years recovering from his physical and emotional injuries from the Kangshung face. He ultimately lost eight fingertips and three toes from our climb. In recent years, he reported "living the dream," working as a guide in Antarctica, hiking with cruise passengers during the day and delivering entertaining lectures at night. He'd become quite a historian and raconteur. He wrote a magnum opus, *Snow in the Kingdom*, about our climb. Published in 2000, it includes stories about other adventures and stunning photographs. He enjoyed family life and, although he feared he'd never climb again, was able to return to this passion.

Upon Stephen's return home, he was greeted with a hero's welcome, as he described in a letter to me shortly after our group dispersed.

At Bombay airport there was a "cock-up" with flights, and I just had to get a transfer, so I told them, "The Great British Public is waiting for me and I have to be in London this afternoon." They put me on a Gulf Air flight and I arrived at Heathrow with one hour in hand—just in time to be whisked through in a wheelchair to the BBC fast car and off to the studio, where there was just time to dab the make-up on the Ishteemy nose, iron the white trousers, polish the crutches and hop on camera to entertain the masses. . . . The following day I was on "Blue Peter," (a children's TV show) to bring a thrill to the hearts of millions of British children. The Blue Peter dog wouldn't stop sniffing my festering toes. . . . P.S. Have you tried your pee bottle in the library yet?

Stephen lost three toes after our climb. We still tease him that he'll be knighted for being the first Brit to summit Everest without supplemental oxygen. Robert likes to add that "Stephen's never had to pay for lunch." Stephen wrote *Everest, The Kangshung Face*, published in 1989 about our expedition, reissued with the title *Alone at the Summit* in 2000. He has written other books, guided climbs, and married the woman he was dating while on our expedition. He is the only one from our team who returned to the Kangshung, leading a trek there.

After the gala, my teammates and I traveled to spend a weekend together at the Pen-Y-Gwryd lodge in Wales, where the first successful Everest team of 1953 had trained. Sitting around a large wooden table in a room decorated with Everest paraphernalia, we drank out of mugs used by the climbers on that team. As I sipped tea from a mug used by Tenzing Norgay, sitting beside his son Norbu, my insides warmed with a flood of gratitude. I felt as if a day hadn't passed since he and I were in thigh-high snow on our way to Base Camp avoiding being mauled by yaks.

All weekend, I was enveloped in an embrace. Our bond from our shared experience in an extreme environment provides me with a unique feeling of being known and appreciated.

Paul remains a mountain man, living in Lake Tahoe, climbing, and skiing. In Wales, he appeared as if he were still twenty-seven with full dark curls and infectious charm. He and Robert have since climbed together on several expeditions.

Robert, who lost half a toe from our climb, continued to be the man of many schemes and dreams, participating frequently in expeditions, including reaching the top of the Seven Summits, the highest peak on each continent. He recently transitioned from his career in advertising to working as a mountaineering guide, leading others up the Seven Summits. He too has authored many books, the latest—*Nine Lives*—about nine of his visits to Everest. Joe accompanied Robert on some of his climbs as the photographer, while continuing his studio work and balancing family life.

Once we reached Lhasa at the end of the expedition, with good food and a warm atmosphere, Robert slowly returned to himself.

"I'm sorry I've been an asshole," he said to me.

"Yeah . . . you don't need to take your shit out on me."

"I'll make it up to you over pizza in Hong Kong." He knew the way to my heart.

We attempted to have a committed relationship following our return. I visited him in New Zealand for an adventure that included glaciers rivaling our first romantic week in Nepal. We called it quits soon after, since neither of us wanted to move, and the distance still didn't make sense.

I will always be grateful to Robert, that he saw something in me I didn't know was there, and for the great fun we had.

Ed was the first teammate I called after finishing this book. He offered to read it and provide me with feedback. Two weeks after our conversation, he died, suddenly and unexpectedly, from natural causes. We are all still processing his loss.

James, my close friend from medical school, reminds me that when I returned from Everest, I was "very grateful for ceilings." The hospitals were full of gifts like heating and air-conditioning, walls, electric lights, and running water. Walking into work felt like a holiday, day after day, a cozy place with people and telephones for connection. To be in an institution with abundance made me feel supported if not also indulged. I wondered what follows fulfilling a big dream at twenty-five.

I ached to write a book about my experience but couldn't manage the commitment while finishing medical training and couldn't take time off because I needed to make student loan payments. What a very different book that would have been. After our climb made a big splash and was featured on the cover of several mountaineering magazines, I was invited on other expeditions, but was never able to make it work.

I plodded ahead to complete school and OB/GYN training, crying often during my first year of residency from the workload and stress, contemplating quitting.

Two weeks after completing residency, in an operating room on a tiny eight-mile-long island called Guam, I peered through surgical goggles, my words garbled under my mask.

"Ready?" I nodded to the anesthesiologist at the head of the table and the expectant pediatrician near the incubators. Overseeing this moment, I asked others if they were ready, even though I didn't feel quite ready. I still often don't feel ready, but I've learned women often underestimate themselves. We can handle more than we think.

"Skin," I said, so the circulating nurse could record the moment my scalpel incised the patient's abdomen. The male general surgeon on the other side of the table, my assistant, watched my steps, retracting the flesh and muscle out of the way, shadowing each of my moves in a perfect dance. After incising the uterus and rupturing the amniotic membrane, a flood of fluid poured over the blue surgical drapes, some dripping on my white paper boots. I slid my hand deeply behind the pubic bone and lifted a baby's head out into the world.

"Baby one, boy," I said, as I suctioned his nostrils and removed his squirmy body, quickly handing him to the surgical nurse. He cried as I reached for the next baby's hips, presenting close to the incision. I grabbed them with two hands like a steering wheel and coaxed him out backwards into view, "Baby two, boy," I said, taking a deep breath. I had to work quickly. These were small babies squeezed into the contractile uterine muscle. Even during a cesarean section, the uterus can curl into itself, into a tight ball of muscle, ensnaring a tiny baby.

The remaining baby had more room to stretch in the uterus now and was slightly sideways when I grabbed her ankles to coax her closer to the incision. I wrapped them in a blue surgical towel for traction, slowly delivered her torso, and gently tucked her chin to safely deliver her head into the world. She was born feet first.

"Baby three, girl," I said as I handed her off and looked up at my assistant. We high-fived knowing the babies were out and safe. I could relax now, since closing the uterine incision from three babies is no different from a singleton. A case like this, done in New York City where I'd just completed training, would have been overseen by multiple obstetricians and pediatricians, probably a neonatologist and perinatologist.

But I was alone again. A sole obstetrician, operating near the deepest oceanic trench on Earth, in the middle of the Pacific Ocean, not long after my stint on the highest mountain. In another isolated place with endless blue, this time the surrounding magnificent waters.

Six months earlier, I'd leafed through a medical magazine when a palm tree caught my eye.

Come practice in Guam.

I presented the idea to my new husband, Jeff. Our mutual friend had set us up on a blind date because we "were both Jewish and loved to travel." We had more than that in common, and I found his dark curly hair, humor, kindness, and artistic sensibility irresistible.

"It would be a great opportunity to travel," was his first response. We could work in Guam, save money, and backpack in Southeast Asia before returning to complete our medical subspecialty fellowships. We would have to figure out how to make our loan payments while traveling, whether Jeff could find work in Guam, whether we could defer our fellowships.

"Plus," he added, "we barely know each other, so it would be good to take a long trip." This was our running joke. We had met and married two years earlier during our residency training while working eighty-plus-hour weeks. How much time had we truly spent together? How well did we really know each other? As it turned out, our energies matched perfectly for reading side by side.

After all our adventures, Jeff and I raised our three children in the suburbs of Atlanta, having moved there for jobs right after training. We would wonder how we ended up in such a manicured place. We arrived with a one-year-old, not knowing a single person, I was pregnant with our second child, starting a new job as the director of a medical service, and panicking—my default response to stress—over my impending oral OB/GYN Boards. Maybe choosing our first jobs in Atlanta instead of New York was a kind of adventure.

I wondered why some people never ventured far from their homes, as much as I wondered why I made choices that should have given me more pause. Despite the sense of being on my own, despite my hurts, despite my wanderings, it was my parents, my grandmother, my ancestors, who were my strength.

My journey to Everest reminds me that taking risks is a path to growth and that I still need to listen for unusual opportunities. To jump in even when I don't feel ready.

To surrender. Just like the glacier told me to.

ACKNOWLEDGMENTS

This book would not be in your hands without my agent, Erin Clyburn, and editor, David Legere, who believed in my story. I'm grateful for their vision.

Thank you to the talented and generous writers, teachers, and editors whom I admire and who guided me in different ways along the way. Tracy Hart taught the first one-hour writing workshop I ever attended. She generously pulled me aside and encouraged me to continue. These little sparks are meaningful and don't always happen. Thank you to Jill Rothenberg, Emily Rapp Black, Steve Almond, Anne Dubuisson, Paula Coomer, Stephanie Gilmore, and Allison K Williams. Thank you to the generous authors who took the time to read this book and endorse it. You all are my heroes, and I'm eternally grateful!

I would never have finished the many revisions of this book without the stalwart company and camaraderie of my writing critique group. You are all models of patience, creativity, and grit, as well as dear and generous friends. I'm indebted to Eileen Vorbach Collins, Karen DeBonis, Lindsey DeLoach Jones, Kirsten Ott Palladino, and Casey Mulligan Walsh.

Thank you to the many early readers who advised me. Your time, insights, and contributions were generous and invaluable. To Beryl Bucher, Kate Lee-DuBon, Amy Schatz, Gaby Sonet, Randie Weseley, Sharon Jarchin, Chris Cline-Cardot, Dena Snyder, Wendy Richter, Stephen Venables, Norbu Tenzing, Barbara Rosenblit, Sharon Lewin, and Dorothy Novick. Thank you to my writing confidante Zinaria Williams, with whom I share all the struggles.

I owe a lot to my climbing team, especially Robert Anderson, who invited me to join the expedition. To my cherished teammates Paul

Teare, Stephen Venables, and our beloved, missing Ed Webster. To Joe, my support team dude, who rocked a Jell-O cheesecake whenever we needed a treat.

Although my grandmother, mother, and father have all passed on, I think about them all the time and aimed to honor them in this book. I am so grateful for the continued presence of my brother, Josh, in my life. To Dr. Robert A. Hatcher and Dr. Roberta Golden, cherished mentors who always offer wise counsel and love and who inspire me to become a better person.

Nothing I say can capture the love and gratitude I have for my children Ari, Noa, Maya, and my bonus daughter Yelli. Your laughter, creativity, brilliance, and kindness go a long way toward improving the world. You have taught me so much. Let's keep dancing together!

Thank you to the sponsors of our expedition. We were endorsed by the American Alpine Club, American Geographical Society, the Explorers Club, American Mountain Foundation, Mount Everest Foundation, National Geographic Society, and the United Nations.

Our major sponsors were also sponsors of the 1953 Everest expedition: Eastman Kodak, Burroughs Wellcome, and Rolex Watches USA.

We received financial donations from American Express, Dow Consumer Products, Kiehl's Pharmacy, Lindblad Travel Inc., Petroconsultants, and Weaver Coat Company.

Equipment was donated by Climb High, Dollond & Aitchison, Duggal Color Projects, Fairydown of New Zealand, Jones Optical, Mountain Equipment, Leki, Metolius Products, Mountain Equipment, Nike, Seranac, Stubai, Omni International Distributors, Ultra Technologies, and Wild Country.

Finally, infinite thanks to my best friend and partner in life. To Jeff, who puts up with my mishugas every day and who loves a good adventure. Without your encouragement, writing this book would not have been possible.

About the Author

Mimi Zieman is a mother, writer, physician, and speaker. In addition to *Tap Dancing on Everest*, she is the author of *The Post-Roe Monologues* and *Managing Contraception*. Her writing has appeared in *The Sun Magazine*, *Ms. Magazine*, *Newsweek*, *Dorothy Parker's Ashes*, *NBCNews THINK*, *The Forward*, and other publications.

Home base is with her husband and dog in Atlanta, far from her New York City roots, with no high mountain in sight, where she eats no grits, biscuits, or collards, and must navigate ten-lane highways. But she loves Southern hospitality, her community of friends, and the canopy of trees that keeps her grounded. Learn more at www.mimiziemanmd.com and follow her social media @mimiziemanmd.